THE RAILWAYS OF LONDON DOCKLANDS

THE RAILWAYS OF LONDON DOCKLANDS

THEIR HISTORY AND DEVELOPMENT

JONATHAN WILLIS

PEN & SWORD
TRANSPORT

AN IMPRINT OF PEN & SWORD BOOKS LTD.
YORKSHIRE – PHILADELPHIA

First published in Great Britain in 2022 by
Pen and Sword Transport
An imprint of
Pen & Sword Books Ltd.
Yorkshire - Philadelphia

ISBN 978 1 52679 058 3

Typeset in Palatino 10.5/14 by SJmagic DESIGN SERVICES, India.

Printed and bound by Printworks Global Ltd, London/Hong Kong.

Pen & Sword Books Ltd incorporates the imprints of Pen & Sword Books Archaeology, Atlas, Aviation, Battleground, Discovery, Family History, History, Maritime, Military, Naval, Politics, Railways, Select, Transport, True Crime, Fiction, Frontline Books, Leo Cooper, Praetorian Press, Seaforth Publishing, Wharncliffe and White Owl.

For a complete list of Pen & Sword titles please contact

PEN & SWORD BOOKS LIMITED
47 Church Street, Barnsley, South Yorkshire, S70 2AS, England
E-mail: enquiries@pen-and-sword.co.uk
Website: www.pen-and-sword.co.uk

or

PEN AND SWORD BOOKS
1950 Lawrence Rd, Havertown, PA 19083, USA
E-mail: Uspen-and-sword@casematepublishers.com
Website: www.penandswordbooks.com

CONTENTS

ACKNOWLEDGEMENTS

Over the 180 years that railways have served London Docklands, some tens of thousands of people have worked on plans, proposals and the implementation of rail projects. Initially to serve the working docks, carrying mainly goods but also people travelling to and from work, the railways in their second incarnation now carry people to new businesses and homes, changing the area beyond recognition.

This book is dedicated to all the people from the initial private railway companies, their engineers and labourers who built the maze of dock railways, to the modern-day planners, engineers and consultants who repeated the task using very different techniques and machines many years later. Not forgetting the long suffering Eastenders who have endured years of upheaval, but hopefully benefit from all that has been done. Without the former dock railways leaving their invaluable legacy of rights of way, it is very likely the modern Docklands would have been very much more modest or maybe not have happened at all.

Taking projects forward is very much a team effort. As well as the colleagues, consultants and contractors I have worked with, I would like to personally thank David Bayliss, Jim Berry, Michael Bryant, Keith Berryman, Cynthia Grant and Simon Bennett for reviewing text and making very useful corrections and comments. Also, I would like to thank Jane Smith Media for assistance in sourcing a number of images and Transport for London, The LT Museum, Canary Wharf Ltd, Crossrail and Miles Willis Photography for giving me permission to freely use their images.

I give particular thanks to Lord Heseltine for his inspiration in creating the London Docklands Development Corporation, his decision to go ahead with the initial Docklands Light Railway and his writing of a foreword to this book.

Finally I must thank my wife Angela for all her support and suggestions during the several years of writing.

FOREWORD BY LORD HESELTINE

As Secretary of State for the Environment, I was closely involved in the redevelopment of London Docklands. During the 1960s with the advent of containerisation it became increasingly obvious that the former London docks were no longer fit for purpose. By 1970 all the working docks had closed. The next ten years saw a multitude of studies and plans prepared by local and transport authorities, but with no concrete agreement on a way forward.

A radical approach was necessary. In 1979 I persuaded Mrs Thatcher to allow me to create the London Docklands Development Corporation (LDDC) to oversee development in a similar manner to the setting up of the New Towns Commission a few years earlier. This would have required a Hybrid Bill and I therefore took general powers and designated Liverpool at the same time. To give Docklands a kick-start, Geoffrey Howe, as Chancellor of the Exchequer, was keen to designate an Enterprise Zone in the Isle of Dogs with freedom from rates for ten years and generous capital allowances.

Improving transport was a key to getting developers interested in the area, physically close to Central London, but with congested roads the journey could take well over an hour. The LDDC had to work closely with London Transport (LT) to develop ideas. An Underground extension was favoured but it would take too long to build, cost a lot of money and at that time the scale of development then envisaged could not remotely justify it. London Transport and LDDC came up with ideas to make use of the old railway rights of way for a lightweight train. Two routes were planned but the evaluation, carried out by this author, showed they could not be justified. My colleagues in the Department of Transport favoured buses but I was convinced that something other than buses was required. Not least it was found that the railway option could potentially generate more jobs. In the end I gave the go ahead for the initial Docklands Light Railway, sharing the funding between our two departments.

Jonathan Willis has been closely involved with the development of railways in Docklands from the start. Within LT he was responsible for the planning of the initial DLR, several of its extensions and then the Jubilee Line extension. The last chapter of Jon's career was Head of Planning of the Crossrail project on its revival at the start of the new millennium. Jon summarises the history of the docks and its original railways and provides a comprehensive record of the planning and development of all these projects. These railway projects have supported Docklands, enabling it to become one of the most important areas of London and a model of successful urban regeneration.

ABOUT THE AUTHOR

Jonathan Willis MSc (Transport), BSc (Engineering), retired.

Following an Engineering Degree at Loughborough University, I joined London Underground as a graduate trainee with the Signal Engineering Department. After helping to get the platform clocks to work on the newly opened Victoria Line, I moved on to help implement a real time location system for buses. Following a Masters degree at Imperial College in 1973, I moved to the Greater London Council (GLC) and after working on a study of the benefits of bus lanes, commenced work on the development of transport solutions for Docklands.

I worked with the GLC and then, on its demise, with London Transport (LT), later to be known as Transport for London (TfL). I was closely involved in the planning, design and evaluation of the initial Docklands Light Railway (DLR), the DLR City extension, the DLR Lewisham and Beckton extensions and the Jubilee Line extension. As Head of Strategy and Planning for LT, I gave evidence at a number of Parliamentary Committees.[1] My final position with TfL was as Head of Planning for the Crossrail project during its revival stage at the start of the twenty-first century.

Transport planning is a job involving a wide range of disciplines including planning, engineering, environmental, social and economic. I was fortunate enough to be involved in a number of major projects which were approved, funded and built.

Docklands occupied much of my career but other projects in which I was involved included the Piccadilly Line to Heathrow Terminal 4, a range of strategic studies including Transport Interchanges and the role of Intermediate Modes, such as guided buses, and the bringing back of trams to London with Croydon Tramlink.

PREFACE

This book is intended to provide a broad summary of the development of railways in East London, focusing on the former London dock areas, now known as London Docklands, including the Isle of Dogs.

Docklands – from its initial creation as working docks from the sixteenth century to its massive expansion in the early nineteenth century, its rise and fall in shipping trade prominence, to its rebirth as a major regeneration and development opportunity, and its associated political and social history, is a fascinating and vast subject, particularly over the last forty to fifty years since the closure of the docks, with many books, articles and reports written covering its history and redevelopment.

Here an attempt is made to bring together in one document the most significant railway proposals and how they were engineered, conceived, planned and implemented. Engineering is often thought of as the construction stage of a project but the true and full engineering of a project is the identification of a problem and the determination and implementation of an appropriate and economic solution. It also includes the operational phase where ideally the project is then reviewed to see if it has met its objectives. Unfortunately too often this last phase is forgotten.

The emphasis here is on the process up to the point where the decision is taken to proceed with the project. Sometimes this can happen in a remarkably short period. The report on the initial DLR was submitted to Government in July 1982, which made the decision to go ahead three months later in October of the same year. At the other end of the scale it can be argued that for Crossrail, with the project having started life in the 1970s, this period has been nearer to fifty years.

The first railways in Docklands were built by private companies to provide mainly for the transport of goods to and from the docks. The more recent railways have all been planned and largely funded by the public sector to carry people. In both cases the investment was seen as critical to the success of London as a growing world city. For the 180 years or so between these two periods, railways have had their ups and downs in political terms. Thankfully, UK investment in railways is now at a much higher level than for many years as governments seek to reduce congestion and pollution from road transport and meet environmental targets.

From the short trips made on such systems as the DLR to the longer distance trips which will be made by Crossrail, rail is seen as having a key role in London's future transport strategy. With projects such as the High Speed 2 (HS2) railway and Crossrail 2, and further upgrades and extensions to the Underground in the pipeline, this is set to continue.

All costs quoted in the book are at historic price levels.

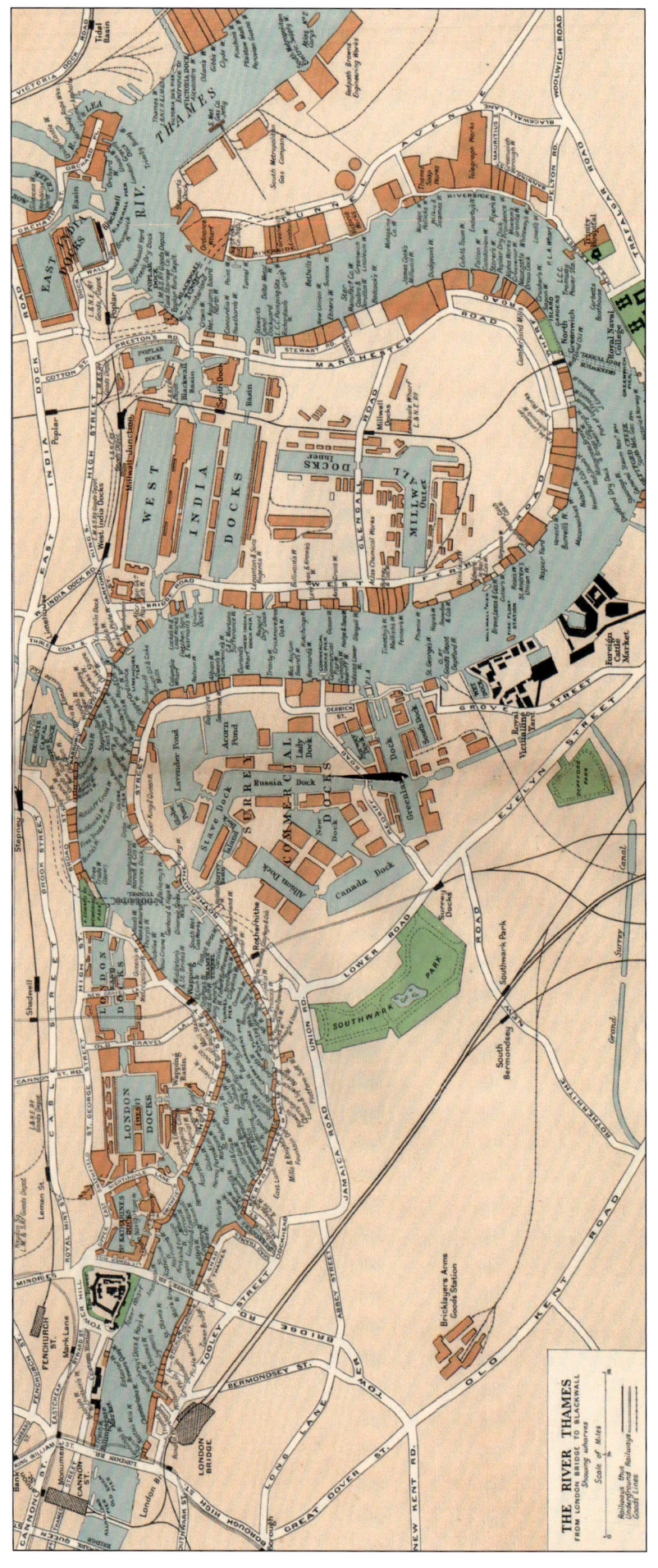

London's docks, c. 1900.

CHAPTER 1

A BRIEF HISTORY OF THE RISE AND FALL OF LONDON'S ENCLOSED DOCKS

Being given the task to 'look at possible transport options for London Docklands', my first impression was gained by a 1950s 6-inch to a mile Ordnance Survey map of the area. The extent of the docks was impressive but it was the miles and miles of former railway lines which caught my attention. Perhaps we could somehow make use of these existing rights of way?

My first visit to Docklands was to the Isle of Dogs around 1970. The number 277 bus served the perimeter of the Isle, giving a glimpse over the wall to another world but a better view was obtained by climbing up the stairs to cross the 'glass bridge'. Built in 1965 to replace a low-level pedestrian right of way, it linked the two sides of the Isle across the Millwall Dock. When I walked across it, the bridge was in a sorry state with the lifts out of order and much of the glass walls shattered. It closed in 1975.

My second visit was into the West India Docks, led by a Port of London official who unlocked a gate in the perimeter wall, where ramshackle warehouses, rusting cranes, stagnant water and the odd vessel created a desolate scene. No one could possibly have imagined what this could become.

The role of the enclosed London Docks in the development of London and the rest of the UK should not be underestimated. From the early eighteenth century onwards, international trade focused on our capital city, growing in line with our influence abroad and our desire to explore the world and seek out new products and markets. At the start of the nineteenth century, shortage of space on the riverside wharves led to a period of major construction of the enclosed docks employing some of the finest engineers of the day, including John Rennie and Thomas Telford.

With the development of the largest port in the world, trade increased dramatically, providing the backbone to the UK economy for about 150 years. Built for sailing ships, many of the smaller docks struggled to survive with the advent of steam and diesel. Closures started in 1967. Even the Royal docks, built to accommodate up to 35,000 ton vessels, could not keep pace with the larger container ships and finally closed in 1981.

Pressure on the Port of London

By the end of the eighteenth century trade to and from London had expanded considerably and the quays and

1.1: The Pool of London, c. 1800.

wharves in the Pool of London below London Bridge were becoming increasingly congested. The unloading and loading of ships was often delayed and the highly organised 'river pirates' and 'night plunderers' took their advantage of cargoes waiting their turn.

Following pressure from the ship owners, the Prime Minister, William Pitt, set up a Select Committee to 'Enquire into the best mode of providing sufficient accommodation for the increased trade and shipping of the Port of London'. The report, published in 1796, favoured enclosed docks at Wapping and Blackwall but it was undecided if they should be run by the City Corporation or by private enterprise such as the powerful West and East India Companies. After much prevarication, the Government gave in to the pressure from the major players and allowed enclosed docks to be built and operated by the private companies.

The West India Company

In 1799 the Dutch West India Dock Company was created, dominating trade with the West Indies, being heavily involved in the slave trade and bringing exotic goods to London. Along with the East India Company these giants developed and supported the UK's growing empire and influence, dramatically improving the prosperity of the country throughout the period.

The West India Company commissioned William Jessop, the canal engineer, to design a new dock at the northern end of the Isle of Dogs. The other great canal engineer John Rennie was called in as a special consultant. The dock system comprised thirty acres of import dock linked by connecting basins at either end to twenty-four acres of export dock, allowing ships to transfer from one to another at all states of the tide.

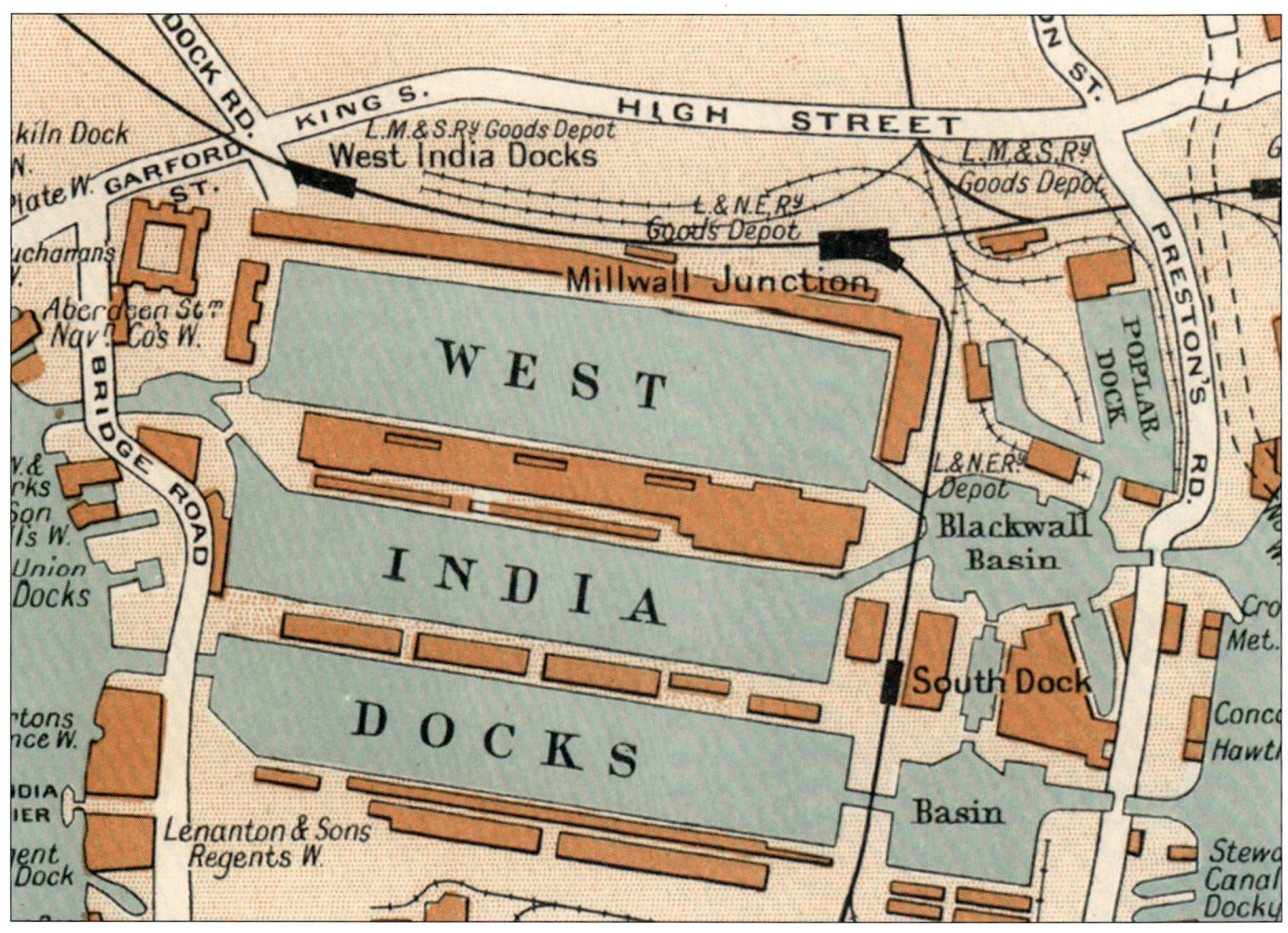

1.2: West India Docks.

The West India Docks opened in 1802 with a monopoly on trade from the West Indies for twenty-one years. Vast five-storey high warehouses surrounded the docks where goods were taken by crane and stored. High security walls surrounded the whole site. Goods were then either distributed by road – the new Commercial Road was constructed at the same time – or by water in lighters to other quays further upstream.

The City of London saw the development of the West India Docks as a serious threat to trade through the Port of London. In an attempt to make it easier for ships to access the area, avoiding the tricky sailing conditions around the Isle of Dogs, they built what was termed the 'City Canal' across the Isle of Dogs, to the south of the West India Dock complex. This was opened in 1806 but proved to be a white elephant as the time saving to ships was minimal. They were required to lock in and out of the canal at either end and then be hauled through by teams of horses. It became a mooring point for waiting ships and was eventually sold to the West India Dock Company which widened it for use as a timber pond.

1.3: West India Docks, c. 1960.

1.4: Goods distribution from West India Dock.

The London Docks

After initial opposition from residents, as the construction required demolition of around 2,000 homes, the City had more success with the setting up of the London Dock Company. The City built in Wapping three main interconnected docks termed the Eastern, Western and Tobacco docks, specialising in the import of tobacco, brandy, rice and wine for which they had

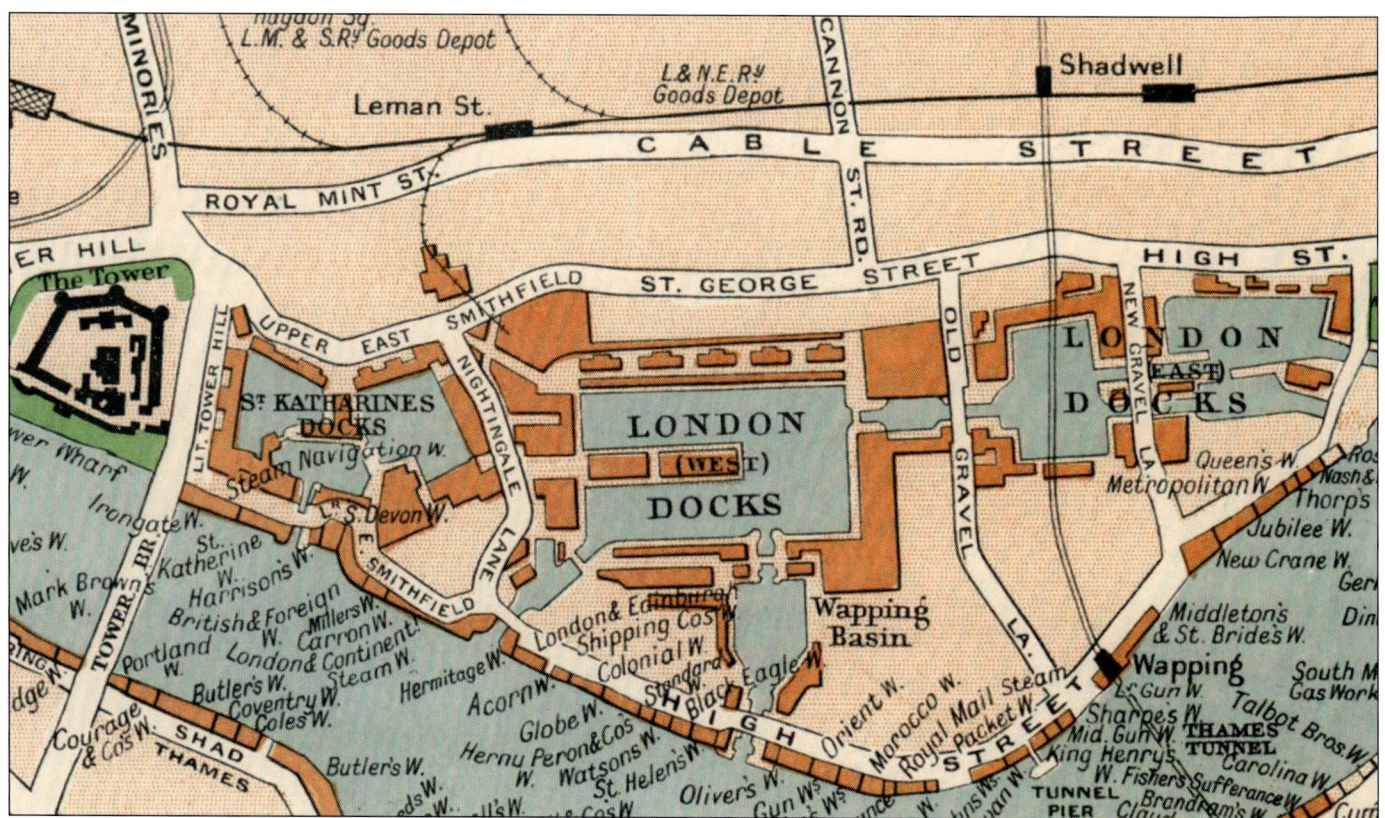

1.5 • London Docks.

been granted a twenty-year monopoly. The London Docks opened in 1805.

The East India Company

The East India Company formed in 1600 to exploit trade in spices, particularly with Indonesia and India, became involved in the slave trade and became part of the political regime in India until the British Empire took over in the mid-nineteenth century. Cotton, tea and opium were staple commodities and its large sailing ships contributed to the congestion in the Pool of London, downstream from London Bridge.

The Company was not to be outdone by its rival the West India Company and using engineers John Rennie and Ralph Walker, who had both worked on the West India Docks, the Company opened two docks and a holding basin in the Blackwall area in 1806. Like its rivals, the Company was granted a twenty-one year monopoly of trade with the East Indies. The complex could handle around 250 ships with large quays but there were few warehouses as the Company preferred

to transfer its high value goods to its own secure warehouses in the City. The large increase in traffic required the construction of a better road between the docks and the City. The East India Dock Road opened in 1827.

However, not long into the nineteenth century, competition between the individual dock companies and wharves started to reduce the business of the East India Dock Company. In 1833 the Government removed the East India Dock Company's monopoly on trade with India and later with China in the same year. The opportunity was quickly taken by the West India Company to offer to purchase the East India Company and the two were amalgamated in 1838 by an Act of Parliament, allowing trade from any source to use both dock systems.

Surrey Docks

South of the river the Commercial Dock Company commenced development around the old seventeenth-century Howland dock, later named Greenland, on

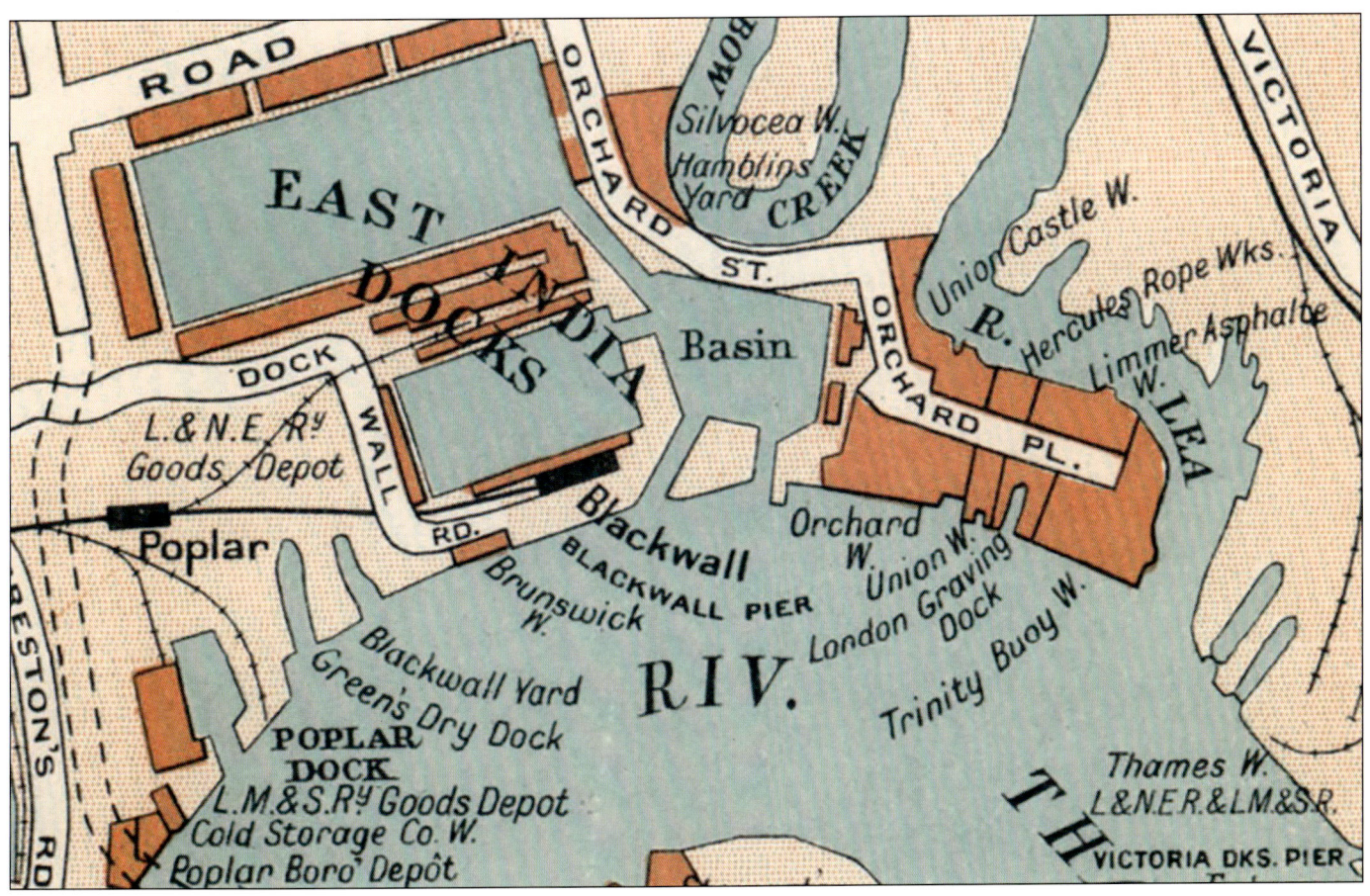

1.6: East India Docks.

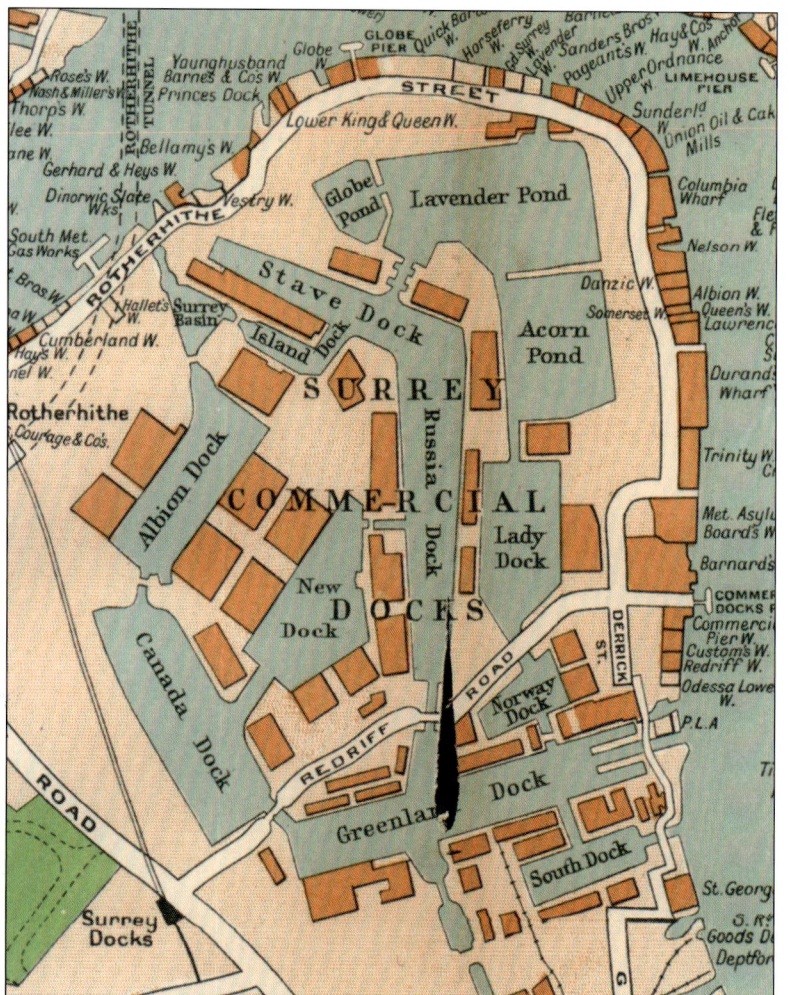

1.7: Surrey Docks.

directly loaded by crane. As the dock was built in an already developed part of the city, a large number of homes had to be demolished along with a church and a hospital. The relatively small St Katharine's Dock chiefly handled tea and wool but its success was short lived. Ships were getting larger and started to be powered by steam rather than wind and in view of their increasing size could no longer be accommodated.

Regent's Canal Basin

Further to the east, opened by the Regent's Canal Company in 1820, the basin was used by smaller seagoing vessels to offload goods onto canal barges for distribution across London and beyond via the nation's extensive canal network. The Regent's Canal running across North London was effectively a bypass to the crowded River Thames as well as serving numerous wharves along its length. The canal and basin were as important for goods in the opposite direction from the rest of the country, particularly coal from the Midlands for London's power stations. It was very successful until the railways took most of its trade away.

the Surrey peninsula, initially for 350 ships mainly importing timber and grain and later whale meat and oil. North of the peninsula the separate Surrey Dock Company built docks to accommodate a further 300 ships. The Surrey docks eventually grew in a fairly haphazard way to cover the major part of the peninsula by the end of the century. These had been created by a number of independent companies which gradually merged and in 1864 the Surrey Commercial Dock Company was formed. It embarked on a programme of linking the various basins, including opening a further basin in 1876 named Canada Dock.

St Katharine's Dock

The last dock to be constructed at the western end of the area was St Katharine's Dock, opened in 1828. Thomas Telford was the chief engineer, designing the dock to accommodate around 130 ships, surrounded by impressive warehouses into which goods could be

Millwall Dock

The overall increase in port activity and the success of the Victoria dock led to further proposals in the Isle of Dogs. In the late 1850s a new company, the Millwall Freehold Land & Dock Company, was formed to develop the southern part of the Isle of Dogs with plans for fifty-two acres of docks. Lack of finance dictated a cutback on the original proposal to thirty-six acres, which opened in 1868. The L-shaped basin connected to the Thames on the west side of the Isle. Spoil from the construction of the dock was deposited on the east side of the dock creating the aptly named area, Mudchute, now home to a city farm. The dock specialised in grain from the Baltic but also handled wool and timber and, as we will see later, was also served by rail. By the end of the century a connection was made into the West India Dock complex at its northern end.

1.8: Millwall Dock.

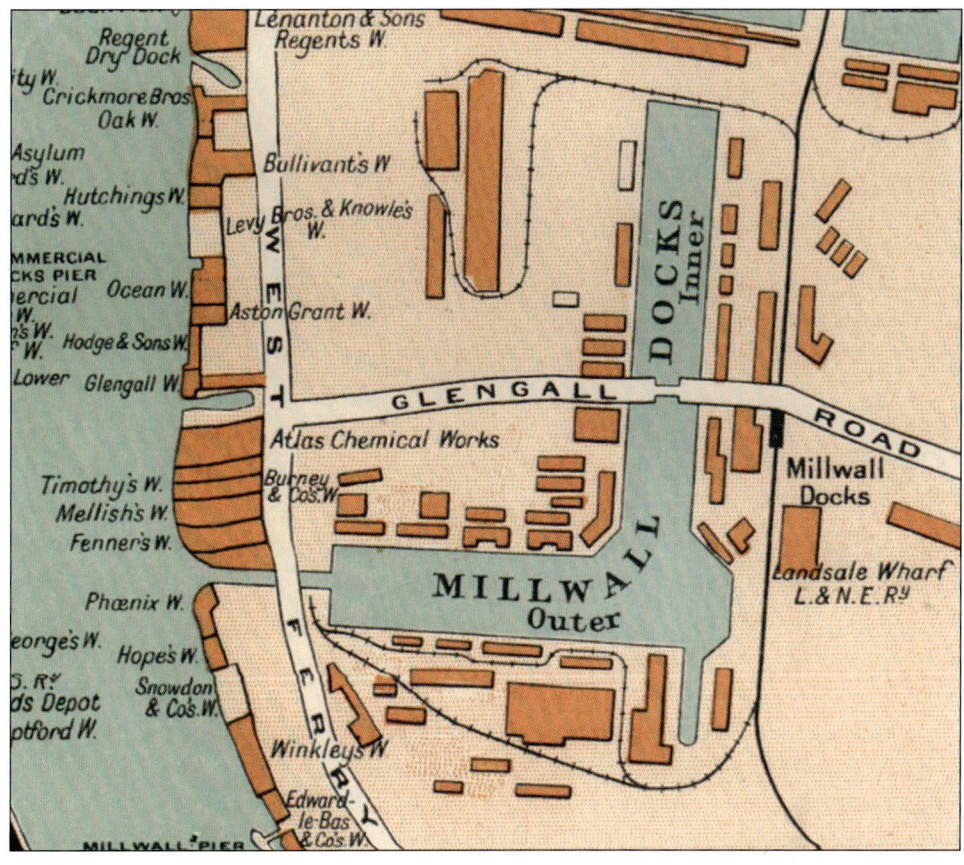

1.9: Glass bridge over Millwall Dock.

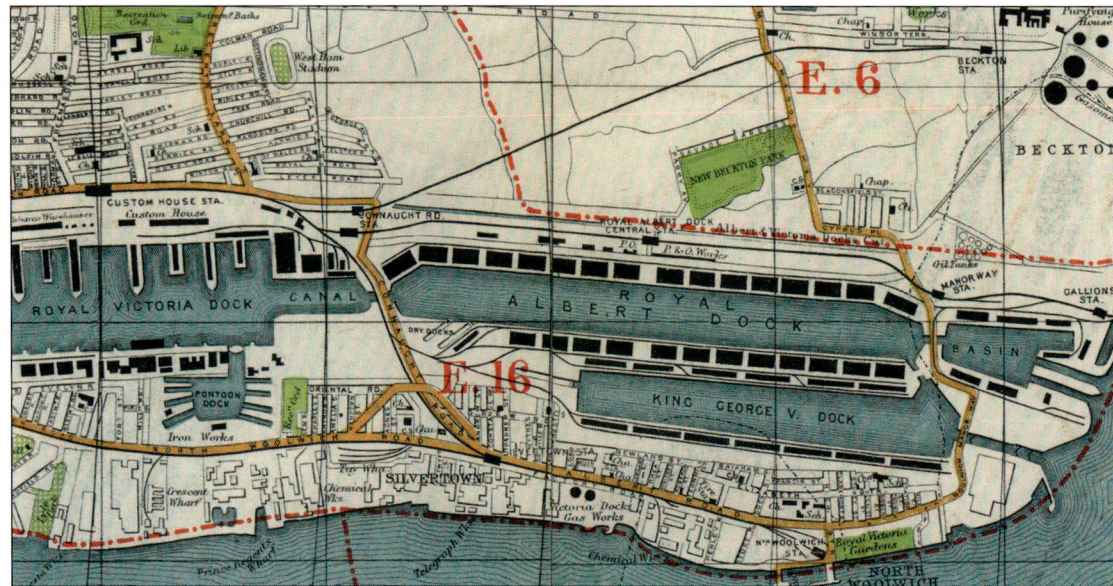

1.10 (left): Royal Docks.

1.11 (below): Royal Docks, c. 1960.

The Royal Docks

All the docks created in the early years of the nineteenth century were designed for sailing ships. From the mid-century onwards the introduction of larger steam driven vessels started to have an impact, but it was not until the 1880s that British-registered steam tonnage exceeded that of sail. Many of the new ships could not enter the old docks and there was little room for railways, which were fast becoming the preferred means of onward transport for goods.

By the middle of the nineteenth century the quays of the Pool of London, the London Docks and St Katharine's were having increasing difficulty in handling the larger ships and this precipitated the formation of a new company to investigate the construction of a new dock on an entirely different scale on the eastern fringe of London, later to be known as the Royal Docks. The Victoria Dock Company sought and obtained an Act of Parliament in 1850 to create a new enclosed dock to accommodate these larger vessels, with a much larger entrance lock and basin than its predecessors. The new Victoria Dock was to be built on marshland, around two miles to the east of the Isle of Dogs, and was the first dock to be linked to the rest of the country by railway.

The dock, opened by Prince Albert in 1855, was an immediate success and by 1866 was already handling double the trade of the London Docks.

Further Impacts

The success of the Victoria Dock further increased the problems for the small London and St Katharine's

Docks and the two agreed to merge in the 1870s. The St Katharine and London Dock Company saw the future in larger ships and went on to purchase the Victoria Dock and adjacent land. With increasing world trade the Company went on to build the adjoining Albert Dock, opened in 1879, which not only provided modern facilities for cargo but also for passengers as international travel was starting to take off. The Company also built railway stations and a hotel for passengers named the Gallions Hotel and provided fresh water supplies and lighting on the quays.

Not wishing to be outdone by the success of the now Royal Docks the East & West India Dock Company attempted to leapfrog the successful Royal Docks and invested in a new facility at Tilbury, another twenty miles downstream. It was not an immediate success as access to London was poor and it would be around seventy years before Tilbury Docks came into its own and was developed to become one of the largest container ports in the UK.

Towards the end of the nineteenth century the smaller enclosed docks were suffering from reduced trade and the East & West India Company was forced to close. Its long term rival, the St Katharine and London Dock Company, offered to buy out the East & West Company and in 1889 the London and East India Joint Committee was formed. The Millwall and Surrey Dock Companies also agreed to participate in discussions and agreement was reached in an attempt to reduce competition and the decline in trade.

The engineering of the early off-river enclosed docks, many concentrated in the short thirty-year period at the start of the nineteenth century, was a fine example of, and contributor to, our burgeoning Industrial Revolution. Engineers such as John Rennie, William Jessop and Thomas Telford, who had learned their skills on the building of our canals, had no problems with scaling up to the construction of the docks, locks and quays. Power from steam for keeping the docks full of water was readily available from Boulton and Watt and similar companies. Massive employment was created as most goods were manhandled to and from the ships into horse-drawn carts or river lighters, for distribution throughout London and later by train to the rest of the country.

The complexity of companies, monopolies and rivalries over the 100 years before the nationalisation of the docks in 1909, the often ruthless ship owners, the warfingers (quay owners), general hands, carriers and lightermen, created a highly volatile society not helped by the frequently appalling living conditions of East London. The 'call on' system where men were chosen, or not, for work by the foremen, up to three times a day, meant they had to live close to the docks. The enclosed nature of the docks meant that many women never saw the 'hidden world' where their husbands worked. For them it was often a hand-to-mouth existence.

The Port of London Authority Era

At the start of the twentieth century the docks were suffering from a lack of facilities for berthing and unloading ships, leading to lengthy delays and congestion. In 1890 the Government set up a Royal Commission to consider the problem. This concluded that there were too many docks of the wrong kind, a lack of coordination between the multitude of docks and no effective authority to manage the river. The port facilities were outdated because of lack of investment and the river was too shallow to allow modern ships to reach the upper docks. The recommendation, published in June 1902, was that a single public authority should be created to manage both the docks and the tidal river from Teddington down to the sea. The Government agreed and an Act of Parliament setting up the Port of London Authority (PLA) came into law in 1908.

The PLA brought some order to the struggling chaos and made significant investments in facilities. It set about removing some of the old company constraints on trade, dredged the river to enable the passage of larger ships and invested in new warehouses and storage, in particular the expansion of the Royal Albert Dock. The result was a significant rise in tonnage. Unfortunately the imminent war with Germany necessitated the requisition of many facilities by the Government and the PLA had to put a hold on investment until after the war was over.

The First World War took its toll on wharfs and quays throughout Docklands, as a result of zeppelin bombing, and also in taking the lives of many dock workers who had gone to fight in the trenches. However after the war, trade quickly returned and the PLA set about further investment, most notably the construction of the King George V dock, south of the Royal Albert Dock and opened in 1919, partly seen as a post-war job creation project. For the next twenty years the investments paid off with overall tonnage growing from 39 to 58m tons per annum despite the recession in the late 1920s.

The Second World War again saw the requisition of many warehouses by the Government and a halt to the further planned improvement works by the PLA. Once the air raids started it was clear that the docks were a prime target for bombing with the resulting massive destruction of docks, warehouses and ships, along with their cargoes. First there were planes, then the V1 flying bombs and V2 rockets, killing around 30,000 Londoners and leaving many parts of the docks totally destroyed.

After the war the PLA tried to restore key docks and facilities but it also had to contend with worsening labour relations, mainly over conditions of work and pay. The traditional 'call on' system where men were picked for work on a daily basis was a continuing contentious issue. The dispute in London spread, eventually affecting most of the major ports in the UK. There was also the rampant problem of 'wastage' or 'pilfering' from the docks which had been a tradition since medieval times. Injuries were common and the health of the workers was at a low ebb.

This combination of issues, coupled with the advent of secure cargo in containers in the 1950s, significantly hastened the demise of the traditional docks. First introduced for the American Army, containers brought with them not only larger ships but the requirement to have large 'back lands' for their storage and mechanisms for transferring the containers from the ships to waiting road or railway trucks. None of the existing docks had this capacity and the inevitable move downstream to Tilbury, starting in the mid-1960s, came much quicker than many expected.

The first casualties were the ancient wharves which lined the banks of the Thames in inner London. St Katharine's and the London Docks were closed in 1968 and most riverside wharfs by 1970. The Surrey Docks also closed in 1970 and the West India and East India Docks in 1975. The first plans for redevelopment of the area, becoming known as the 'London Docklands', produced in 1976, still assumed that part of the Royal Docks would remain operational. However the inexorable decline continued with the final closure of the remaining Royal Albert Dock in 1981. Over the ten years from 1966 to 1976 more than 150,000 jobs had been lost in East London resulting in increasing hardship, deprivation and increasing poverty for the people of the area.

Initially the docks were served by horse and cart and river lighters but from the 1850s onwards, for well over 100 years, the major docks were served by railways, enabling the much wider collection and distribution of goods. The next chapter looks at this first development of the docks' rail network and the legacy this would leave us to later exploit.

1.12: Tilbury Docks.

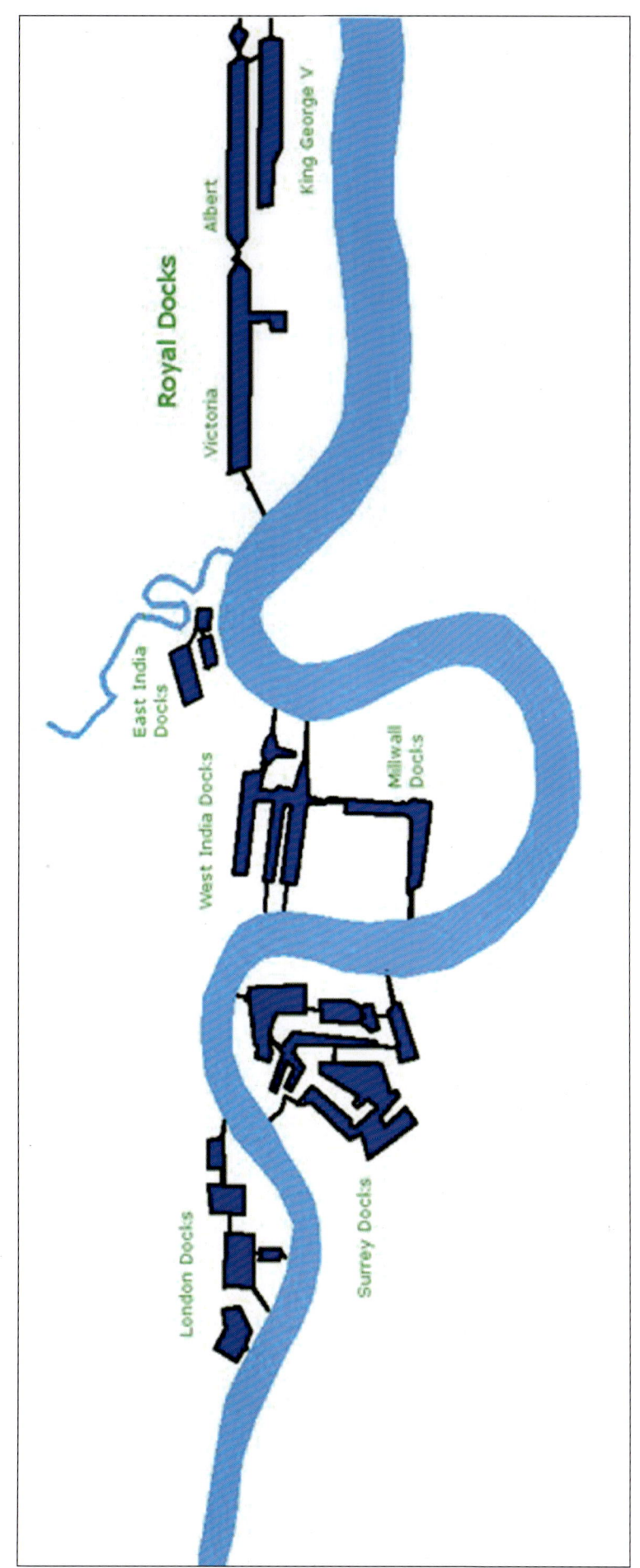

1.13: London Docks c. 1900.

CHAPTER 2

RAILWAYS TO SERVE THE WORKING DOCKS (1840–1970)

In 1970 three of the railways on my 1950s OS map were still operational – the freight only line from Victoria Park to Poplar, LT's East London line and the very isolated British Rail (BR) passenger line from Stratford to North Woolwich. I remember standing on the remains of the platform of Millwall Junction station at the head of the Isle of Dogs, surrounded by rusting freight lines and a plethora of wagons.

Later, when walking along part of the old Limehouse viaduct, I was reminded that 130 years earlier this had carried the 1840 cable-hauled railway in which Stephenson was involved. The viaduct had not been used for thirty years and the substantial buddleia bushes and nettles had firmly taken control. The viaduct gave a good view of prominent local buildings including Hawksmoor's, St Anne's Church, Limehouse and the pressure tower of the hydraulic main system formerly used to power the cranes and lock gates of the docks.

Railways have played a crucial role in supporting the economy of Docklands in both the earlier and recent periods of development. The year 1840 saw the first railway supporting the trading docks with progressive and extensive expansion from the mid-nineteenth century until the demise of the enclosed docks some 130 years later. New twentieth and twenty-first century railways, often using the rights of way of the original services, have supported Docklands in its new role as a major centre for new homes and offices, with many banks and financial businesses also trading with the world but in a rather different format. This chapter provides a summary of the principal railways constructed to serve the docks over the period 1840 to their effective closure in 1970.

The London and Blackwall Railway

The London and Blackwall Railway (L&BR) was not the first in London. That honour fell to the London and Greenwich Railway (L&GR) opened between 1836 and 1838. At the start of the intense rush to build railways everywhere throughout the UK, the L&BR obtained permission to start construction in 1836. Like all railways, until the advent of the Transport and Works Act in 1992, a Private Members Bill had to be submitted to Parliament, which, after due consideration, hopefully obtained Royal Assent of the Act, in other words it was

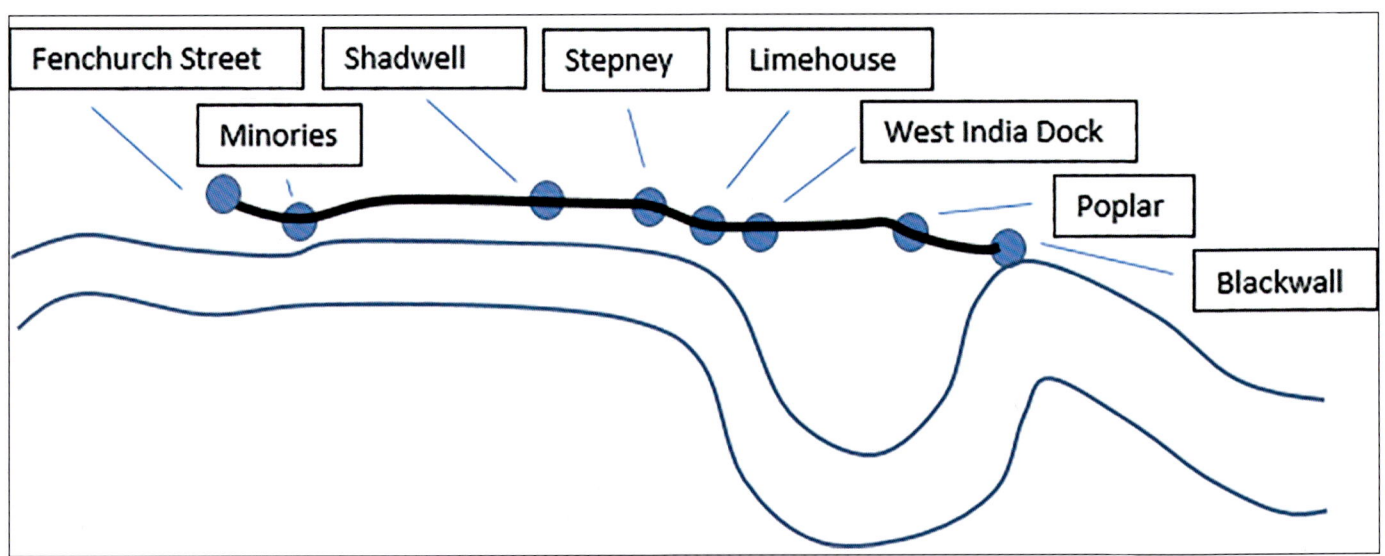

2.1: London and Blackwall Railway.

2.2: Cabled-hauled London and Blackwall train.

'signed off' by the reigning monarch. The Act, most importantly, gave the railway company powers to compulsory purchase rights over land and property but significantly not for land speculation.

The London and Blackwall Bill of 1839 was presented to the House of Lords with the debate focusing on a number of objections to the original proposal which had a terminus within the City walls.

During its passage through Parliament, Lord Ashburton objected to the Bill. According to John Christopher (Ref 2.1), he stated:

Because the railway would come into the very heart of the metropolis, and if that were allowed in this case, there was no reason why the termini of other railroads, such as the Birmingham Railway, should not also have the same permission.

He further considered:

That it was not merely particular parties who would be injured, but the whole neighbourhood would be affected by the railway, in consequence of the rattling

of the carriages upon the arches, whether moved by steam or anything else. All railways should have their termini at the skirts of the metropolis, for otherwise a great general nuisance might be committed to persons in the city, although they might not be able to produce evidence of any specific injury.

The Bishop of London stated (Ref. 2.1):

That under no circumstances, would he give his assent to bringing a railway into the heart of the metropolis. The proposed terminus of the Blackwall Railway was equidistant from three churches, and the collection of many thousands of persons on a Sunday at this terminus, together with the noise of the carriages, would prove a serious interference with the decency of divine service.[1]

However Lord Ellenborough, the proposer of the Bill, responded (Ref. 2.1):

The railway for which the bill on the Table was wanted, was not a railway on which it was proposed to work

2.3: West India Dock station.

machines by means of steam; and he understood that the company were prepared to introduce a clause prohibiting the use of steam or locomotive machines on it. It was to be a railway on a viaduct, supported by arches; and along its side there was to be a pathway for foot passengers, so that it would add to the communications of the metropolis, instead of restricting them.

Interestingly, after only one year of operation and in spite of these objections, the promoters did obtain permission to extend the railway from its initial terminus at Minories, just outside the City boundary, to Fenchurch Street, a few hundred yards within the City walls. However the petitioners' requirements would set precedents for most railways entering the capital. Much to the annoyance of the railway companies they all had to settle for termini on the edge of the central area.

The railway, initially called the Commercial Railway, opened in 1840 to a curious design in which both the illustrious engineers Robert Stephenson and John Rennie were involved. It ran from Minories, just east of the City, to Blackwall, some three and a half miles downstream. The trains were cabled-hauled by means of a seven-mile long five-inch diameter hemp cable (later metal as rats enjoyed eating the hemp), driven by a steam engine at either end. The carriages were gripped to the rope by a member of staff on each car operating a lever, in a similar manner to the San Francisco cable cars. The men would release the rear carriages one by one at the intermediate stations and on the return journey they would be successively added to the train. This made travel between intermediate stations somewhat tortuous requiring a journey to the

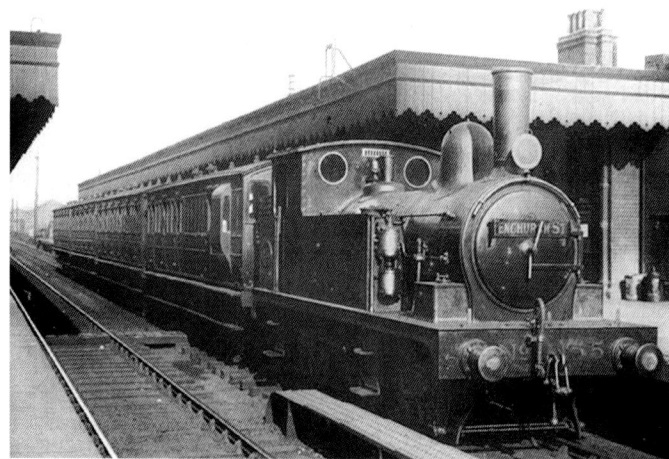

2.4 • Leman Street station.

end of the line and then back. An electrical signal was used to inform the engine drivers to reverse the cable. This is believed to be one of the first times electricity had been used for the signalling of trains.

The railway opened with six intermediate stations at Minories, Shadwell, Stepney, Limehouse, West India Dock and Poplar with cable hauling lasting until 1849 when steam trains took over. Initially only carrying passengers, the railway was very popular, carrying workers to and from the docks and leisure passengers to meet the river steamers at Blackwall Quay running to Southend and Margate. Around 9,000 people travelled each day.[2] Ten years after opening, the London and Blackwall line was joined to the growing East London railway network with an eastern extension to Bow and extended with a number of freight yards on short branches clustered around the fringe of the City near Minories. An additional station at Leman Street was opened in 1877.

By the start of the twentieth century passenger numbers were in decline following the rapid development of London's bus network. Closure was proposed in 1926 around the time of a general strike which was effectively the nail in the coffin for the passenger service. However freight continued to use the line via the Stepney East connection until 1951, after which trains ran via Limehouse Junction until 1963.

The Millwall Extension

In 1863 the L&BR sought permission for a railway into the Isle of Dogs, across the western entrances of the West India Docks, employing engineer George Berkeley. However the project was opposed by the dock company and rejected by Parliament because of its impact on the working docks. When, a few years later, the proposals were bought forward to construct the Millwall Docks, the railway project was resurrected by the Great Eastern Railway Company, which in 1864 had taken over control of the proposal. The company had to tailor the project to suit the dock company, agreeing either to build a tunnel under the docks or a line on the east side, with the right

2.5: Millwall Extension Railway.

2.6: Millwall Junction station.

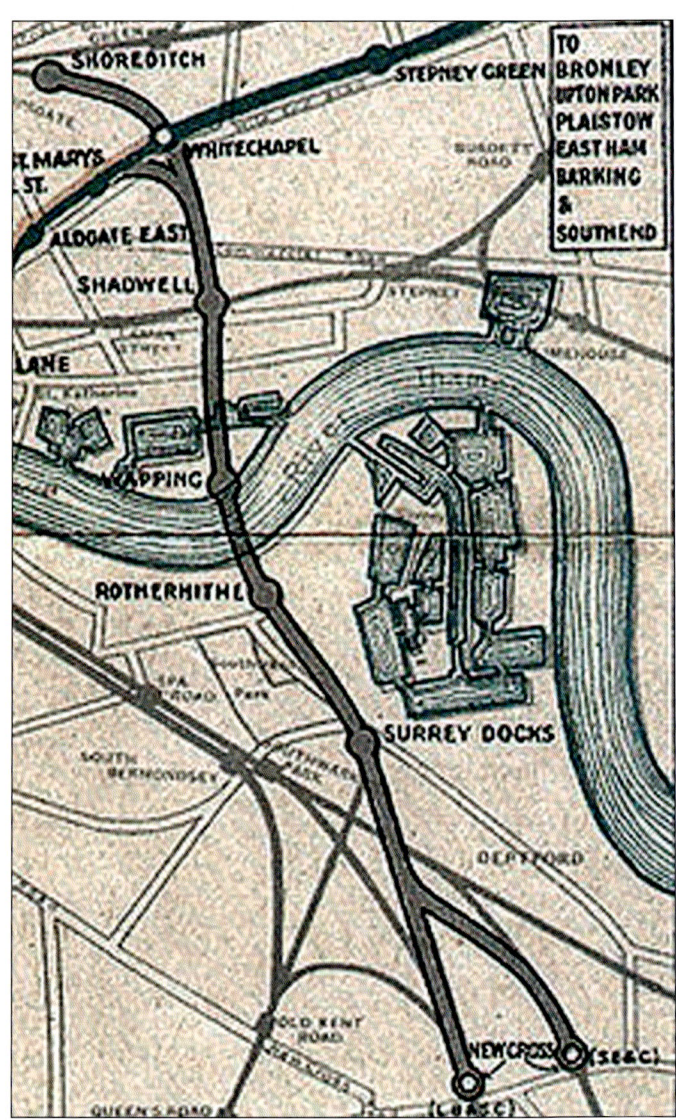

2.7: East London line.

to exclude passengers and locomotives to reduce the risk of fire.

Financing of the railway proved difficult and the rebuilding of the West India South dock in 1867 made the tunnel option impractical. Construction did not start until 1868 when it was agreed that the Great Eastern Company would build the northern section and the Millwall Dock Company the southern section on an eastern alignment involving swing bridges across the dock entrances. Initially the railway was for a single line branch from a junction with the existing railway at Millwall Junction, between Stepney and Limehouse stations, with horses pulling wagons through the West India Dock area. It was not until 1880 that locomotives were used but ownership of the line remained divided. Stations were built to serve South Dock and on the southern section at Millwall Dock and North Greenwich. As with the later North Woolwich station, although on the north side of the river their names were obviously chosen to emphasise the proximity to their respective towns, albeit via a ferry.

Both freight and passenger trains used the line. Passenger services ran every half an hour or more, taking only nine minutes to run from Millwall Junction station to North Greenwich, mostly carrying dock workers. Numerous freight services also ran from the docks to the City rail yards around Minories. At the foot of the Isle of Dogs, the ferry service across the Thames, which was operated by the railway company, lasted until the start of the twentieth century when the London County Council (LCC) constructed the Greenwich foot

tunnel from close to the North Greenwich station under the Thames, near to the future resting place of the *Cutty Sark*. The general strike in 1926 saw closure of the passenger service on the line but freight was retained as far as Millwall Dock until 1966.

The East London Line

The East London line was initially designed and built for use by main line trains. It was then used for many years as part of London Underground (LU) and more recently converted back to a main line as part of the London Overground in 2007.

The tunnel under the Thames, notable as the first tunnel under a tidal river, was started in 1825 by Marc Brunel – father of the more famous Isambard Kingdom

Brunel. Although built for trains the tunnel was initially to be used by road traffic, with spiral ramps descending from the surface at either end. Severe problems were encountered during its construction including several inundations of the river and fatalities.

The tunnel finally opened in 1843 as a pedestrian tunnel. However twenty-two years later, in 1865, the East London Railway purchased it to form part of an underground rail link running connecting services across the river, including services from Liverpool Street to as far as Brighton. Over the coming years it was used by a few through-running passenger services, some to Hammersmith, but seen mainly as a cross river route for freight services. On nationalisation LT took over ownership of the line and ran passenger services from Shoreditch to New Cross and New Cross Gate.

2.8 (left): The Thames tunnel.

2.9 (below): Shoreditch station.

2.10: Broad Street station.

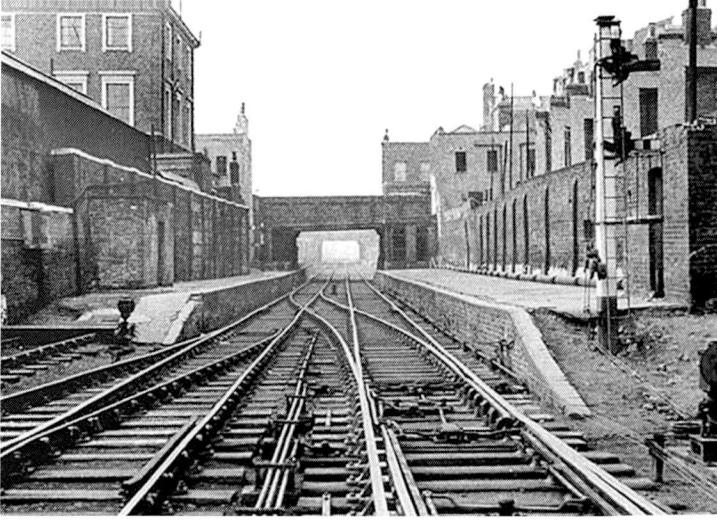

2.12: Poplar station.

The North London Line

The North London line had its origins in the London and Birmingham Railway (also the L&BR) which wanted to connect its growing network with the docks. In 1846 the London and Birmingham obtained permission for a new line running from Camden Town to Poplar via Dalston and Hackney which opened in 1852, initially only for freight. By 1866 it had developed into a frequent and popular passenger service, with an extension in 1870 at its southern end to Blackwall to also link with the pleasure steamers. With its good connection into the main UK rail network it carried substantial freight to and from the docks and also coal in the reverse direction from the Midlands to London.

In 1854, with the line now owned by the London and North Western Railway (LNWR), the company linked the line to Stratford. In 1865 a branch was built from Dalston into a new City station at Broad Street, allowing services to run from Poplar to the City. Broad Street was also used for North London line services to Richmond and Watford, and in the earliest part of the twentieth century was one of London's busiest stations as well as being a major goods terminal.

The line to Poplar was heavily damaged in the Second World War and was closed to passenger services in 1944 but remained open for freight servicing Polar Dock until 1966. The line to Richmond had been electrified and survived Dr Beeching's proposed closure in the 1960s. As we will see in the

2.11: Bow station.

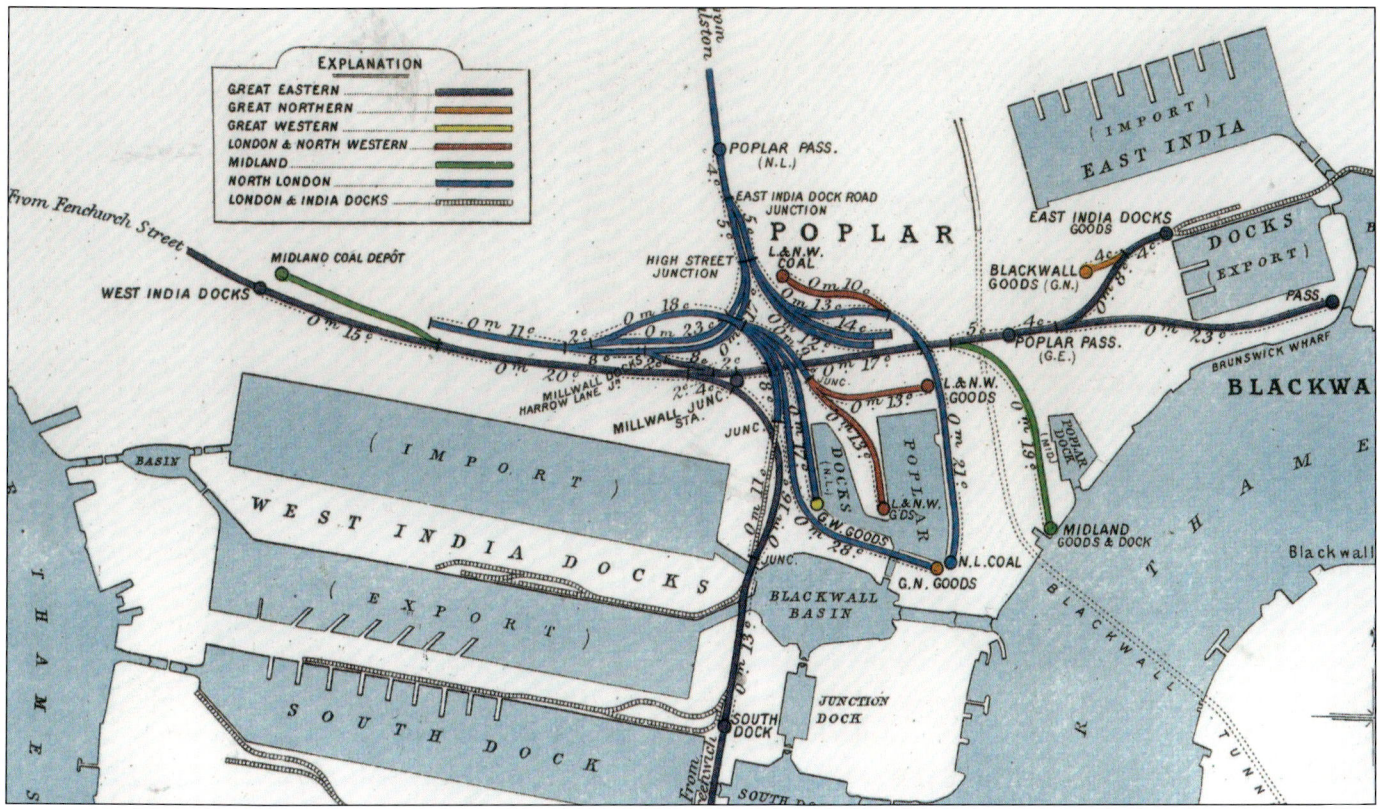

2.13: Poplar area railways, 1914.

next chapter the closure of Broad Street station, adjacent to Liverpool Street, and the diversion of its remaining services in 1986, signified the end of the decline of railways in East London and the start of their revival.

The North Woolwich Line

The third major rail connection to the docks was at the eastern end, with a line running from Stratford to North Woolwich opened in 1846 for freight as far as Thames Wharf. It had intermediate stations at Stratford Market and Canning Town and was built in anticipation of the opening of Victoria Dock, the first of London's docks to be planned around railway access rather than the tracks being added later. There was also a connection across Bow Creek to serve the East India Docks. The line was extended to North Woolwich, initially running south of the Victoria Dock along a route later known as the Silvertown Tramway. This required the crossing of a swing bridge at the entrance to the Victoria Dock so an alternative route via the northern side was opened in 1855 with a new station at Custom House. With the connection from Stratford to the North London line at Victoria Park, the line soon became the main means of taking goods to and from the developing docks.

The Albert Dock opened in 1880, linked to the Victoria Dock thus necessitating a swing bridge to carry the railway and a road across the connection between the two docks. To avoid the disruption to both railway and shipping, in 1878 the 600-yard long Connaught rail tunnel was constructed under the link.

There were two branches of the railway. The first to Beckton Gas Works, which opened in 1870 and was

2.14: North Woolwich.

2.15: Gallions Hotel.

2.16: PLA freight train.

served by a two-mile railway connection to Custom House, opened in 1873. It carried coal and for a short time around the end of the century, workers and passengers. Within the works was a complex layout of lines at two different levels to serve the gas producing plants. The line was officially closed in 1971 following closure of the works and the end of gas production from coal. The derelict site was famously used in the films *Full Metal Jacket* and *For Your Eyes Only*.

The Gallions branch also ran from Custom House along the north side of the docks to the Gallions Hotel, opened in 1881 for passengers awaiting the steamers in the adjoining dock. Through trains ran to Fenchurch Street station in the City. Although less than two miles in length the branch had intermediate stations at Central and Manor Way.

Port of London Authority Railways

The creation of the PLA in 1909 saw the transfer of the remaining dock railways to the new authority. It was an extensive railway system with around seventy miles of track, steam and later diesel locomotives, engine sheds, and its own signal boxes and level crossings. At the height of trade in the 1950s some fifty goods trains a day were serving the Royal Docks and at its peak the network carried nearly a million passengers a year, including services at Tilbury.

After the First World War most of the passenger services to the London based docks had ceased, leaving only the line from Stratford to North Woolwich operational. When the PLA decided to deepen the Royal docks to accommodate larger shipping it needed to increase the depth of water above the Connaught tunnel. To achieve

this the tunnel was lined with cast steel segments and the brickwork surrounding the tunnel removed.[3] The surface swing bridge was kept operational as a diversionary route until the 1960s. Freight services remained on the Bow to Poplar line until 1984 and passenger services to North Woolwich until 2006.

More information on the former railways of Docklands is available on the excellent website 'Disused Stations' (www.disused-stations.org.uk).

Trams to the Docks

The other rail-based transport system serving the docks was the tram network. The 1870 Tramways Act allowed local authorities to purchase privately owned tram services and by 1899 most of London's horse-drawn trams were owned and operated by the LCC. By 1915 all were run on electricity with LT taking responsibility in 1933 and power provided by Greenwich power station.[4]

A number of routes served the docks both north and south of the river with two routes penetrating the dock complexes – Route 47 in the London Docks and Route 77 in the West India Docks. All London's original trams had been withdrawn by 1952.[5]

As we will see in the following chapters, the many miles of redundant industrial railway left by the PLA have proved to be an invaluable asset in the regeneration of Docklands. Without these rights of way, which fortunately remained in public ownership, it would have proved far more difficult to provide a low cost transport solution to support the initial regeneration process. The outcome for the area would most probably have been very different.

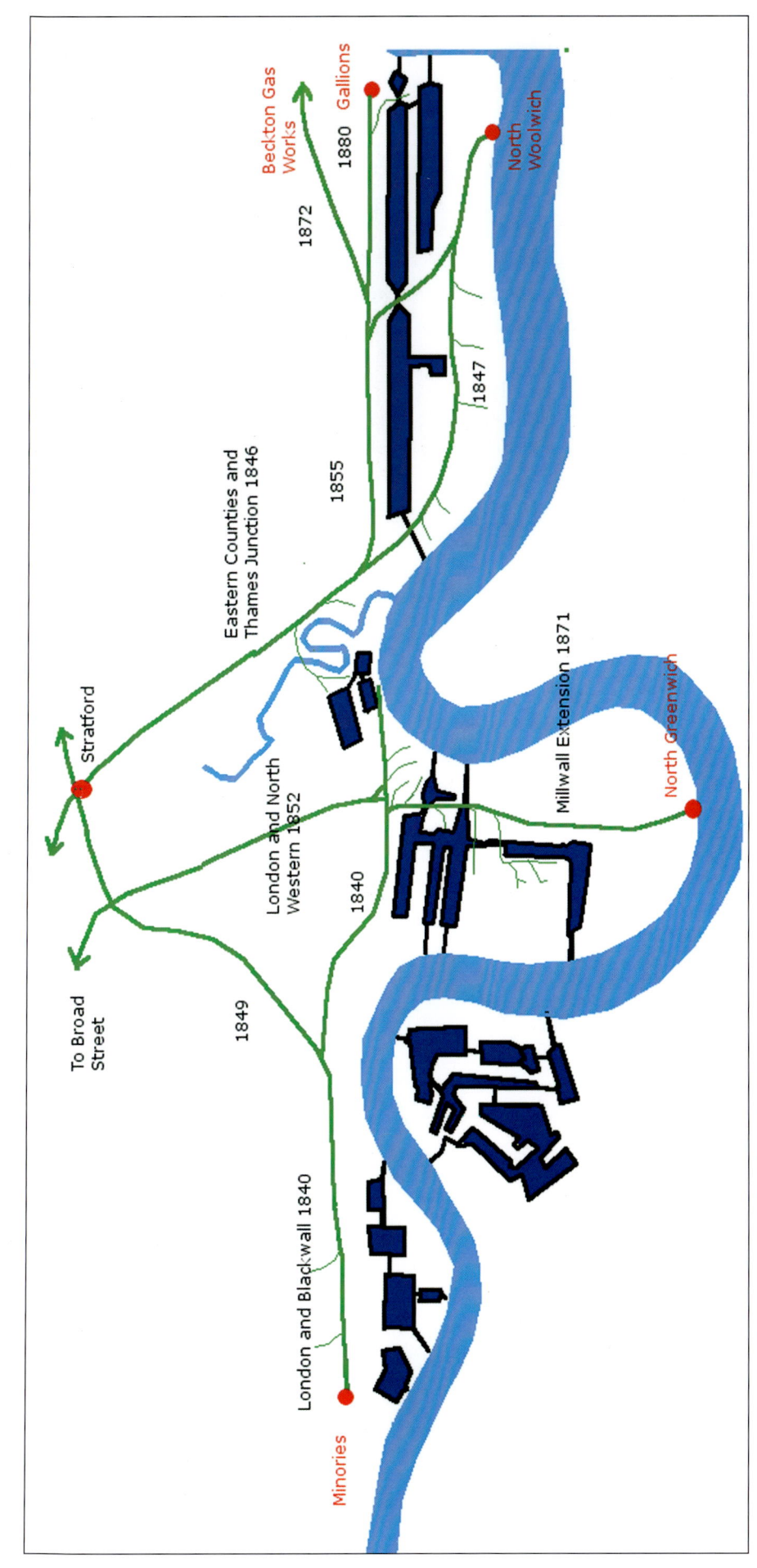

2.17: Dock railways and opening dates.

CHAPTER 3

EARLY PLANS AND PROPOSALS

My first involvement in the development and evaluation of possible transport solutions was a contribution to *The Docklands Spine* report of 1976. The GLC had set up the Docklands Joint Committee (DJC) to try to reach agreement with the five local boroughs and needed to include the transport proposals in the 1976 Strategic Plan. LT had already done some work on light rail options and these were compared against bus options and six alternatives for an Underground extension. It was my first serious foray into the esoteric world of transport computer modelling and cost-benefit analysis. It was also my first experience of the prerogative of politicians to not always accept the results of a professional analysis.

London's Post-war Developments

However, the first official proposals for bringing new railways to East London emerged much earlier as part of the plans for post-Second World War reconstruction and development. A plan was published for the administrative County of London in 1943 that made limited references to the need to improve railways (Ref. 3.1).

3.1: 1946 Rail Plan.

Whilst the plan contained some tentative proposals including a new Underground link between Waterloo, London Bridge and Surrey Docks, part of the future route of the Jubilee Line extension, the main recommendation was that there should be a separate investigation into London's railway requirements. This suggestion was taken up by the Ministry of War Transport which was then responsible for London's railways and proposals for improvements were published in 1946 (Ref. 3.2).

These plans contained a variety of new railway lines, including an Underground line from the north-east to the south-east of London that, for most of its length under the central area, followed an alignment later to be adopted by the Fleet line proposal. Priority, however, was given to a new route from the north-east to the south-west, which became the Victoria Line, opened in 1968.

Once the Victoria line was under construction, attention turned to other possibilities. In 1965

A Railway Plan for London was prepared by a Working Party for the LT Board and the BR Board (Ref. 3.3). The report was concerned with increasing capacity to meet expected future demand. The introduction to the report stated:

> It is of at least equal importance that transport factors should influence the basic planning decisions on land use and the location of population and employment which will determine the scale and pattern of the future commuter demand.

Underground proposals in the report included the extension of the Victoria Line from Victoria to Brixton and an extension of the Piccadilly Line shuttle between Holborn and Aldwych (closed in 1994) to Waterloo. But the major project, costing £57m out of a £100m package of improvements, was for a new line from Baker Street to New Cross and Lewisham – to be called after the long buried river it roughly

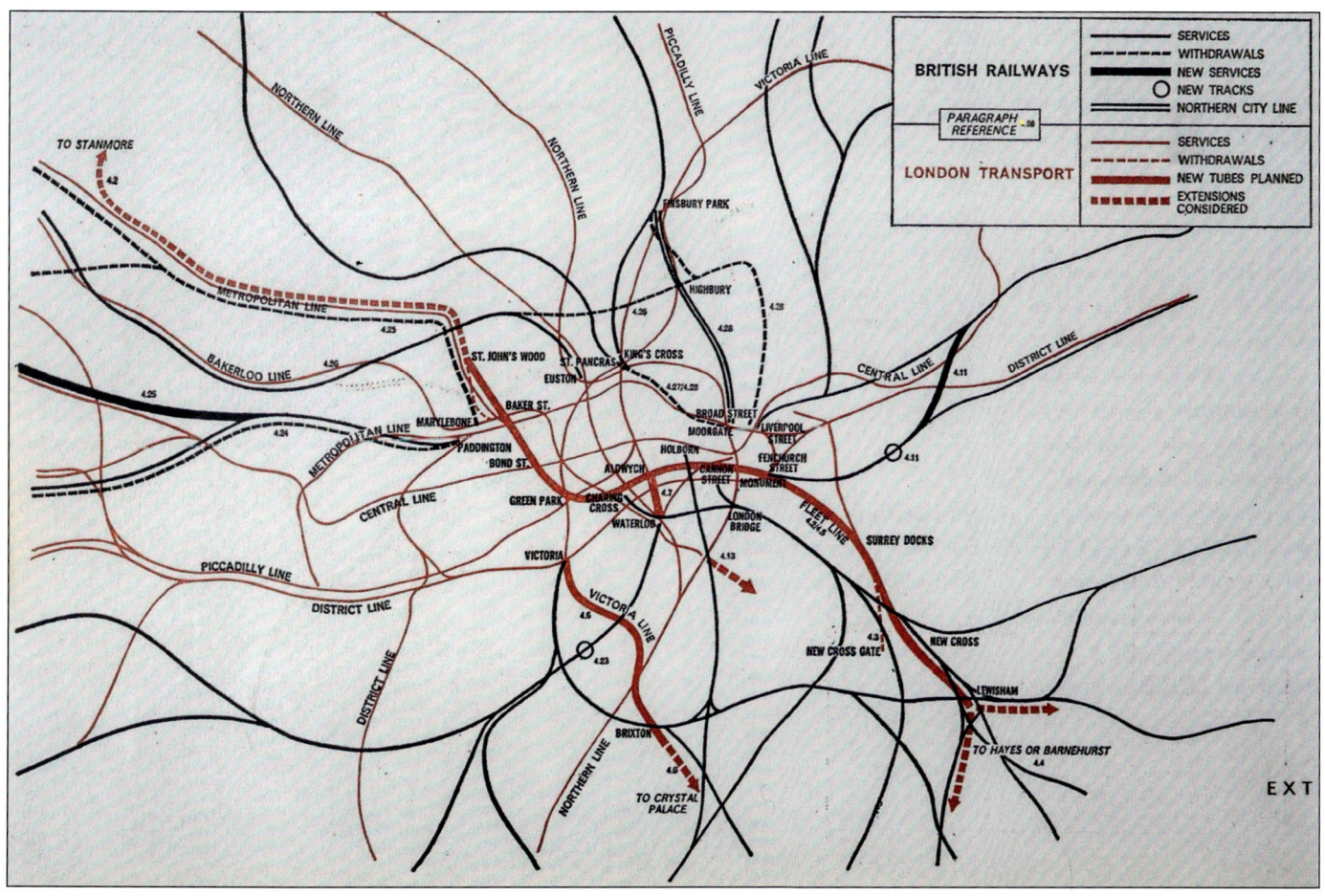

3.2: 1965 Rail Plan.

followed – the Fleet line. The report stated that the new line would:

Relieve the Bakerloo Line and contribute to the relief of the Central Line and the District Line; relieve the hard pressed South-Eastern Division of the Southern Region by taking over a branch line, and releasing capacity at the London Bridge bottleneck and assist in distributing and collecting commuter traffic via subway interchange facilities at Charing Cross and Fenchurch Street terminal.

The Fleet line was to be constructed in four stages. Stage 1 would take over the Stanmore branch of the Bakerloo Line, diverting from it at Baker Street along a new alignment to Charing Cross. Stage 2 would extend from Charing Cross to the only main line terminus not on the Underground at Fenchurch Street. Stage 3 would run via the East London line to Surrey Docks, take over the New Cross branch and then terminate at the BR station at Lewisham. A possible further Stage 4 was an extension to Hayes and Addiscombe over BR tracks.

The final economic evaluation of the Fleet line was carried out by LT (Ref. 3.4) and produced a benefit to cost ratio of 0.9 to 1.0, by coincidence almost exactly the same figure for the Jubilee Line extension at its time of approval. Various quantified and unquantified additional benefits, not included in the main analysis, were put forward to back the case for investment. These included the use of a higher value of leisure time, and the wider values of: 'sustaining the dynamic role of Central London', promoting development, and allowing higher density development around stations to help solve London's housing problems and the increase in land values.

Parliamentary powers were granted for construction of the Baker Street to Charing Cross section of the Fleet line in 1969 with work getting underway two years later. In 1977 the line was renamed the Jubilee Line to mark twenty-five years of the reign of HM Queen Elizabeth II. Funding for the works was split between the Government and the GLC and the first stage opened for passenger service on 1 May 1979.

The new line took over the Stanmore branch of the Bakerloo Line and a new depot was built at Stonebridge Park. At Baker Street a new station tunnel was constructed to allow cross-platform interchange with the Bakerloo Line. The line then ran to Green Park with an interchange with the Central Line. At Charing Cross the opportunity was taken to link the former Strand (Northern Line) and Trafalgar Square (Bakerloo Line) stations into a single complex, together with the new Jubilee Line station and rename it Charing Cross. The former Charing Cross station was renamed Embankment.

At the time of its approval it was assumed that progress on Stage 2 of the Fleet line to the City would

3.3: Charing Cross Jubilee Line station.

3.4: The first Jubilee Line train.

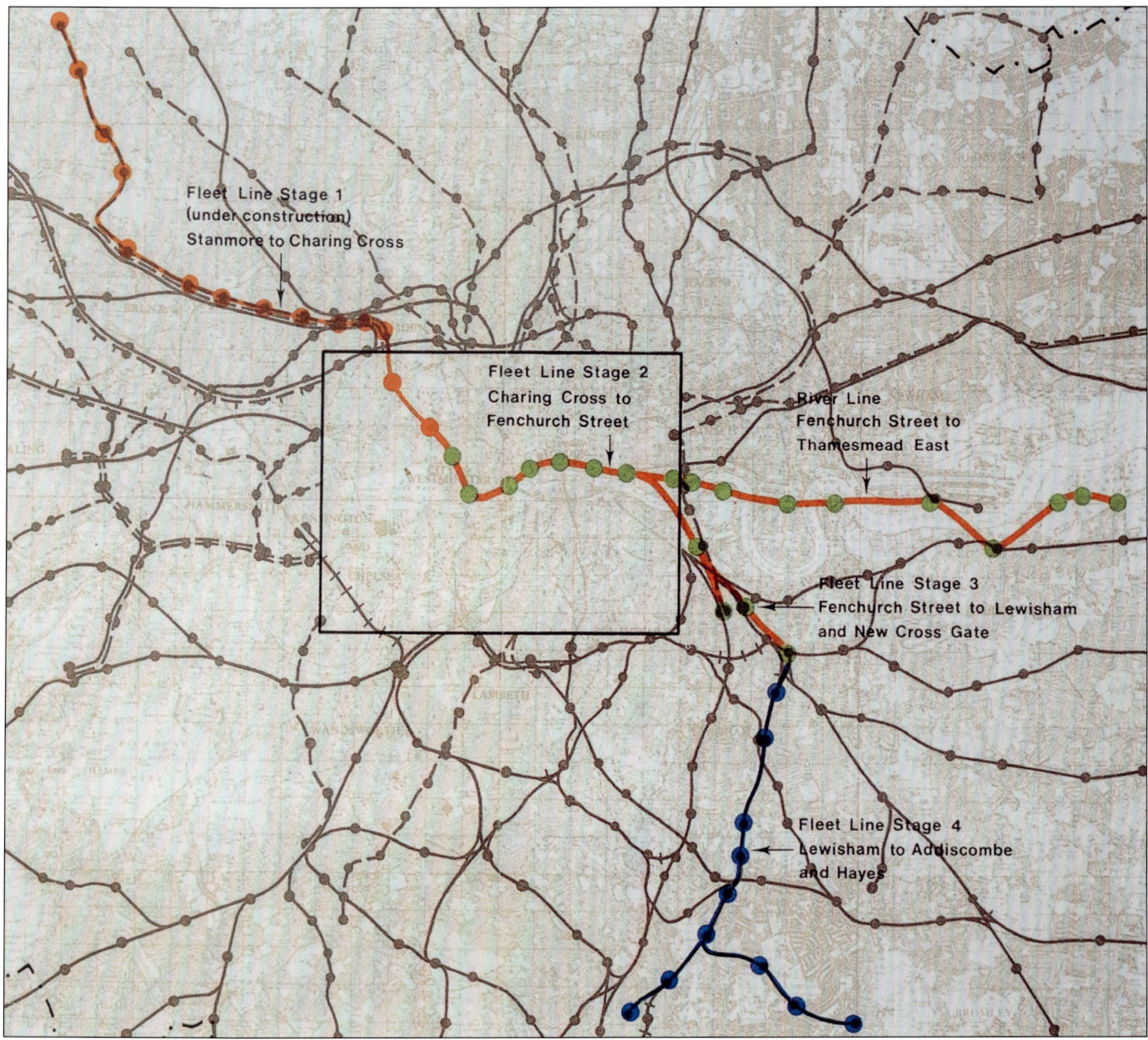

3.5: The Fleet line proposal.

quickly follow on, but Government funding was not forthcoming. However, Parliamentary approval for Stage 2 was obtained by LT with GLC support in 1971 and by 1975 a significant amount of money was being spent on safeguarding the line through the City. This was just the time when deep-piled foundations for new office blocks were becoming the norm and it was essential to preserve an Underground route. By 1980 the amount spent on safeguarding had risen to £10m. Works included partial construction of the ticket halls at Fenchurch Street and Ludgate Circus and a major

structural change to the design of Bush House adjacent to Cannon Street station. The cost of obtaining the powers and safeguarding the line were high and the expenditure was to prove abortive.

Docklands Regeneration – the Beginning

Other than to take over part of the East London line through Surrey Docks, serving Docklands was not seen as a major function of the Fleet line. In the early 1960s the East and West India Docks and Millwall Docks were still functioning largely as they had done for well over a century. The Royal Docks complex had been completed only forty years previously and was seen as having a useful life for many years to come. However redevelopment of some areas had started. The interesting buildings around St Katharine's Dock were being preserved and the London Docks were being filled to enable new housing, former water areas not yet being seen as attractive features.

On a larger scale most of the former Surrey Docks south of the river were also filled, initially as a landfill site, with many ideas but no firm proposals for what kind of development should take place. An international 'Trade Mart' was favoured and proposals reached an advanced stage, but the GLC was also considering siting the London terminal of the proposed Channel Tunnel rail link in the area, one of several possible sites in East London.

In 1973, in an attempt to encourage progress, LT commissioned a report into the potential impact on land use and development south of the river of the proposed Stage 3 of the Fleet line (Ref. 3.5). It claimed the report was: 'One of the first post-war attempts to use public transport as a framework for the development of a sector of London'.

The report concluded that the Fleet line would affect the study area in a number of ways including that: 'It would be a catalyst for substantial intensification of land use' and 'It should open up this neglected sector of London through provision of greater accessibility to and from central London'. The authors believed the potential for the area could only be fully realised if 'The process of land use and public transport are conceived as a whole, and that the phasing of the line

3.6: St Katharine's Dock.

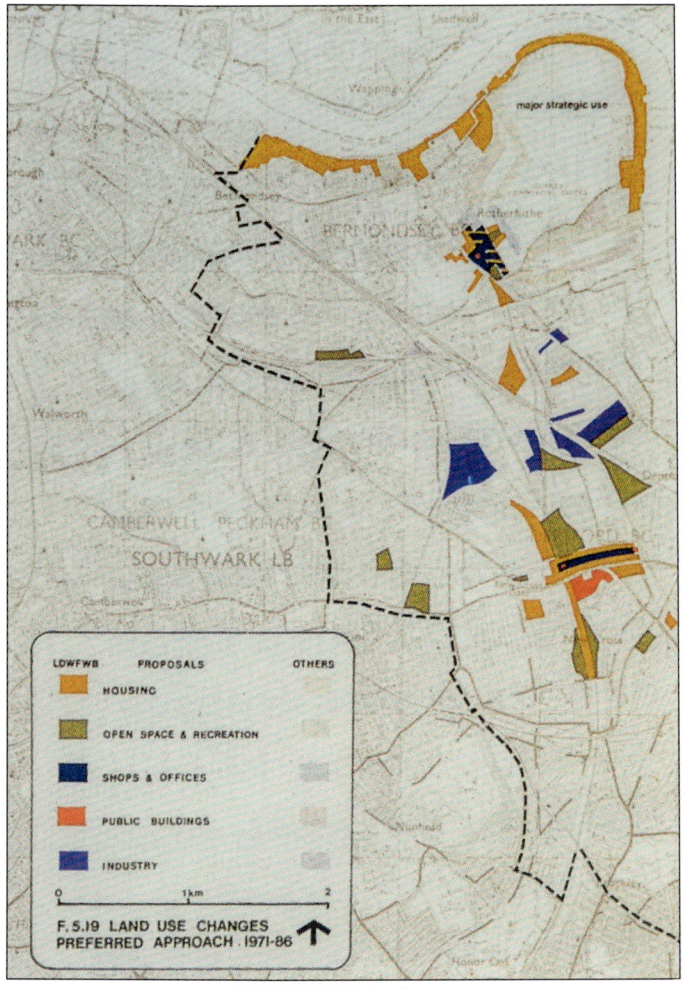

3.7: Fleet line land use assessment.

construction and redevelopment are similarly closely co-ordinated'.

Until this time the majority of Docklands was not seen as an area requiring better public transport, in particular new rail access. As we have seen, the former docks had an extensive rail network and some passenger services, but traditionally the majority of people who worked there lived locally and walked, cycled or used the bus or tram. In the late 1950s some of the highest bus passenger flows in London were seen on routes serving the docks. There was little longer-distance commuting and certainly no need to provide better connections to Central London. The area was self-contained and there was little reason for anyone not connected with the port activities to travel to the area – indeed they were positively discouraged by high walls and heavy security.

However, by the early 1970s it was realised that even the large traditional docks might only have a limited

future. In 1967 the casual employment of dock workers ceased but very poor industrial relations remained. Other factors were at work – containerisation was the new technology, bringing much faster loading and largely eliminating theft, which had been prevalent in the docks since their creation. But containerisation needed extensive 'back lands' and good rail or road access which the traditional docks lacked. There was growing competition from Rotterdam's Europoort. Ships were getting larger and it was no longer economical to bring them far up the Thames, even if they could fit into the nineteenth-century docks. London's shipping activities were fast transferring to Tilbury and although initially it was thought some trade would continue in the Royal Docks, vast areas were rapidly becoming wastelands. Thoughts were starting to be given to the future of this eight and half square miles of potential development land, physically close, but very inaccessible to the centre of London.

First Plans

In 1973 the Department of the Environment (DoE) and the GLC commissioned a report from consultants Travers Morgan with the title *Docklands Redevelopment Proposals for East London* (Ref.3.6). The emphasis, particularly from the local boroughs, was on retaining as much as possible of the traditional employment and river-related activities. Where new areas became available, housing, mostly to be constructed by the local authorities, was proposed. Improved transport access was seen only as a secondary issue.

The report suggested a broad range of land use options from a traditional employment/residential/open space scenario, to one which included major new commercial offices/recreational and 'people draw' uses. Demand for public transport was seen as rising to a maximum of 9,000 work trips an hour – well below that which might justify a new Underground line. The consultants did however propose a low cost 'minitram' system – small automatic electric trams carrying fourteen to twenty people – crossing the Thames twice and interchanging with the assumed Fleet line Stage 2 at Fenchurch Street. Extensions to Barking and Thamesmead were also suggested. The proposals were not popular with everyone as a separate system unconnected from the Underground and using new unproven technology would be needed.

3.8: GEC minitram.

The report was in the mould of the 1960s comprehensive land use and transport planning prevalent at the time, but there was a growing body of opinion against such ideas which many felt paid little regard to the needs and wishes of the indigenous population. The strongest reaction was from the Dockland's boroughs who felt that the people of the area should have been consulted. They wanted a plan which was more sympathetic to the residents and respecting of the strong traditions of the area.

The London Rail Study

In parallel with the growing interest in Docklands, the 1973/4 *London Rail Study* was addressing a wider issue relating to the future of the rail network in London as a whole (Ref. 3.7). The first Stage of the Fleet line to Charing Cross was under construction. Stage 2 to Fenchurch Street was at an advanced state of planning and Stage 3 to Lewisham was assumed to follow. However beyond Stage 2 the report identified a possible new route – the River line.

Quoting from the report:

The purpose of the River Line would be to serve the Docklands area. This area is to be redeveloped

following the removal of the focus of docks activities downstream to Tilbury. A study is being conducted jointly by the GLC and the London Boroughs most closely involved, to determine what form new development should take. We evaluated two routes for the River Line, one aligned to the north of the river, the other, a more southerly alignment crossing the Thames a number of times. River Line North would begin at Fenchurch Street and run through Stepney East and Poplar before crossing the River Lea to connect with the existing British Rail line at Custom House and continue to Beckton. Up to this point its alignment would be principally on the surface using disused railway rights of way. Beyond Beckton the line would go in tunnel under the Thames to serve Thamesmead. River Line South would be an underground line. It would also run from Fenchurch Street to Thamesmead and could cross the Thames up to four times serving Surrey Docks, the Isle of Dogs, North Greenwich, Custom House and Woolwich.

3.9: London Rail Study report.

The report concluded that River line south would be the most suitable alignment and significantly went on to say:

As we have found with the other proposals for extending London's railway system, neither the Fleet Line (to Lewisham) nor the River Line can be justified either on financial grounds or a conventional cost-benefit assessment of their transport effects. But in the case of the River Line there are strong grounds on general planning grounds for a new line to link the proposed development areas of Docklands to central London and at the same time give the growing new community of Thamesmead a direct rail connection to central London. The line would knit together communities which would otherwise be divided by the river, it would support public investment in Docklands and help attract private capital (indeed a commitment to build the line would have a considerable effect here) and would provide a major opportunity to integrate land use and development with public transport.

On timing the report stated:

Construction should not await the completion of development, and in order to obtain the maximum benefits from the line, the development should be consciously and intensively planned and phased to make the fullest possible use of it.

The London Rail Study set the ball firmly rolling as far as an Underground extension to Docklands was concerned. It also recognised that the line could do more than just provide a transport service and was unlikely to be justified in conventional cost-benefit terms. The outstanding question to be addressed was what form and scale of development was necessary to remotely justify such major investment?

The Docklands Strategic Plan of 1976

On 1 January 1974 the GLC and the five boroughs of Greenwich, Lewisham, Newham, Southwark and Tower Hamlets joined forces to establish the Docklands Joint Committee (DJC) with, in their words: 'A major responsibility for formulating a strategy for the 8.5 square miles of London's Docklands'.

One of the Committee's first publications – *A Strategy for Docklands: Setting the Scene* – went on to say (Ref.3.8):

3.10: Strategic Plan report.

This is the largest area to become available in London since the Great Fire; the largest area for urban development available in Europe today; and will encompass a large proportion of any changes in London between now and the end of the century.

The Committee set itself two objectives:

To see the Docklands redeveloped as quickly as possible in a way which makes it a better place to live and work and bring up your children, and which helps to solve the wider problems of the area of East London whose heart it is; and in planning and carrying out this development, to ensure that the people whose lives it will affect have a full opportunity to give their views and to have them taken into account in what is done.

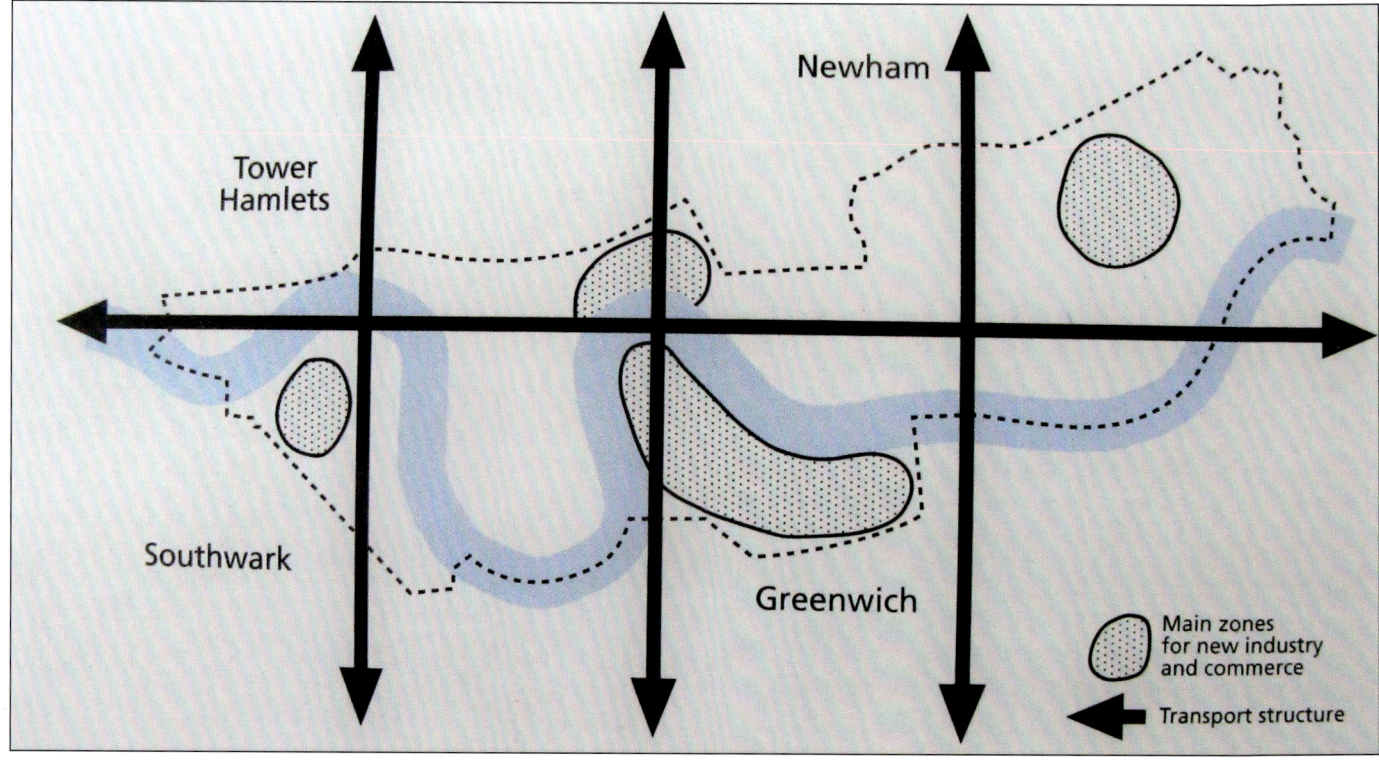

3.11: Transport and Development areas.

The approach of the DJC was to consult local people on the key elements of the proposed strategy including housing, transport and employment and a series of discussion documents were produced, one for each topic. The background to the planning of the area was laid out in *Setting the Scene*. This document:

Outlined a general structure for Docklands development as a framework for further work on the development of the Strategy. The structure included four major zones for future industrial and commercial development – Greenwich peninsula, Surrey Docks, Blackwall and East Beckton. Outside these zones it was proposed that land would be used mainly for housing, open space, recreation, education, shops, etc.

Setting the Scene also outlined a structure for the public transport network proposing that:

The whole area including the Surrey Docks, which is already served by the East London Line, could be knitted together and joined to the central area by a spinal east-west public transport link. Bus services could provide the essential north-south links with the

adjacent major office and shopping areas, with easy interchange points with the east-west spinal link. These interchanges would then be natural centres for local communities.

The four industrial/commercial zones and the strategy for public transport were illustrated by means of a simple diagram.

The Transport Options in 1976

A consultation document, *The Docklands Spine – Tube, Bus or Tram?*, was one of the first to analyse transport options, and looked at the relative advantages and disadvantages of different routes and modes for the spinal link (Ref. 3.9). It considered the existing transport network and concluded that it was more difficult to travel to and from Docklands by public transport than to any other part of Inner London.[1] The following options were examined:

- **Bus services on existing roads:** the report concluded that even with extensive bus lanes, buses could not provide the required journey time and capacity improvements.

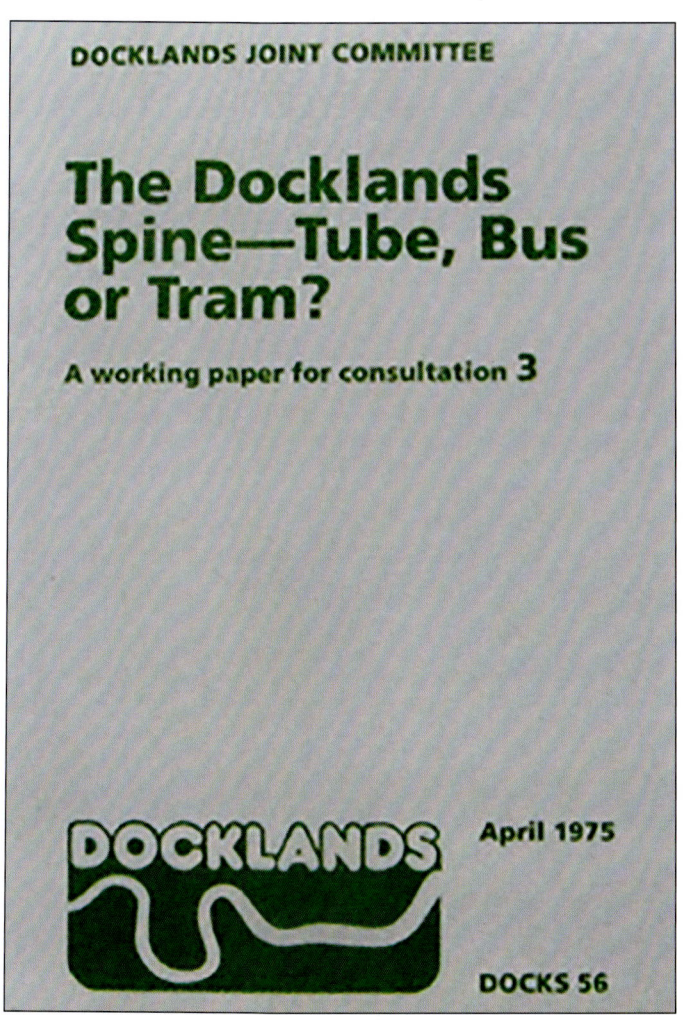

3.12 (above): *Docklands Spine report.*

- **Buses on reserved roads or busways:** the report said that parts of Docklands were particularly suited to this concept as existing disused railway tracks could be used. If the second stage of the Fleet line to Fenchurch Street was constructed the busway services could interchange at Tower Hill, or services could extend on ordinary roads into the central area.
- **Light rail – minitram:** this was the system recommended in the earlier Travers Morgan report using small guided automatic vehicles. Again these could use existing disused railway rights of way.
- **Light rail – trams:** these could run on the disused railway lines and also on the streets.
- **Light rail – light rapid transit:** these were seen as the modern combination of the other two light rail systems – fully segregated using vehicles carrying 160 people. All the light rail systems were assumed to have an interchange with Stage 2 of the Fleet line at Fenchurch Street or at Tower Hill with the District and Circle Lines.
- **Underground lines:** the report considered six 'River line' routes, all extensions from the assumed Fleet line at Fenchurch Street and using similar technology to the Victoria Line opened in 1968.

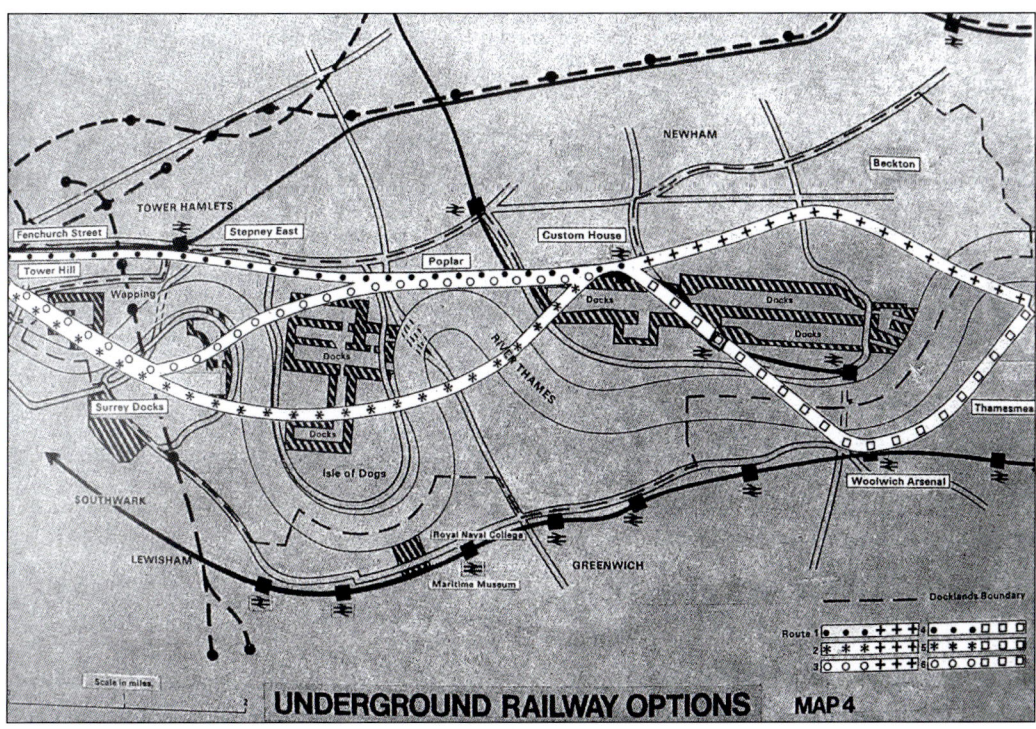

3.13 (right): 'River line' options.

The report found that the cost of a busway and a minitram system would be about the same and a light rail system would cost more. The busway had a higher capacity than minitram and it would be easier to provide an interchange with the Underground at Tower Hill. The first conclusion was that: 'The Busway option appears to be better than Minitram or Light Rail.'

The final choice was therefore between the busway and the Underground and the report went on to assess these in terms of their costs and debt charges and the number of passengers carried. Also assessed was the likely increase in land values. The conclusions were that the Underground could create value of £35m against that of a busway at £5m. Also:

More people would use the Underground (19,000 compared with 13,000).

The Underground would be more reliable and the busway concept was untried in London.

The Underground would provide a better link with industrial and residential areas and the rest of the network. It would open up employment opportunities and stimulate the economy of London. The Underground would better serve Thamesmead and potentially reduce overcrowding on the North Kent line.[2]

Publication of the London *Docklands Strategic Plan*

The DJC published the *Plan* in 1976 (Ref. 3.10). It envisaged substantial filling of the docks, retention of existing industry and large-scale new, mainly local authority housing. Population in the eight and a half square mile area covered by the plan was forecast to increase from 56,000 in 1975 to 120,000 by the end state during the

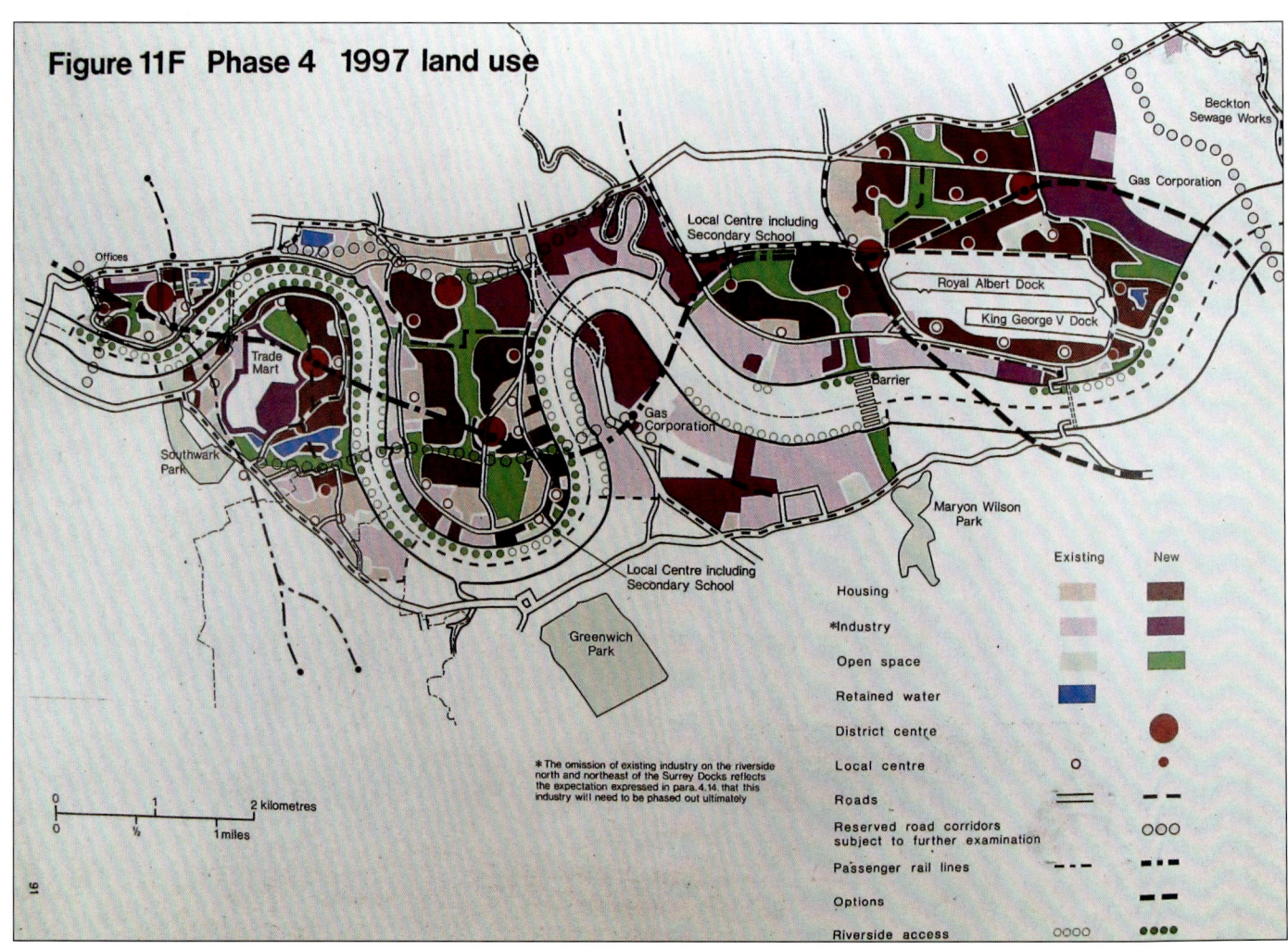

3.14: *Strategic Plan* land use.

1990s. In the four areas (Isle of Dogs, Silvertown, North Woolwich and Beckton), jobs were forecast to increase by 25,000 to 32,700 over a similar period.

Improved transport provision had now moved up the priority list and the report stated: 'Improvements in all aspects of transport are the key to regenerating the economy of East London and to making Docklands an attractive place to live in.'

The strategy recommended construction of the River line running from Fenchurch Street (optimistically assuming that the second stage of the original Fleet line had already arrived there), through Surrey Docks, the Isle of Dogs, North Greenwich and Custom House. A choice was left as to whether the line should continue to Beckton or to cross the river again to Woolwich and Thamesmead. The mismatch between the scale of the proposed development and the level of passenger demand to justify a new railway was obvious to many at the time, but did not seem to worry the politicians.

The Report identified three levels of priority for rail investment. The First Priority proposals were for improvements to the East London line, the North Woolwich passenger service and through running of the North Woolwich service onto the North London line, being pursued by the GLC and BR, as we will see in the next chapter.

The Second Priority included a reinstatement of the freight line to Beckton and construction of the River line from the Strand to Fenchurch Street, through Docklands to Thamesmead. The Third Priority included extensions to the East London line both north and south, and the electrification of the North Woolwich line.

In 1978 there was an attempt by the GLC to secure the Olympic Games for London in the Royal Docks area (Ref. 3.11). Central to the application was the Underground extension. With their backing LT obtained the necessary Parliamentary Powers for a line to Woolwich and a branch for a depot at Beckton.

In March 1979 the GLC considered a report (Ref. 3.12) on funding of the line. It was estimated to cost £103m at then current prices and gave LT the authority to: 'authorise the initiation of arrangements for proceeding with the construction and to seek a sum of £12m in the 1979-80 Money Bill to cover the first 18 months of planning and design'.

A number of boreholes were dug along the route and a short section of trial tunnel constructed in Surrey

3.15: Chairmen of GLC and LT 'start' construction.

Docks to test the new 'Bentonite Shield' method of construction.

In the event there was a change of Government and money to start the project was not made available. Apart from a symbolic hole dug in the ground to mark the 'start of construction' by the then leader of the GLC, Sir Horace Cutler, on 4 April 1978, nothing happened.

Lower Cost Alternatives

By 1979 the potential opportunities created by the decline of the traditional dock activities, including by now the end of commercial activities in the Royal Docks, were becoming clearer. The new Minister of Transport, Norman Fowler, in Margaret Thatcher's newly elected Government, informed the GLC that:

He was committed to getting the right links for Docklands and was prepared to earmark resources for a specific programme of road and rail improvements in the area... however in view of the financial constraints only about £100m at then prices was available for both road and rail construction ...and commitment to the construction of the full Jubilee Line extension would pose great problems.

The Government and the GLC therefore agreed that there should be a pause whilst the possibility of lower cost options for transport investment were examined. The GLC and the Docklands Development Organisation (DDO) initiated a study focusing on the impact of the various means of transport on the regeneration of housing and employment in the area (Ref. 3.13). Five alternatives to the full Jubilee Line were assessed including diversion of the East London line, a branch from the District Line and a largely surface alignment, all rejected at an early stage.

The main 'lower cost alternatives' considered were:

- **Express buses and busway I:** on-street buses from Aldgate East to the Isle of Dogs and Canning Town via a busway to Beckton and North Woolwich.
- **Express buses and busway II:** as above but replacing most of the street running with a busway on the old railway alignments.
- **Street tramway:** on-street from Aldgate East to Poplar and then segregated to the Isle of Dogs and Beckton.
- **Automatic light rail:** segregated system from Aldgate East to the Isle of Dogs and Beckton.

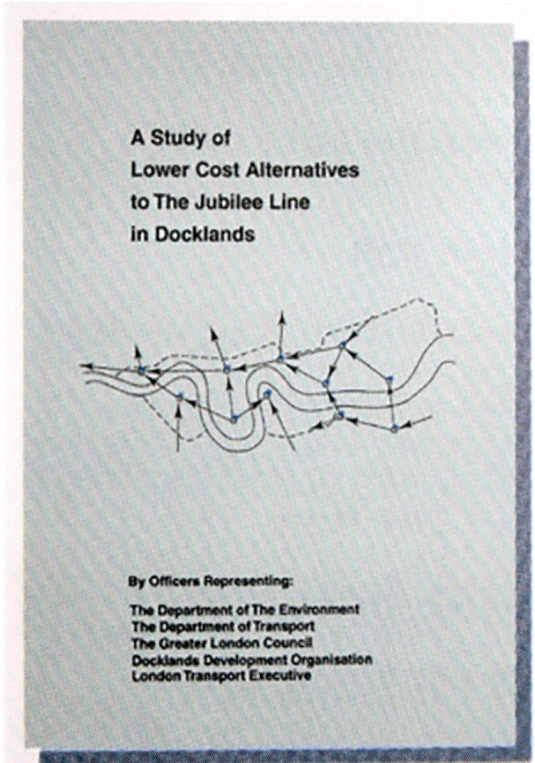

3.16: *Lower Cost Alternatives* report.

- **Interim Jubilee Line from Charing Cross to Beckton:** excluding the extension to Woolwich Arsenal and Thamesmead.

At the time, the planning framework for the area still largely reflected the aspiration of the 1976 Strategic Plan and whilst the evaluation showed that all options would cater for the likely passenger demand under the 'full Docklands strategy' and all would bring significant improvements in accessibility, none could be justified in terms of travel benefits. Wider social and/or development benefits would be required to make them worthwhile. At this time development in the Isle of Dogs was assumed to be largely completed by 1990.

The report, which was agreed with the Department of Transport, Department of the Environment, GLC, DJC and LT, concluded that the transport benefits did not increase in proportion to investment and none of the options would cover their operating costs or contribute to the recovery of capital costs. It concluded:

> The case for implementation of any of them must accordingly rest on other grounds including the wider social planning and economic benefits which they may encourage, which will vary significantly between the options.

It was thought that the Government might be more receptive to a package approach with a balance of investment between public transport and new roads. Various packages ranging from £100–£300m were put together (Ref. 3.14) and Government tentatively indicated that funds of around £100m – for a busway and road package – might be available.

At this time the road proposal for a Docklands Northern Relief Road conflicted with the automatic light rail option as both assumed use of the former railway right of way through Limehouse to the Isle of Dogs. If the road had proceeded faster, the opportunity for building a low cost railway or busway would have been lost. [3]

However, Margaret Thatcher's new Government in 1979 had plans for changing the planning regime in Docklands and any decisions on funding had to await the setting up of a new planning authority for the area. Fortunately the GLC remained active in working with LT and BR to develop the two remaining railway lines serving the area.

CHAPTER 4

DEVELOPMENT OF THE EAST LONDON AND NORTH LONDON LINES

I was not significantly involved in the development of the East and North London lines, this being led by my colleague in the GLC, David Warren. However I undertook an analysis of the costs and benefits of reopening Kentish Town West station on the North London line which had burnt down in 1971. BR wanted to permanently close it but it was reopened with GLC money in 1981, and used by around 2m passengers a year.

During the 1970s the passenger numbers on several Inner London services were falling in line with a decline in London's population. The developing new towns were encouraging people to move and the Government had a policy to relocate offices out of the capital. Closure of some lines was seriously considered by BR, including the North London line between Richmond and Broad Street and the line between Stratford and North Woolwich. However the recently created GLC was more interested in making better use of underused inner London lines than closing them, including the East London line owned by LT and the North London lines owned by BR. Also a number of options for developing the North London line were considered in the *London Rail Study* of 1974 (Ref. 3.7).

North London Line Developments

At the start of the 1970s Broad Street station, on the west side of Liverpool Street station, was the City terminus of the North London line with third rail 750V electric trains running in the peak every 20 minutes to Richmond and Watford. In East London diesel trains ran from North Woolwich to Stratford every thirty minutes.

Rising land values in the City prompted BR to proceed with the closure of Broad Street station allowing the large Broadgate office development to take over

the site. The initial proposal for the remaining services was to divert the Watford and Richmond services into Liverpool Street.

The first proposal initiated by the GLC was the improvement of stations on the North Woolwich line and its extension from Stratford to Camden Town over the North London freight line. The service opened in 1979 initially without any intermediate stations. At the start, the service was provided by diesel multiple units but in 1985 the GLC and BR, together with the Inner City Partnership, funded the electrification of the line and with the closure of Broad Street station a through service from North Woolwich to Richmond was established. Over the next few years stations were opened at Hackney Wick (1980), Dalston Kingsland (1983) and Homerton (1985). The stations between Stratford and North Woolwich at West Ham, Canning Town, Custom House and Silvertown were upgraded, with this section of line also electrified. This effectively

4.1: Relocated Canning Town BR station.

4.2: Original Hackney Wick station.

4.3: Rotherhithe station.

restored a passenger service between the Royal Docks and North London which had been withdrawn some forty years before.

In 1988, as part of a review of transport proposals for Docklands in the light of the growing employment in the area, the GLC and BR undertook a study of a possible 'Woolwich Metro' to serve the Royal Docks development area and extend the North London line with a new river crossing to Woolwich Arsenal. However the impending privatisation of the National Rail network and the need to show such investment was financially worthwhile, quickly put a stop to this proposal. Much later this link was to be provided by the DLR and more recently also by Crossrail.

The line between North Woolwich and Stratford was closed in 2006 in preparation for the takeover by a new DLR service opened in 2010.

East London Line Developments

By the 1970s, at the other end of Docklands, the East London line was the poor relation of LT's Underground services. With the decline of the docks, passenger numbers had fallen significantly and the stations were in very poor and deteriorating condition. Services sometimes using tube stock and sometimes ex-Metropolitan Line stock ran from Shoreditch to New Cross or New Cross Gate. Water ingress was a particular problem at Wapping and Rotherhithe stations, either side of Brunel's Thames Tunnel, and the tunnel itself required 24-hour pumping. There were no lifts at any of the deep stations at Wapping, Shadwell or Rotherhithe with Shadwell station for example having over ninety steps to the platforms.

Again the GLC was prepared to invest in the line. There was also an investigation into restoring the original connection from the East London line from Shoreditch into Liverpool Street station, but this proved to be unworkable as a major upgrading of the main line station was on the cards. However in 1983 the GLC and LT embarked on a programme of improvements including station refurbishment and the installation of lifts. These were provided at Rotherhithe, Wapping and Shadwell and the entrance of Shadwell station moved a short distance onto Cable Street so that lifts could be provided. Unfortunately by doing so the opportunity was lost to provide a direct interchange with the Shadwell station DLR, opened only a few years later.

The East London line was closed in 1995 to carry out various repair work and to construct Canada Water station on the Jubilee Line extension. The most significant part of the work was to reduce the leaking of the tunnel section and strengthen the brickwork by 'shotcreting' – spraying the brick-lined tunnel with a concrete lining. However just before the work commenced Listed Building status was imposed following a number of protests. This delayed the works

4.4: Wapping station.

4.5: Recent modernisation of Whitechapel station.

but eventually it was agreed that a short section of the original tunnel brickwork would be restored but left unlined. The route reopened in 1998. New linings were added to the platforms at Wapping and Rotherhithe. However, water ingress continues to this day requiring continuous pumping of the Thames Tunnel.

London Overground

In 2007, TfL took over the North London Railway routes from Silverlink Metro, forming the start of the London Overground network. In the same year the East London line was closed for extensive refurbishment, opening again in 2010 as part of the new network with northern extensions to Dalston and Hackney, partly over the old Broad Street alignment, and to West Croydon and later to Clapham Junction to the south.

With refurbished stations, new trains and much improved train frequencies the former East London line and the former North London line now provide secondary links into Docklands via Canada Water, giving interchange with the Jubilee Line opened in 2000. The London Overground route to Stratford also provides interchange with the Jubilee Line as well as the DLR. Crossrail provides further connections with the Overground at Whitechapel and Stratford.

In 2019, as part of the Government's Housing Infrastructure Fund, initiated in 2017 to help unlock 320,000 homes in the period up to 2024, the East London Overground was awarded £80m to enhance signalling on the line, allowing up to twenty trains per hour to run, and to provide a new station at Surrey Canal Road. The fund is seen as unlocking around 14,000 new homes in the area.

All these improvements to the existing local network have led to significantly improved transport links around Docklands. The question at the time was could the new LDDC help progress a solution to serve the heart of the area?

4.6: Hackney Wick Overground station.

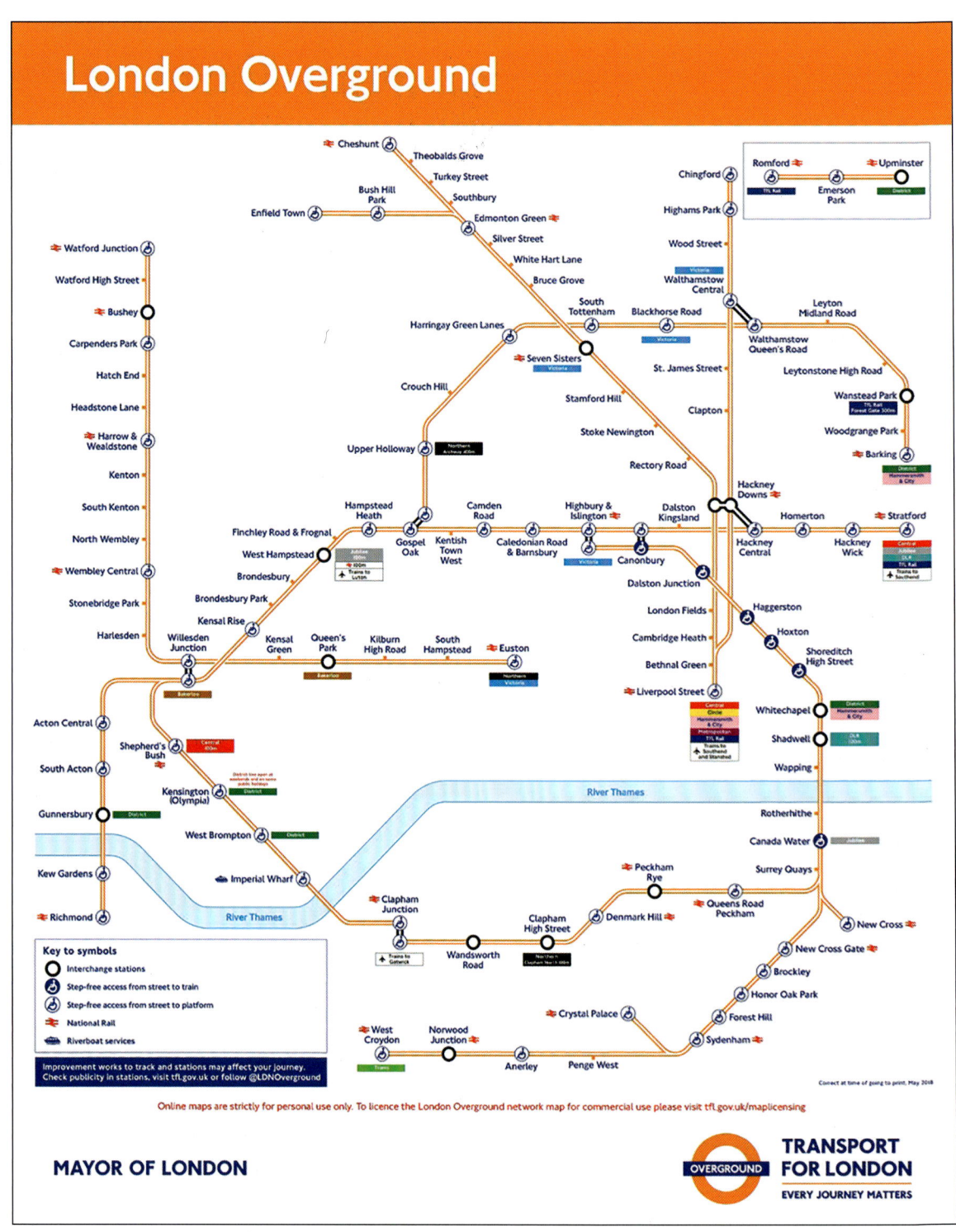

4.7: London Overground map.

CHAPTER 5

CREATION OF THE LONDON DOCKLANDS DEVELOPMENT CORPORATION (1981–1998)

The setting up of the LDDC in 1981 was vigorously opposed by the Labour controlled GLC, where I worked at the time. I was invited to join the team preparing the case to oppose the Parliamentary Bill but declined as I believed my future career was in transport planning and not in political campaigning. In the early days working with the LDDC was a little difficult. Indeed initially we were told by the GLC politicians not to speak to them. However improvements in transport, which they recognised were necessary to attract redevelopment, had to be implemented by LT under GLC control and joint working arrangements were eventually established. I was involved in making a number of presentations to the LDDC Board and at public meetings about the plans for the DLR. My key contacts in the LDDC were with the town and transport planners Howard Potter and later Cynthia Grant, with whom I worked closely over the coming years.

It was clear that the vast areas left after the closure of the working docks were a unique opportunity for London. Few cities of the world would have such an opportunity so close to the central area. But what type of development was appropriate and how would it be possible to get the local authorities and the GLC to agree what should be done? The Second World War and the impact of containers on the closure of the enclosed docks had given a major blow to East London employment. Was it appropriate to try and hang on to, and recreate, some of the traditional manufacturing and construction jobs, many associated with the river, or was it time to start again as Sir Christopher Wren had advocated for the City after the Fire of London some 300 years earlier? One thing was certain – the more radical the ideas for change, the more difficult it was going to be to achieve a consensus on the way forward.

A Radical New Approach

Margaret Thatcher's new Government of 1979 recognised that it was going to be very difficult to achieve substantial progress within the existing planning framework. Even if the GLC was interested in looking at the area as an asset to exploit for London as a whole, the five London boroughs affected, with their own local agendas, largely supported by the strong traditions of the East End communities, had other ideas. However, the Government decided that the only way forward was a radical approach.

The creation of the LDDC was an idea from Michael Heseltine, then Secretary of State for the Environment. The plan was to transfer the planning powers of the local authorities to a new corporation, run by an appointed Board which alone would decide the form and scale of development. The idea nearly came unstuck when it was realised that the Act of Parliament necessary to create such a body would be 'Hybrid', and therefore unlawful as it would only apply to a specific area. Heseltine's answer to this problem was to promote a General Bill which could also be applied to other areas, Liverpool

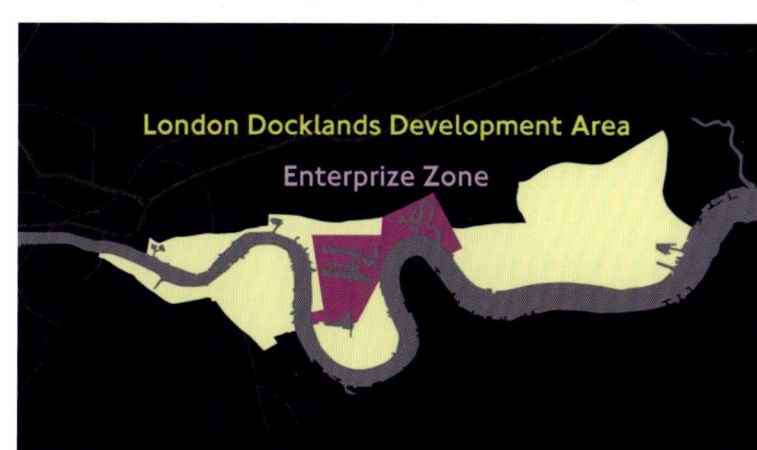

5.1: LDDC designated area.

being the other such development corporation created at the same time. The idea was broadly based on plans for the creation of the New Towns some thirty years earlier.

The adverse reaction from the boroughs and the GLC was virulent and a massive campaign was created to try to stop the Government's Bill, but to no avail. The LDDC was set up in 1981, initially for a ten-year period, with the simple but broad remit to regenerate Docklands. Its planning powers were wide ranging. Principally it could assemble land from the local authorities, the PLA and where necessary compulsory purchase privately-owned land. The docks in the Isle of Dogs were already closed by the time the LDDC was created. This was the same year the PLA announced the closure of the Royal Docks, adding significantly to the land available for redevelopment.

The Government created an Enterprise Zone for a large part of the Isle of Dogs, the main area seen for early development. Prospective developers were exempt from local authority rates for a ten-year period along with generous tax allowances on buildings under construction during this period. And of course a greatly simplified planning approval process.

An early initiative was the creation of London City Airport by the construction company John Mowlem on land sandwiched between two of the Royal Docks. The practicality of a 'STOL' (Short Take-Off and Landing) airport was spectacularly demonstrated in 1982 by the landing and take-off of a Dash 7 aircraft on a cleared Heron Quay in the centre of the Isle of Dogs. A huge site to the north of the airport adjacent to the Victoria Dock became the ExCeL Exhibition Centre, a vast modern venue.

Initially it was assumed that the LDDC's success would rest on trying to identify and encourage 'suitable' alternative industrial uses for the vast sites it administered. Those unemployed former dock workers and their families, who had not moved to work at Tilbury docks, wanted equivalent skilled trades in warehousing or manufacturing to replace their lost jobs.

In the early years the relationship between the LDDC, the boroughs and the local people was very poor. In the Isle of Dogs a strong residents' group was formed under the leadership of the late Ted Johns, who fought for improved transport, education and shops. Slowly the relationships improved. By 1989 the LDDC had developed an 'Accord' with the Borough of Tower Hamlets following a Memorandum of Agreement with the Borough of Newham in 1987. In 1998 the Corporation reported that it had spent just over 7 per cent of its total budget on community infrastructure and activities. Of this £120m, about half had been invested in education and training and half in health and other community activities. In addition, the Corporation spent in the region of £8m on grants to voluntary bodies in London Docklands.

The LDDC's powers enabled it to take over development control responsibility from three boroughs – Newham, Tower Hamlets and Southwark – and to spend Government money on preparing the area for development. There were however significant gaps in its powers, notably relating to transport, with the GLC remaining the strategic highway and public transport authority, LT and BR the transport operators and the London boroughs responsible for local roads. For a time there was a stand-off, with little communication,

5.2: Isle of Dogs development framework.

5.3: London City Airport dwarfed by the Tate & Lyle sugar refinery.

5.4: Early low-rise development dwarfed by recent buildings.

particularly between the then Labour controlled GLC and the unelected LDDC.[1] However, plans for improving public transport were of interest to all parties and led to the opening up of dialogue and eventually joint working between the authorities.

The LDDC's Influence on Development and Transport

The creation of the LDDC, and this short ten-year opportunity timescale, gave fresh impetus to the search for a public transport solution. Development forecasts at this time were still modest – up to 25,000 jobs in the Isle of Dogs[2] with fewer in the former Royal Docks areas. It was initially assumed by Government that redevelopment would largely consist of business parks and housing. However the LDDC also took a very different and dynamic approach to development.

There was to be no strategic or master plan with land use and its scale predetermined. The theme was 'market led' development, through use of development frameworks and design guidelines. It was recognised that if the area was to benefit from Enterprise Zone status something had to happen quickly. But did anyone at the time actually realise *what* might happen?

An immediate priority for the LDDC was to open up the area, clear abandoned sites and install utility services. One of the first real signs of something happening on the ground was the construction of a very modest 'Red Brick Road' improving access from the Commercial Road into the heart of the potential development area in the Isle of Dogs.

However it still took well over an hour to travel from Central London to the Enterprise Zone by public transport and all agreed that improving access by road and public transport was a must. Improved bus services were a start and the LDDC sponsored a shuttle bus to Mile End station, the nearest Underground. The anticipated scale of development could not remotely justify an Underground extension and even if it could, funds were simply not going to be available. But if anything other than more 'back land' and warehousing development was to be persuaded to come to the area, improved accessibility to the central area and to the neighbouring population catchment was essential. It was not surprising that soon after its inauguration the LDDC asked LT to dust off and review the earlier plans for transport solutions which would open up the area and stimulate development.

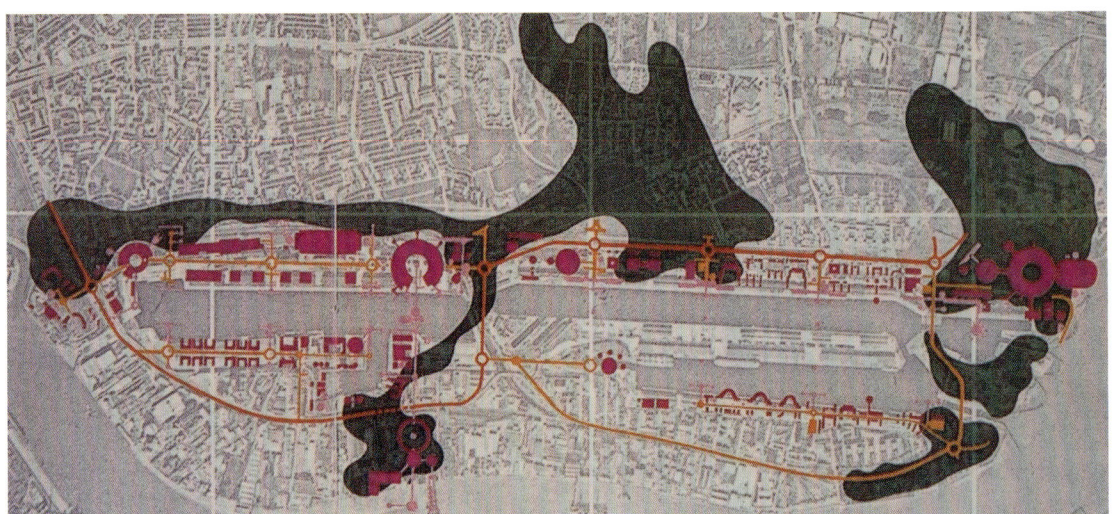

5.5: Royal Docks development framework.

In its eighteen years of existence the LDDC had a major influence on the development of public transport in the area. It played a significant role in the development of the DLR and its extensions to the City, Lewisham and Beckton, where the railway was integrated with a new road, wholly funded by the LDDC, the Jubilee Line extension, and a major new road (The Highway) partly running under the water at Limehouse Basin.

In April 1992 ownership of the DLR transferred from LT to the LDDC. The DLR was enduring a period of unreliability causing concern from the Corporation and developers. Pressure on the Government resulted in the transfer. Funding for further extensions consequently passed from the Department of Transport to the Department of the Environment.

Without Michael Heseltine's involvement, the LDDC's powers granted by Government and their influence on change, backed up by the pressure from major developers, together with the inspirational first Chief Executive Reg Ward and architect Ted Hollamby, Docklands would be a very different place today.

The proximity to the City and the attractiveness of the riverside soon made the area attractive to developers of upmarket offices and apartments, often using very modern architecture. By encouraging the development of attractive waterside apartments along the River Thames and the old docks, the LDDC brought new, middle-class residents into the area, closely followed by shops, restaurants and bars. Docklands suddenly became a new and exciting place to live for Londoners.

Their ability to welcome and foster the Canary Wharf development, massively exceeding the original expectations for the area, was a major success story for the organisation. Canary Wharf is now one of the most important supporters of the UK economy and one of the most accessible areas of Inner London, enhanced by the DLR, the Jubilee Line extension and further with the arrival of Crossrail.

In 1998 the LDDC produced a monograph document entitled *Attracting Development, Creating Value*, summarising its achievements over the eighteen years of its existence (Ref. 5.4). These included disposing of over 1,000 acres of land to all kinds of development, with sales of 185 acres to developers, raising an income of £63m; 24,000 homes completed with a further 27,000 underway; and 2.33m square metres of commercial and industrial floorspace completed.

Winding Up the LDDC

In 1998 the LDDC was wound up with assets mainly transferred to the London boroughs. Responsibility for the DLR passed back to LT and two years later, following the Greater London Authority (GLA) Act of 1999, to the new organisation TfL (Transport for London) under the responsibility of the newly created Mayor, Ken Livingstone.

The creation of the LDDC, with its specific remit to regenerate the area within a tight ten-year timescale, meant attention could be focused on transport solutions. But, as we will see in the next chapter, the LDDC had to work in close cooperation with the official transport authorities to achieve this.

5.6: Canary Wharf master plan.

CHAPTER 6

INITIAL DOCKLANDS LIGHT RAILWAY

eveloping plans for the initial DLR was a significant and highly enjoyable period of my career. Following the go-ahead from Government, LT set up a small team led by the engineer David Catling,[1] together with Ben Harding and Roger Jones. I was the transport planner representative from the GLC. We used railway consultants Kennedy & Donkin to help develop the project. Chris Johnson was their lead engineer who helped with a range of projects in which I was involved. We worked closely with the first Director of the railway, Bill Clarke, and then with Cliff Bonnet who stepped into the role following Bill's promotion as Operations Director of the Underground.

Walking the old railway rights of way, identifying possible station locations, estimating the passenger demand, undertaking the cost-benefit analysis and making a wide range of presentations was not the only work. This was a new concept for London and unexpectedly I found myself involved in issues as diverse as station and train design and noise policies. I was also involved in the sometimes difficult dialogues between the LDDC, the local boroughs and local groups such as the Docklands Forum.

Planning and Approval

In 1981/82, LT, the GLC and the LDDC developed further joint studies of light rail and busway options in response to the need to consider alternatives to an Underground extension to Docklands. The busway option was along similar lines to the earlier proposals, essentially running from the central area along existing roads as far as Limehouse where a segregated alignment would be created along the former L&BR route to Poplar and then to Beckton. Elsewhere, such as through the Isle of Dogs, the buses would run on the ordinary roads.

A wider range of light rail options was considered in an attempt to better link the Isle of Dogs to the Central Area including:

- a street option running along the Commercial Road from the edge of the city at Minories to the Isle of Dogs
- two different underground termini in the City, one underneath Tower Hill station and the other under Minories bus station to the north
- a street-running option from Mile End Underground station southwards along Burdett Road to the Isle of Dogs

6.1: DLR assessment reports.

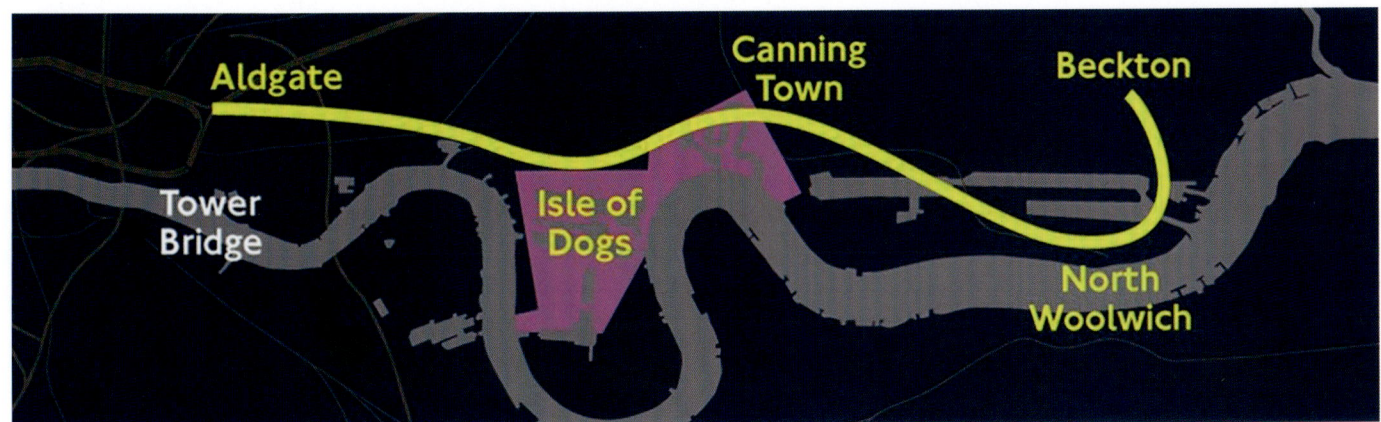

6.2: Busway route.

- an option running from the Isle of Dogs northwards along the former Poplar branch railway to Bow Road and then westwards on the south side of Bow Road to Mile End station.

None of these options would have provided an ideal solution, most involving interaction with normal traffic and congestion.

Seen at the time as a long shot, discussions were held with BR about the possible relinquishing of two of their London, Tilbury and Southend (LT&S) lines between Fenchurch Street terminal and Limehouse, where the disused alignment of the former L&BR commenced. Rather surprisingly this was agreed, making available a continuously segregated alignment from Minories, a short distance from the Fenchurch Street terminal, to the north of the Isle of Dogs.[2] A station at Minories, to be named Tower Gateway, was as close to the City that any system could reach without expensive tunnelling, giving a short three-minute walk to the Underground station at Tower Hill. Limehouse DLR station was adjacent to the main line LT&S lines but funds could not extend to a direct link, leaving a very unsatisfactory interchange via the street level and back.[3]

Within the Isle of Dogs, options for street running were also explored on several alignments either side of the West India Docks and then largely following the former Millwall railway alignment to join the disused viaduct to the southern point at Island Gardens, almost entirely following the working dock railway alignment.

The LDDC was however concerned about the impact of the street running options on the development areas in the Isle of Dogs. The chief architect, Ted Hollamby, advocated a bold approach suggesting an elevated route

6.3: Busway on Limehouse viaduct impression.

across the northern docks to create, 'a dramatic entrance to the area'.

Four options were taken to a joint full evaluation by the LDDC, LT and the GLC:

1. The busway option running from Minories to Beckton.
2. A fully segregated light rail running from the City at Minories to Island Gardens, almost entirely on former railway rights of way except across the new elevated crossing of the West India Docks.
3. A light rail running from Mile End on-street to Bow Road and then fully segregated using the former Poplar branch railway and then as Option 2 to Island Gardens.
4. The combination of Options 2 and 3 above, joining at the top end of the Isle of Dogs.

The appraisal again showed that only the busway option was likely to be justified in conventional cost-benefit terms. The light rail options typically showed only half of the costs covered by the transport benefits. However a potential land use exercise, conducted in conjunction with developers and estate agents, concluded that the light rail options would potentially bring 9,300 more jobs to the area. At the time the maximum number of jobs in the Isle of Dogs was forecast to be only 25,000 on completion of development. In a novel evaluation, the value which needed to be placed on these extra jobs to close the transport economic gap was estimated at £3,100 per job created. This was well below the cost of job creation in other regional development projects in the country at the time.

The joint report concluded:

There is a clear need for better public transport in Docklands, both to improve access to and mobility within the area and as a consequence, to improve its attraction to potential developers … The immediate decision is whether a rail link of the type described in the report should be provided. That decision turns on a subjective judgement to be placed on the unquantified benefits – mainly those affecting the probable pattern of development in Docklands – which the schemes would be expected to bring.

The two alternative light rail options were seen as having different roles. The City branch connecting the Isle of Dogs to the Central Area was viewed as having the best influence on developers, with the Mile End street-running branch seen as predominantly bringing people to work in the development areas from east and north-east London. Although the conventional cost-benefit evaluation showed that only half of the costs could be justified by the transport benefits, the report concluded on the combination of both routes: 'From the point of view of capturing all the transport benefits identified in the study and in the context of the overall strategy for Dockland, this [combination of the two routes] is the ideal scheme.'

The GLC and LDDC produced informative leaflets and consulted local people on the proposal and a number of public meetings were held. The ideas met with much scepticism and on more than one occasion people had heard someone from LT was coming and they just came along to complain about the local bus services!

The final report was submitted to Government in June 1982 (Ref. 6.1). The Secretary of State for the Environment, Michael Heseltine, was enthusiastic about

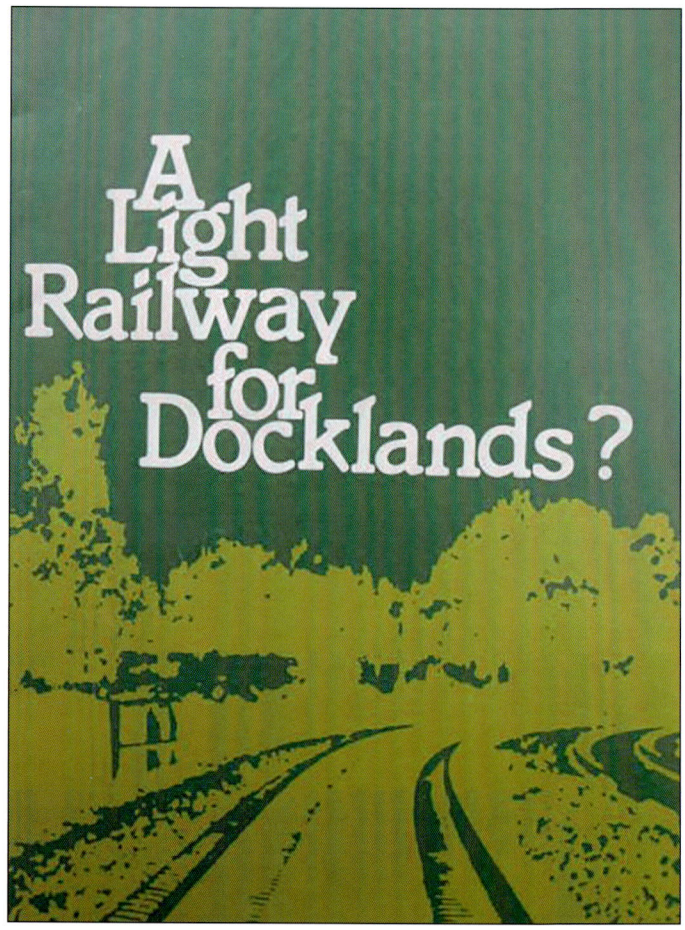

6.4: Public consultation leaflet.

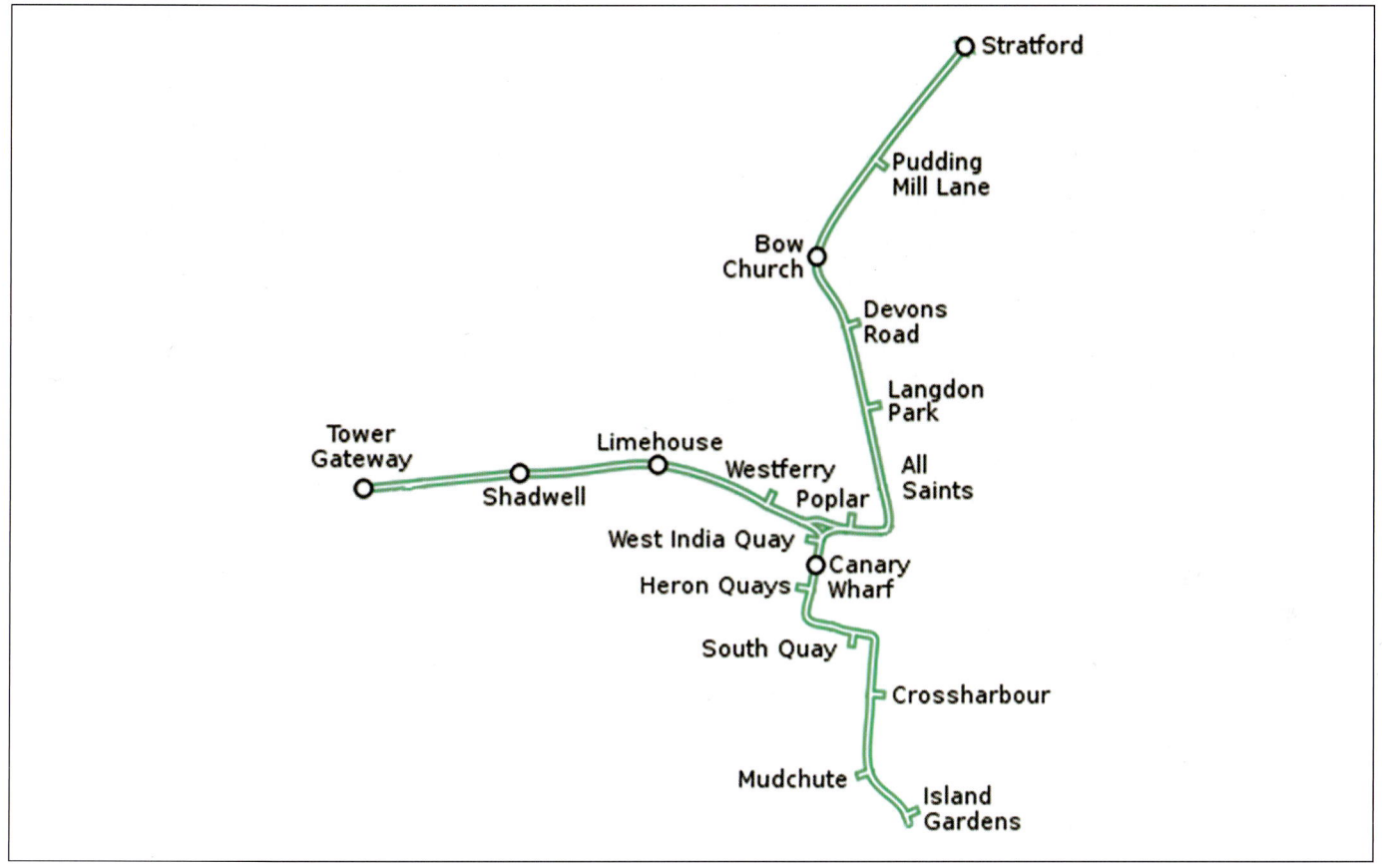

6.5: DLR Initial Railway.

the plans. Not so his counterpart for Transport, David Howell. However in an extraordinary short time – at the Conservative Party Conference in October of the same year – Michael Heseltine gave the go-ahead for the project.[4]

A Parliamentary Bill for the railway was submitted by LT in November 1982 for the first route to Tower Gateway, with the proposed prominent viaduct running across the West India Docks. The LDDC was increasingly concerned at the impact of the overhead wires, as required by the street-running to Mile End on the northern branch. Interest was growing in a possible system which could have low-level rail current collection and to operate fully automatically, this being seen as a first for the UK and a symbol for the 'new world' of Docklands.[5] A possible choice for Docklands was the Vancouver Skytrain, developed by the Canadian Bombardier Company, which was under construction and opened in 1985.

Fortunately for Docklands an alternative to the street-running Mile End route and a better destination was

suggested, with the line continuing further to the north on the former Poplar railway alignment and then rising steeply on a short new stretch of line to run alongside the Liverpool Street main lines to Stratford, where a disused bay platform was available. Parliamentary Powers were sought for the Stratford branch in 1983 and Powers obtained in 1984.

Until 1992 the statutory process for nationalised industries to obtain authority for major projects, including railways, was via a Parliamentary Bill through the Private Bill process, resulting in an Act of Parliament. The principal purpose of obtaining powers was to:

1. Obtain outline planning permission.
2. Compulsorily acquire land.
3. Obtain various incidental powers (e.g. temporary or permanent road closures, general interference with streets, etc.).
4. Construct the works.
5. Operate the railway.

6.6: First DLR train.

This was exactly the same procedure that the various railway companies had to follow for the multitude of earlier railways serving London and the rest of the country for the previous 150 years or more. The process involves all the rigmarole of a Government Bill with a first and second reading in the Commons and a Commons Committee followed by a House of Lords reading and Committee. The Bill then finally returns to the Commons for approval, as amended, if found necessary during the proceedings, by the Committee members.

Anyone with a legitimate interest in the scheme can petition in favour, or much more commonly, oppose the Bill. Their grievances are heard by the various Committees, conducted as in a formal court of law with barristers or Queen's Counsel, a daunting process for any

6.7: Tower Gateway station.

lay person involved.[6] The Committees have the power to make any changes to the Bill in the light of petitions, and frequently did, often incurring the promoters extra costs and time for the project. As with any Government proposal, the Bill only becomes an Act, and therefore the law, after it has cleared all the procedures and has been duly signed by the monarch.

However, being a rather obscure process there was little concern or opposition to the first DLR Bill. The Parliamentary Plans included a set of drawings at 1:1,250 scale showing 'limits of deviation', within which the Act gave powers to the promoter for compulsory property purchase, land required for work sites and land to build and operate the actual railway. Accompanying the drawings was a list of the affected property owners.[7] There was no requirement to indicate where the stations might be or what they might look like and how they might relate to the surround areas. Also at this time there was also no such thing as an Environmental Survey or Impact Assessment.[8]

The second DLR Bill was for the line to Stratford. The London Borough of Newham petitioned against the Bill demanding that an additional station should be built at Pudding Mill Lane on the single line approach to Stratford. Although the promoters stated that the station could not be justified, the House of Commons Committee found in the petitioner's favour requiring a further Bill to be submitted a year later.[9]

Funding for the initial DLR was to be provided jointly by the Department of Transport and the Department of the Environment via LT and the LDDC. This reflected the fact that 50 per cent of the railway was justified on transport grounds and 50 per cent on development grounds. Funding was provided on the condition that the initial cost estimate of £65m (£77m at out-turn prices) would not be exceeded. This required some hard thinking about how the design and construction of the railway would proceed. Two potential stations were deleted from the plans, one on the Stratford branch next to the Landsbury Estate and the other on the City Branch between Limehouse and Shadwell. However these were safeguarded for possible later addition. There was considerable thought as to what the railway should be called, including DART and ELRT (Docklands Area and East London Rapid Transit). In the end no one came up with anything better than the DLR.[10]

Design and Construction

At an early stage the then Managing Director, London Underground, Tony Ridley, agreed with Government that the DLR would be built and operated as a separate organisation from the Underground. Indeed the thinking would go a stage further in proposing that the design and build stages of the railway should together be put out to tender to the private sector. LT would specify the basics for the track layout, the position of stations, number of trains and service levels. The private sector would build to this specification and hand over a working railway to the operator, DLR Ltd, a wholly owned subsidiary of LT. This was the first time that a private sector company had been involved in building a UK railway for a great number of years.

The £77m out-turn cost presented a very tight limit on the design of the railway. It had been produced on a fairly preliminary basis and necessitated some difficult decisions to be made. As well as the elimination of two stations, escalators could only be afforded at Tower Gateway. Station designs were to be as simple as possible with a view to later upgrading – for example, platform canopies were shortened to only a few metres in length.

However, issues concerning access for disabled people were becoming more important and following the success of the recently opened fully accessible Tyne and Wear Metro, hydraulic lifts were to be provided at all elevated stations.

Much thought was given to the nature of the junction of the two branches on North Quay at the head of the Isle of Dogs. Various options were considered including a rather unusual idea to build a roundabout with the station in the centre and trains stopping in three positions around the circumference. In the end a more practical solution emerged with a triangular or delta junction, as it became known, between the three branches, albeit involving very tight radii of 25 metres. A separate station, North Quay, was located to the south of the junction. The elevated tracks across the docks were built on steel beams on concrete supports. Other elevated sections were on concrete twin support columns. At South Quay a tortuous 'S' bend was required to avoid a building which at the time was to be retained, but was later demolished.[11]

Stations were to be designed to take a single articulated car which needed to be able to negotiate the 25-metre radius curves of the delta junction and

6.8 (above): DLR alongside C2C train at Shadwell.

6.9 (left): Limehouse viaduct.

negotiate the steep climb up to the Liverpool Street line. A service of four trains per hour was specified to meet the anticipated demand of a peak load of 1,500 passengers per hour, requiring the purchase of eleven vehicles. A stabling and maintenance depot, a control room and offices were built adjacent to Poplar station.

The viaduct section over the former L&BR between Limehouse and Poplar was by then over a hundred years old and had not been used for over thirty years.

Replacement of the road bridges and drainage improvements would need to be carried out, but essentially the structure was sound for the proposed lightweight vehicles. The other old, single track railway viaduct structure at the foot of the Isle of Dogs last used in 1928 needed some cross strengthening but otherwise was also sound.

Taking over the former Poplar branch, the line then had to rise via a 100-metre radius and a 5 per cent gradient to then run parallel to the main line to Stratford station on a single track, where fortunately there was a disused bay platform that could be reused.

With the elimination of street running, the need for overhead wires was no longer required. Power supply to trains via an exposed third or fourth rail is common throughout London but not seen as appropriate by the Railway Inspectorate for a modern system. A top-protected third rail was therefore designed with the current picked up from underneath the rail. A 750V DC supply was used, similar to that of the Underground.

Following a competition, a Design and Construct contract was let to a consortium of GEC and Mowlem

6.11: Author's impression of West Ferry station.

6.12: West Ferry DLR station.

6.10: Site of West Ferry station.

6.13: All Saint's station.

in August 1984. The trains were manufactured by the German company Linke Hofmann Busch. The project was completed on time and within budget and was opened by HM Queen Elizabeth II and subsequently for the public on 31 August 1987.

Operations

The initial DLR was designed to accommodate 23,000 passengers a day on completion of development and in the first weeks of operation over 18,000 passengers a day were estimated to be travelling.[12] The railway proved not only popular with local people now able, for example, to travel to the Stratford shopping centre (eventually transformed with the Westfield development) without a long bus ride, but also with the growing number of construction workers employed in the area. It was also somewhat surprisingly seen as a tourist attraction in itself, the elevated sections giving views over the former hidden docks and a new route to Greenwich attractions

via the Victorian pedestrian subway under the Thames at the foot of the Isle of Dogs. Providing the first accessible means of transport in London was also seen as a major step forward and a number of passengers in wheelchairs were seen travelling in the first weeks of operation.

The trains were fully automatic, requiring only a 'train captain' to close the doors after each station stop, after receiving a 'ready to start' indication. Three computers controlled the signalling, requiring two out of three to agree before any command could be given to the trains. The system was a first for the UK and had not been installed before on a busy urban railway. With hindsight, insufficient time was given to testing. Reliability proved a major problem in the early days causing the computer system to crash regularly, safely stopping all trains. Train captains could then manually drive the trains at very low speed but all too often it took a long time, sometimes over an hour, to get the system working properly again.

6.14: DLR under construction in 1986.

A number of other issues arose with the system, including the need for passengers to 'composite' their tickets after purchase, a system used all over the Continent but which proved to be beyond the comprehension of the British. The inward folding doors on the trains also proved problematic. These and the signalling problems would persist for some time and its unreliability did not give the initial DLR a very good name. One local councillor called it a 'Mickey Mouse' railway which was unfortunately picked up and used by the press whenever something went wrong.

Over the years that followed, with the City and the other four major extensions described later and the substantial increase in patronage, the initial DLR was subject to massive change and improvements. One major problem which had to be overcome related to the design of the steel bridges straddling the docks. Such modern structures are designed for a specific lifespan, typically 120 years, taking into account the loadings and fatigue stresses caused by the passage of trains. When the calculations were repeated for the longer and more frequent trains anticipated in the future it was found that the lifespan of the structures might reduce by three quarters to only thirty years. The solution was to strengthen the structures with additional riveted plating which can now be clearly seen attached to the beams.

Over the coming years stations were extended to take first two and then three-car trains. Station and passenger facilities were improved, and escalators installed. Stratford, Pudding Mill Lane, Minories, North Quay, Canary Wharf, Herons Quay, South Quay, Mudchute and Island Gardens were all completely rebuilt, the delta junction at North Quay replaced and new tracks added, giving additional capacity to Canary Wharf. Additional intermediate train sidings were added and the signalling system totally replaced. It seemed that the railway was being pulled apart and rebuilt on a never ending programme. However in spite of all these changes the railway managed to play an increasingly important role in stimulating development and carrying the increasing numbers of people to work in the area. By 2011, with the running of a three-car service throughout the system, a degree of completion had thankfully been reached, some twenty-four years after the opening in 1987.

However, even with these improvements the DLR could not conceivably cope on its own with the scale of things to come at Canary Wharf.

Postscript

In 1987, soon after the initial DLR had opened, the author wrote an article for the *Journal of the Institute of Highways and Transportation* on the planning of the railway (Ref. 6.3). It started in the following way:

Less than five years ago a public meeting was arranged to discuss the new idea for transport in Docklands. Several thousand leaflets had been distributed, posters displayed and notices published in the local press. On the night about eight members of the public turned up, outnumbered by officials two to one. The concept of a light rail was explained and how it could dramatically improve accessibility to the area and exciting impressions of things to come were produced. But of course none of the eight members of the public believed a word of it. They had heard that someone from LT was talking about transport in Docklands and all they were really interested in was why there was a 25-minute gap in the 277 bus a week last Thursday – and it was raining!

Planners, architects and engineers must always be optimists, identifying problems, seeking and analysing possible solutions and bringing forward ideas which at the time might seem highly improbable to many people. The original dock railways were constructed by entrepreneurs who simply obtained the powers and went ahead with no thought or compensation for the unfortunate people living in their path. Thankfully today this is no longer the case and presenting and discussing proposals with the wider public is an essential part of any project, however sceptical they may be.

The initial DLR was an act of faith, thought up as a simple and cheap solution to an identified access problem, seized by the inspirational politician Michael Heseltine to stimulate redevelopment. I am sure that he, like me trying to explain to those few members of the public what the railway might look like and the benefits it could bring, had absolutely no inkling of what the railway might trigger in the area and the value it now has for the thousands of local people and commuters it can carry every day in the twenty-first century.

CHAPTER 7

CANARY WHARF DEVELOPMENT

In 1985, a year before the demise of the GLC, I transferred to work for LT in their Planning Department under the Director of Planning, David Bayliss.

My first encounter with the prospective Canary Wharf developers was an early morning meeting in September 1986 in the office of the then Managing Director of London Underground, Tony Ridley, with the American developer Mr G. Ware Travelstead and his transport consultants. What a dynamic and significant meeting that proved to be!

The developers had approached the LDDC in the summer of 1986 before the initial DLR had opened. Their plans would result in more than a doubling of jobs in the Isle of Dogs to around 50,000. Everyone was taken aback by the development proposals which would change dramatically the scale and type of land use and above all the transport requirements for the Isle of Dogs.

Over the next fifteen years or so working with Canary Wharf Ltd, I developed a close working relationship with its experts, particularly the architect Jim Berry. This proved to be significant during the planning of the Jubilee Line extension.

Without the Canary Wharf development the Docklands of today would have looked very different. Any offices would most likely be 'back-office' rather than headquarters and much smaller. Small businesses would be greater in number and housing would be of a much more modest scale. Early developments such as the initial low-rise housing on South Quay, later

7.1: Canary Wharf 1986.

redeveloped as high-rise offices, remained until recently as an example of what might have been.

The DLR was already under construction as Canary Wharf appeared on the scene and it is almost certain that the area would not have been considered at this time for such a major development if this had not been the case. In its absence the DLR would probably have been extended to the Royal Docks and possibly Lewisham but the expensive Bank extension may not have happened. Canary Wharf Ltd has had such a major influence on the development of railways throughout Docklands that a brief summary of its development is in order.

All Change in the City

The 1980s was a period of rapid development in the financial world and London was having to compete with the likes of Paris and Frankfurt for the key financial position, sitting midway between the New York and Tokyo trading time zones. In 1986 the 'Big Bang' in the UK gave the banks more independence and encouraged the creation of a range of new financial enterprises. The traditional open-floor trading of the stock market and other financial institutions and businesses was being replaced by technology and computers. London needed to respond quickly to create more space for people and machines. This was difficult in the very traditional City of London where the planning authority was initially reluctant to allow substantial changes to existing buildings and redevelopment. The availability of Docklands land, the timing of the setting up of the LDDC, the creation of the Enterprise Zone status with its financial incentives and the fact that transport improvements were already underway could not have come at a better time for the future of London's financial business sector.

Big Plans for the Wharf

The proposal, first laid on the table by the American Mr Gooch Ware Travelstead for 1m square metres of development on the former banana wharfs of Canary Wharf, in the summer of 1986, took everyone by surprise, including the LDDC. The plans, first promoted by Mr Travelstead and bankers Credit Suisse and First Boston, later taken over by Canadian developers Olympia and York (O&Y), would comprise ten hectares of a range of buildings largely within the Enterprise Zone, employing up to 50,000 people. It would be the largest such commercial development in Europe.

The initial plan included buildings constructed to the latest international standards within a high quality environment. It was directly aimed at the new requirements of the City financial trading companies with the need for large open plan offices, fully equipped with modern power and telecommunication systems.

An international group of consultants was retained by the developers to create a master plan and to produce

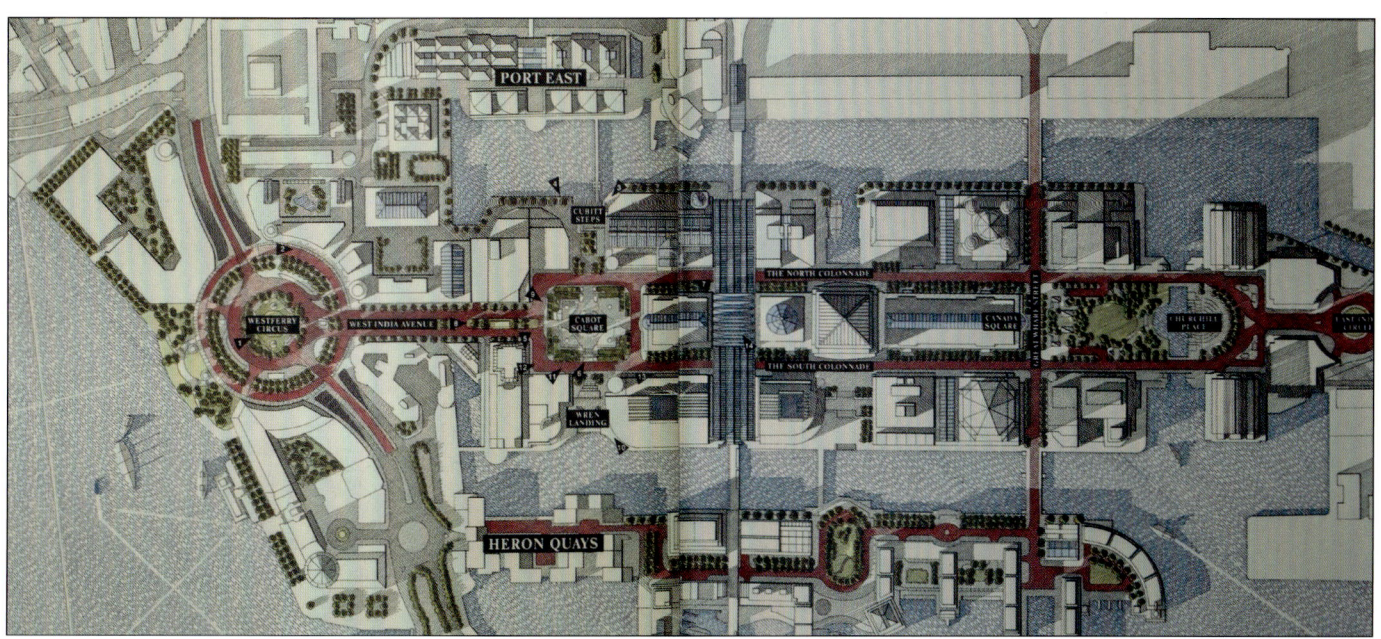

7.2: Canary Wharf first master plan.

design guidelines which would set a high standard throughout the project. As an illustration of the calibre of the design sought, all street furniture on the site (lamp posts, benches, railings, handrails, telephone kiosks, street signs and even litter bins) was to be custom designed. The plan comprised 1m sq. metres of office space, 0.5m sq. metres of retail, restaurants and leisure, a hotel with associated conference and banqueting and over 6,500 above-ground car parking spaces. Twenty-four separate buildings were planned with three identified for high-rise office towers.

When O&Y took over the project in 1987, the outline of the plans was retained but the layout of buildings changed, the road system was lowered and the parking placed underground. Britain's tallest office block was

intended to give a sense of place and identity and to be, in the developer's words: 'a constant reminder to Londoners that a whole new district existed in the capital'. The signing of a master building agreement between the LDDC and O&Y for 12.2m sq. ft (1.1m sq. m) of new offices took place in July 1987 only a month before the DLR opened.

The entire replanning process took only four months and included the complete redesign of Canary Wharf DLR station, then under construction. In fact, when the railway opened later in 1987 the computer system required that trains had to briefly stop at the site of Canary Wharf station but without access for passengers. The station redesign was a crucial element of the new plans and a number of options were explored including

7.3: West Ferry Circus, artist impression.

accessing the platforms from above the station. In a furious few days the design was finalised with three tracks, two island and two side platforms. The island platforms were accessed from a concourse below and the side platforms directly from developments either side. It was an opportunity, seldom achieved, to closely integrate a public transport facility in the heart of a new development. With the doors opening on both sides of the trains, allowing multiple platform access points for passengers, it is a fine example which can be achieved when planners, operators and developers work closely together.

The developers of Canary Wharf brought something unique to London, a concept of a purpose-built financial centre, built in an extraordinarily short time by means of a novel construction process. Five key people were at the heart of the project. Richard Griffiths, the builder; Paul Reichmann, President of O&Y; Chief Executive Michael Dennis; Planner Tony Coombes and George Iacobescu, the Financial Director who went on to be Chief Executive and later Chairman of the Canary Wharf Group.

Conventional building practices were thrown out of the window. To meet the timescale of the Enterprise Zone, construction started at the same time on a group of seven tower blocks. These included No.1 Canada Place, then the tallest building in Europe, at 236 metres. Access to the site over East London's crowded roads was tortuous and space for storage at the site was non-existent. Rapid fast-track construction was only possible by means of a sophisticated

7.4: Canary Wharf DLR station, artist impression.

'just-in-time' logistical operation, with boats carrying 80 per cent of the building materials from a holding site at Tilbury, dramatically reducing the number of lorry movements. Sophisticated programming halved normal construction time.

Most of the first buildings were let before construction had been completed, having been built within their surroundings to a quality unusual for London. The late Sir Roy Strong, former Director of the Victoria and Albert Museum, stated:

> Canary Wharf is a return to the Grand Tradition … I was astonished by the attention to detail … it wasn't at all like we have done for years. You came away feeling this whole thing had been carefully worked out and integrated.

The first buildings were completed in 1991 but unfortunately by the time they opened the London property market had collapsed and O&Y filed for bankruptcy in May 1992.

Initially the City of London saw the development as a threat and proceeded to modify its planning laws to allow more expansion of offices in its province. It has been argued that the resulting oversupply of office space in the capital contributed to the temporary failure of the Canary Wharf project. As we will see later, as a consequence, the Jubilee Line extension project was put on hold until the property market recovered and the banks managing the Canary Wharf assets could be persuaded to see the synergy between the projects, allowing them both to proceed.

Today, in 2022, the Canary Wharf Group is owned by Brookfield Property Partners and the Qatari Investment Authority. 1.5m sq. m. of offices and retail have already been built employing over 120,000 people, including three major shopping areas and many restaurants and bars. Planning is underway for a further 1m sq. m. of development with more emphasis on housing than in the initial stages. Forecasts suggest that employment could eventually rise to over 200,000.

A significant area, currently at the planning stage in 2021, is North Quay, where a mixed development is proposed. Most importantly a key element in the plan is improvement to pedestrian links. The area to the north of the quay houses traditional East London communities with, currently, access only to Poplar DLR station. The plans include extension of the pedestrian overbridge

7.5 • Canary Wharf under construction.

7.6: Canary Wharf today (compare with the Wharf in 1986 shown at the beginning of this chapter).

at the station and new routes through the site leading onto Canary Wharf, via the Crossrail station. This will help to overcome the 'barrier' between the new and old developments and provide much improved access to the railway network at West Ferry, Crossrail and Jubilee line stations from the Poplar area.

Normally at similar locations in Inner London around 50 per cent of people travel to work by public transport. To plan for the continuation of this pattern in the Isle of Dogs would have required many new roads which was unrealistic. Even with the modest new road construction and the provision of large car parks it was envisaged that a much higher modal split in favour of public transport would be required. Today, with the DLR, Jubilee Line extension and many bus services, over 95 per cent of people travel to work in the Isle of Dogs by public transport, reflecting a typical share in Central London. This modal share to public transport has resulted in an under-utilisation of the car parking provided by the first two phases of Canary Wharf, to the extent that some of the upper levels of car parking have been converted to retail to meet changing demand. The continuing improvement brought by Crossrail will allow this proportion to be maintained in the future if not increased.

However, before all this happened, the first transport project to be prioritised by O&Y was the City extension of the DLR.

7.7: Canada Square.

CHAPTER 8

DLR CITY EXTENSION

My involvement in the City extension project included the development of an alternative station layout, the sizing of passage ways and escalators, passenger and revenue forecasts and the cost-benefit analysis which showed a small positive result.

At the first meeting with the Canary Wharf developers in September 1986, their transport consultants, Steer Davies and Gleave, led by Peter Twelftree, put forward a proposal to extend the DLR into the City at Bank which the developers were willing to contribute to. Parliamentary Bills have to be deposited in November of each year but Tony Ridley decided the opportunity was too good to miss and contrary to the normally cautious approach of LT it was decided to pull out all the stops and prepare a Bill for deposit that year. The decision triggered a major piece of work including the preparation of plans for the construction and operation of the extension and the 'Book of Reference' which identified all the property owners involved.

The timing was fortunate as a deep-piled building was planned on the route close to Tower Hill. A later Bill could well have missed the opportunity to negotiate a change of foundations for the building, allowing DLR tunnels to pass between the piles of the building.

Bank station is one of the more complex stations on the Underground network with the Central, Northern and Waterloo & City Lines and an interchange connection from the Northern Line platforms to the District and Circle Lines at Monument. The DLR would have to enter the complex, passing under the Northern Line, therefore making it the deepest railway in Central London at that time, around 42 metres below the surface. Also being in the centre of the City the availability of surface land for a work site was almost non-existent.

The proposal submitted in the Parliamentary Plans in November 1986 was for a DLR station situated beneath the Mansion House to the west of the existing station. However early discussions with the City Corporation revealed two significant concerns. The first was that the Mansion House, built in the 1740s, was known to have very poor foundations and the concern was that tunnelling beneath, particularly for the large platform

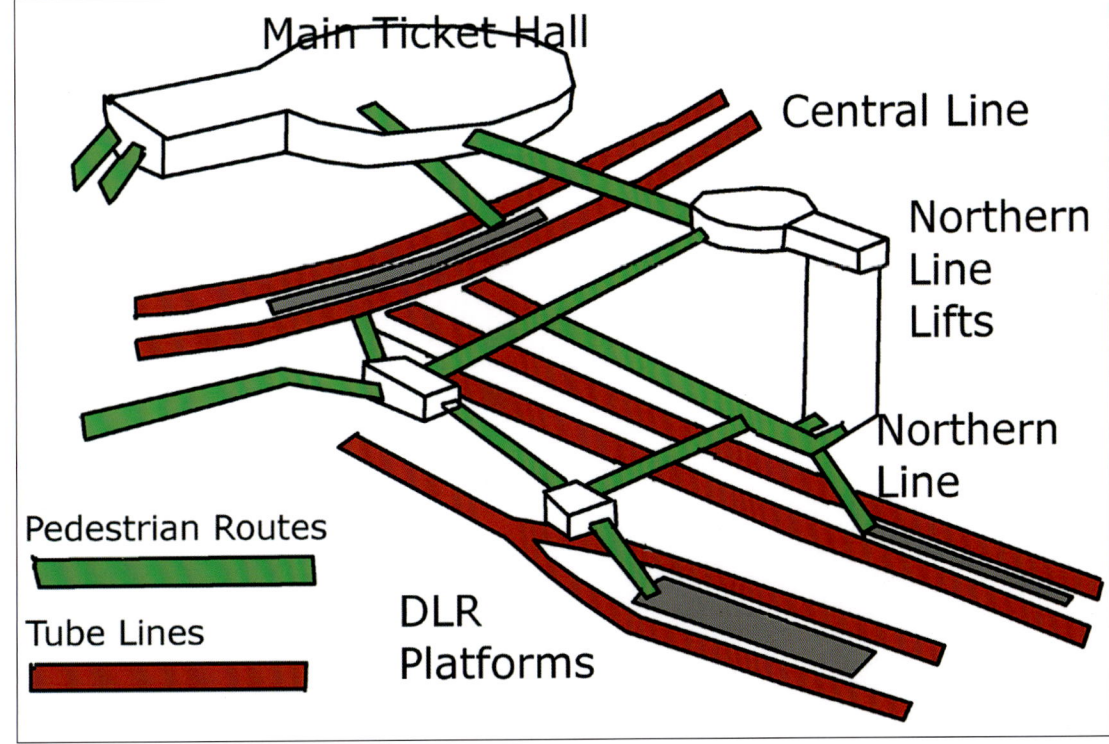

8.1: Author's original sketch of Bank station.

Main Ticket Hall

Central Line

Northern Line Lifts

Northern Line

Pedestrian Routes

Tube Lines

DLR Platforms

8.2: DLR Bank station platforms.

tunnels required, could cause significant damage to the building. The second was that major works in this area would undoubtedly impinge on the resident of the Mansion House, the Lord Mayor of London. It was explained that this position was the pinnacle of the career of the incumbent and to have their whole year disrupted by major works would be, at least, most unfortunate.

Although the Bill had already been deposited an alternative site urgently needed to be found. Fortunately one was produced which moved the platforms to the east directly below the Northern Line platforms above. This had the advantage of allowing construction of an interchange link directly from the DLR to the District & Circle Lines at Monument.[1] Fortunately this proposal fitted within the original Bill's 'Limits of Deviation' and an amended Bill was not required.

The conventional cost-benefit evaluation of the Bank extension produced a much better result than for the initial DLR with a benefit to cost ratio of 1.1 to 1. The final cost at £295m (including works to upgrade the rest of the railway) was more than double the cost of the whole initial DLR and funded between the Department of Transport and the developers O&Y, who contributed £95m. This was the first time a private company had invested in a railway in the UK for many years.

Design and Construction

Bank station was the first new Underground station to have been built since the first stage of the Jubilee Line opened in 1979 and new techniques had to be developed to assess passenger flows on passages, stairs and escalators and produce design guidelines – for example, for the width of stairs. Several aspects of the design of the station were less than ideal resulting from constraints on the budget. The main problem from the operational point of view was the single track overrun beyond the station for the reversal of trains, meaning that the integrity of service was totally dependent on a single set of points.[2] A twin track overrun, as is normal for such termini, would have been far more satisfactory.

Another issue was the design of the escalators with only two constructed in each shaft. Later on, the space between these was modified to create a rather narrow staircase which could be used during escalator maintenance or failure. Also the original interchange

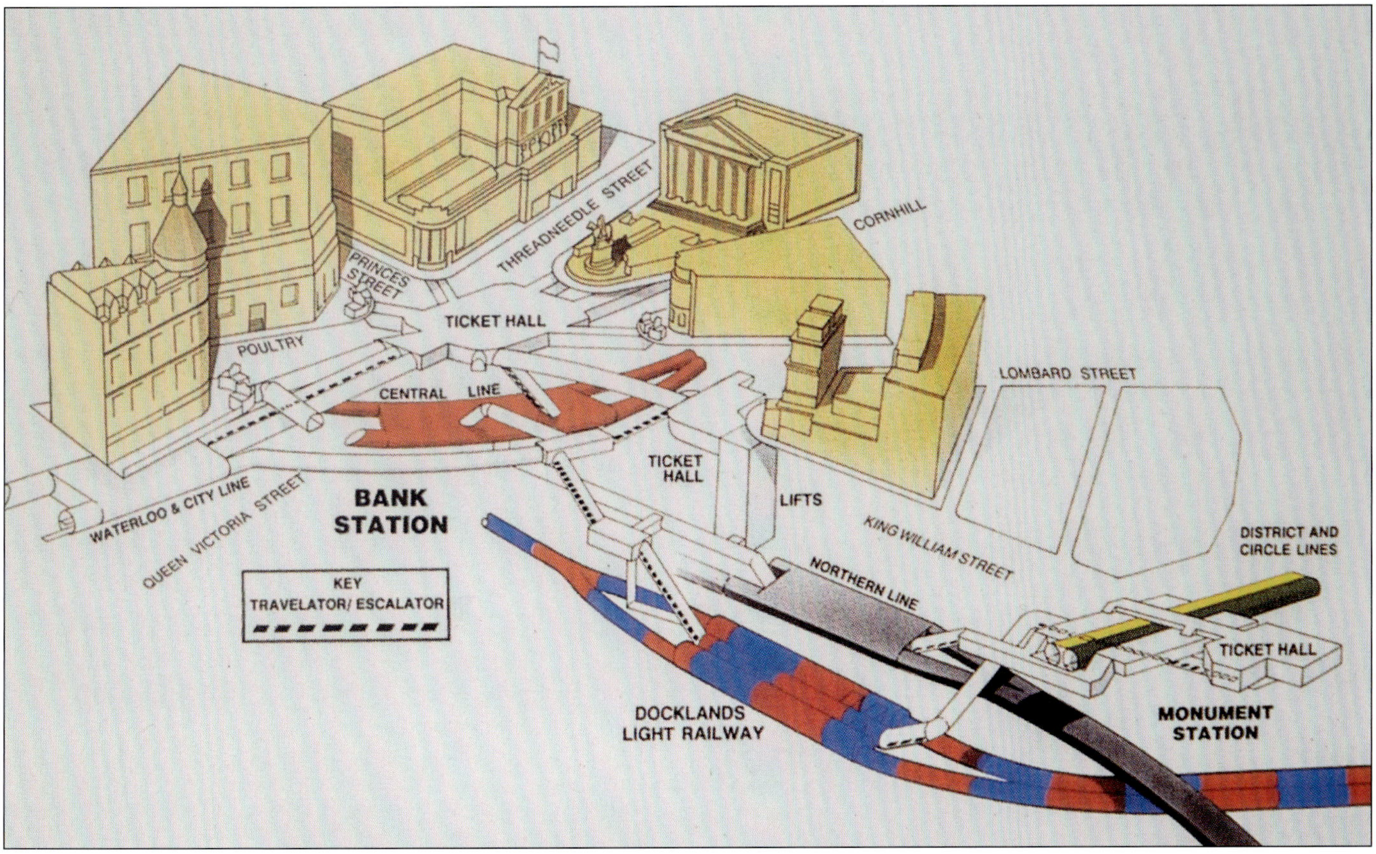

8.3 (above): Bank station, built layout.

8.4 (right): Section of passage under the Mansion House.

to the Central Line proposed to 'slice' through the top of the Central Line station tunnel, giving a short route for passengers. Cost saving eliminated this option requiring passengers to climb stairs up and down over the line.

On the positive side a new low-level pedestrian connection between the Northern Line and the DLR line to the Waterloo & City Line was opened. The latter used to be a running tunnel connection through to the Central Line. This link was used during the DLR station construction, as the main access to a work site on the west side of the Mansion House. On completion this was made a permanent pedestrian connection, although as it passed under the poor foundations of the Mansion House a section of the tunnel was narrowed with extra reinforcements. Passengers passing though the link can today see this section and also the remains of a Greathead tunnelling shield, discovered during the works, which was used to excavate the original link to the Central Line.

Perhaps the most important planning decision made for the station was to construct it so as to enable the future operation of three-car trains. Whilst at the time only two-car trains were necessary to meet the demand forecasts, this decision enabled the railway to expand in the future without substantially changing the station.

The tunnels were bored at 5 metres diameter to allow for maintenance and an emergency access walkway along one side. As the alignment of the running tunnels to join the initial DLR pass quite close to Tower Hill Underground station, thought was given to providing an interchange station. This was ruled out on cost grounds but a length of the tunnels was built on a straight and level alignment to allow the possibility in the future.[3] This section of the railway also had to have permission from the Tower of London authorities as it 'lay within a bowshot range of the Tower'!

The ramp from the tunnel section up to viaduct level on the initial DLR east of Tower Gateway had to be constructed at a gradient of 6 per cent and there were some concerns as to whether the requirement to be able to restart a fully loaded train in wet conditions on the ramp could be met. A design was prepared for a form of canopy to cover the ramp but in the end the test of

8.5: Remains of Greathead tunnelling shield.

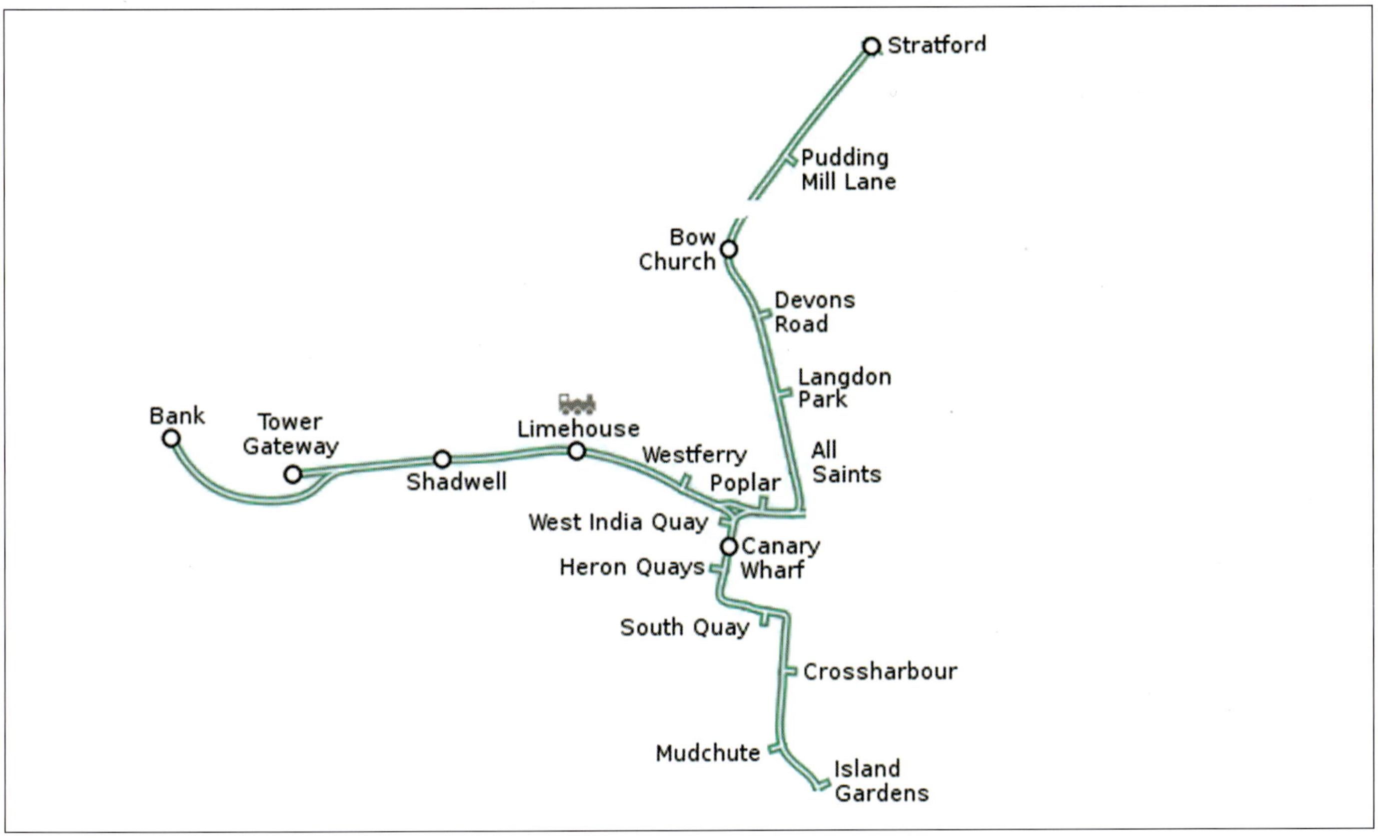

8.6: DLR with Bank extension.

8.7: Ramp leading to Bank extension tunnel.

a new train, artificially fully loaded, proved entirely satisfactory and the canopy was not required.

In July 1987, a month before the initial Docklands Railway opened, a contract was let to Edmund Nuttall Ltd for the Bank extension civil works and to GEC-Mowlem for the electrical works and for upgrading the existing system and new vehicles. These contracts were for Design and Construct as for the initial DLR.

Operations

As demand grew there was significant congestion on the link from the DLR platforms to the Northern Line. To relieve this a direct staircase link was constructed from the centre of the Northern Line platforms down to the DLR platforms below. This was a difficult operation as the Northern platforms are rather narrow, but did succeed in reducing congestion at the northern end of the DLR station.

The eleven trains running on the initial DLR did not meet with modern fire regulations for tunnel operation. Ten new compliant trains were ordered from BR Engineering with a number of improvements over the original design including better door operation. The original trains were eventually sold to Essen in Germany for operation on their system.

The new trains allowed train services to increase to five to six-minute intervals and with the much improved connection into the City, passenger demand on the railway quickly doubled. With the improved signalling in place, trains can now run into either platform at Bank if required.

Upgrading the DLR

The DLR City extension was undertaken at the same time as the upgrading of the rest of the railway with a contract let to GEC-Mowlem, the original builders of the railway. This included extending the station platforms to take two-car trains, upgrading the signalling to allow for a more frequent service and the complete rebuilding of Canary Wharf station. Later, the very constraining 'delta' junction with tight radius curves at the north end of the Isle of Dogs was also rebuilt. The extensive work and overlap between the various contracts created a range of problems for the DLR which resulted in a period of poor reliability for many months as well as necessitating evening and weekend closure of the railway.

Bank Station Expansion

At the time of writing in 2021 construction is well underway on a major upgrading of Bank station. Passenger flows through the station have increased significantly since the DLR opened and congestion regularly occurs throughout the complex. In 2015, TfL obtained a Transport and Works Order (Ref. 8.1) which included a new tunnel alignment for the Northern Line alongside the existing line giving space for new escalators serving the DLR and Northern Line. Also, new escalators and a moving walkway will serve the Central Line and new station entrances opened on Walbrook and Canon Street.

With passenger forecasts still rising in line with the planned growth in employment in the Isle of Dogs, after the City extension thoughts turned to how to improve access to the Royal Docks area – to serve the growing population in Beckton, to stimulate development around the former docks and to open up a new route to Central London via the Isle of Dogs. The extension to Lewisham was principally to widen the catchment of the Isle of Dogs employment area.

8.8: New station entrance on Walbrook Street.

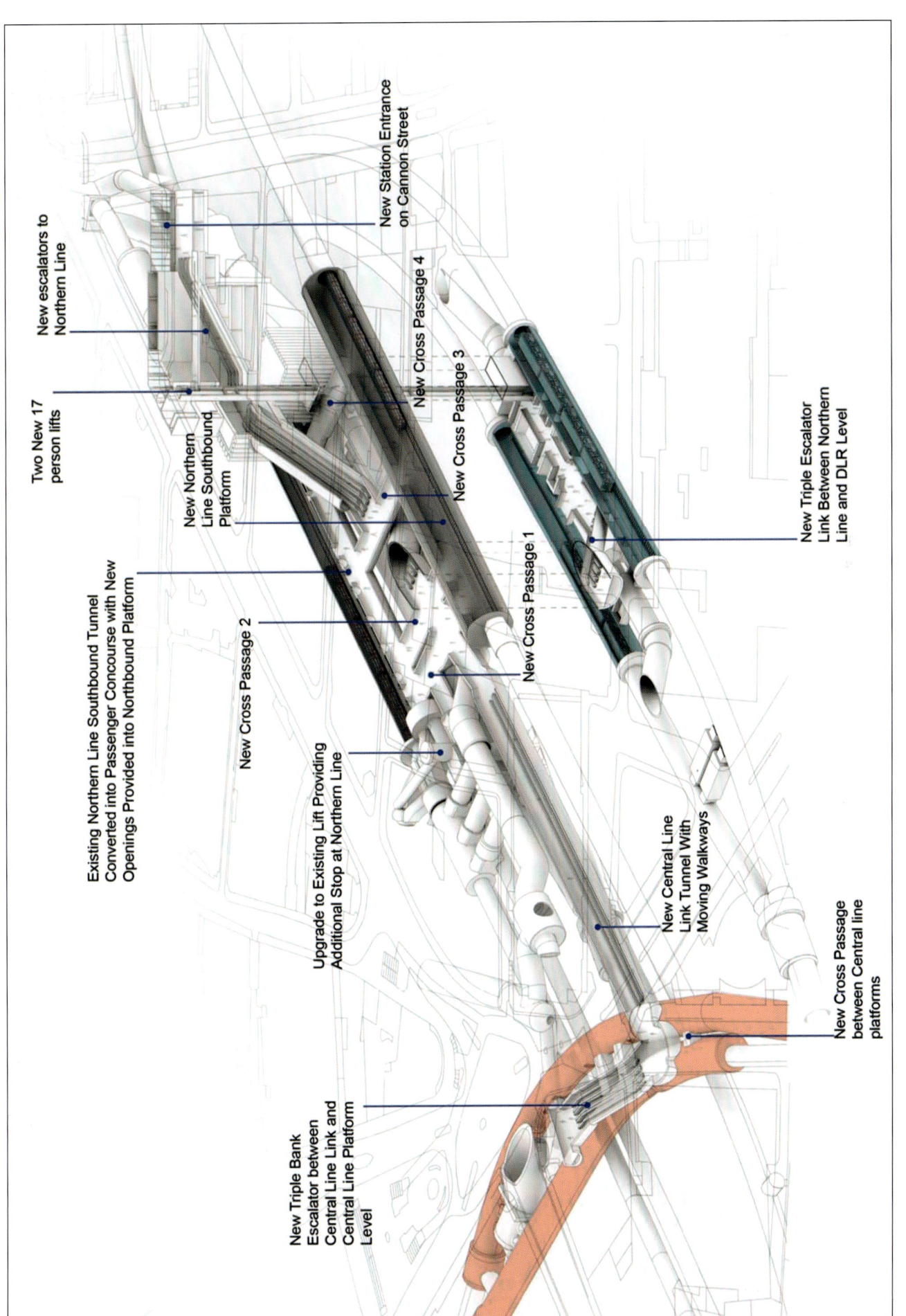

New escalators to Northern Line

Two New 17 person lifts

Existing Northern Line Southbound Tunnel Converted into Passenger Concourse with New Openings Provided into Northbound Platform

New Northern Line Southbound Platform

New Station Entrance on Cannon Street

New Cross Passage 4

New Cross Passage 3

New Cross Passage 2

New Cross Passage 1

Upgrade to Existing Lift Providing Additional Stop at Northern Line

New Triple Escalator Link Between Northern Line and DLR Level

New Triple Bank Escalator between Central Line Link and Central Line Platform Level

New Central Line Link Tunnel With Moving Walkways

New Cross Passage between Central line platforms

8.9: Current improvements to Bank station.

CHAPTER 9

DLR BECKTON AND LEWISHAM EXTENSIONS

Although Beckton and Lewisham extensions were eventually funded by the Department of the Environment via the LDDC, LT was responsible for obtaining the Parliamentary Powers to construct and operate the railways. I was responsible for the planning within LT, being involved in the determination of the routes, the station locations and designs, demand and revenue forecasts, the project appraisal and giving evidence to the Parliamentary Committees.

The Beckton Extension

Following the approval to go ahead with the City extension of the DLR in 1987, the LDDC's thoughts turned to the other large area for potential development, namely the Royal Docks. Land values were rising quickly and it was thought that the development momentum experienced in the Isle of Dogs would be continued in the 'Royals'.

The proposed route was to extend from the existing railway at Poplar and then rise to cross the River Lea before descending to run parallel to the Victoria and Albert Docks on the north side. By this time the London City Airport had started operation on the quay between the Albert Dock and the King George V Dock. The airport was served by the North Woolwich line with a station at Silvertown which was assumed to be satisfactory at the time. There was a choice of route to the Beckton local centre, either along the former 'gas line' which directly ran to the former Beckton gas works, or staying parallel to the end of the Albert Dock towards the old Gallions Hotel and then to turn north to Beckton.

Following the success of attracting new development to the Isle of Dogs, the LDDC worked with a number of developers planning a regional shopping centre, a science and commercial park, a 23,000-seat arena and over 1,000 homes alongside the Royal Docks.

9.1: Poplar station.

The developers were also prepared to invest in the infrastructure and the LDDC envisaged that the DLR extension could be largely paid for by the proceeds of land sales, anticipating a significant increase in value, as had occurred in the Isle of Dogs. The estimates had shown that such a funding mechanism would be viable with the funds being managed by an independent land-holding company. However the newly appointed Environment Secretary Nicholas Ridley did not agree with the LDDC's development proposals, preferring mainly housing. This effectively brought the plans to a full stop until further evaluations had been undertaken. In the end the Government gave the go-ahead on the basis of the extension serving a population of 65,000 and employment of 45,000. These figures have yet to be fully realised.

A Parliamentary Bill was submitted by LT in November 1989 for the Beckton extension but was opposed by the London Borough of Newham which favoured a route via Canning Town rather than running directly across the River Lea. The LDDC favoured the more direct route which would provide quicker journey times to the central area. Promoting the Bill, LT was inclined to accept Newham's point of view but was in a difficult position as it was promoting the Bill on behalf of the Development Corporation. In the end the House of Commons Committee decided that the Bill could not proceed without adopting the alternative route and the promoters had to agree with the decision. The Bill was finally approved but had to be amended by means of an 'Additional Provision', incurring time and cost penalties.[1]

9.2: Canning Town station.

9.3 (left): Prince Regent station.

9.4 (below): Royal Albert station.

However, also in 1989, soon after the contract for construction of the extension was let, London's property development bubble burst and the funding mechanism collapsed. The railway extension was delayed but did eventually go ahead and had to be paid from public funds by the Department for the Environment through the LDDC at a cost of £280m. At the same time a new signalling and control system was introduced at a cost of £56m.

Design and Construction

All the stations on the extension were constructed to take two-car trains, later extended to three cars. At Poplar the opportunity was taken to reconfigure the two side platforms of the initial DLR to form island platforms with the Beckton lines running on the outside. As services were to run from the Isle of Dogs to Stratford and from Tower Gateway to Beckton, this arrangement gave cross-platform interchange in the most used directions between the two services at Poplar.

From Poplar to Canning Town a single concrete column structure was used, being somewhat more elegant and robust than the two-column concrete and steel structures used in the Isle of Dogs. New elevated stations were constructed at Blackwall, East India and Prince Regent.

The route via Canning Town then had to adopt a circuitous loop running across one of the bends of the River Lea and then via a very narrow peninsula formed by the river to provide a station adjacent to the North London line station at Canning Town. Although difficult at the time, the decision to route the railway in this way was able to create a very satisfactory interchange with the Jubilee Line some ten years later.[2] A possible future station at Thames Wharf was safeguarded and at the time of writing is being considered for construction. From Canning Town to Connaught Crossing the line was constructed alongside the North London line with surface stations at Royal Victoria, Custom House, providing interchange with the North London line, and Prince Regent. Beyond Royal Albert a new highway was also to be constructed on a similar alignment so the opportunity arose to integrate the two designs along with two

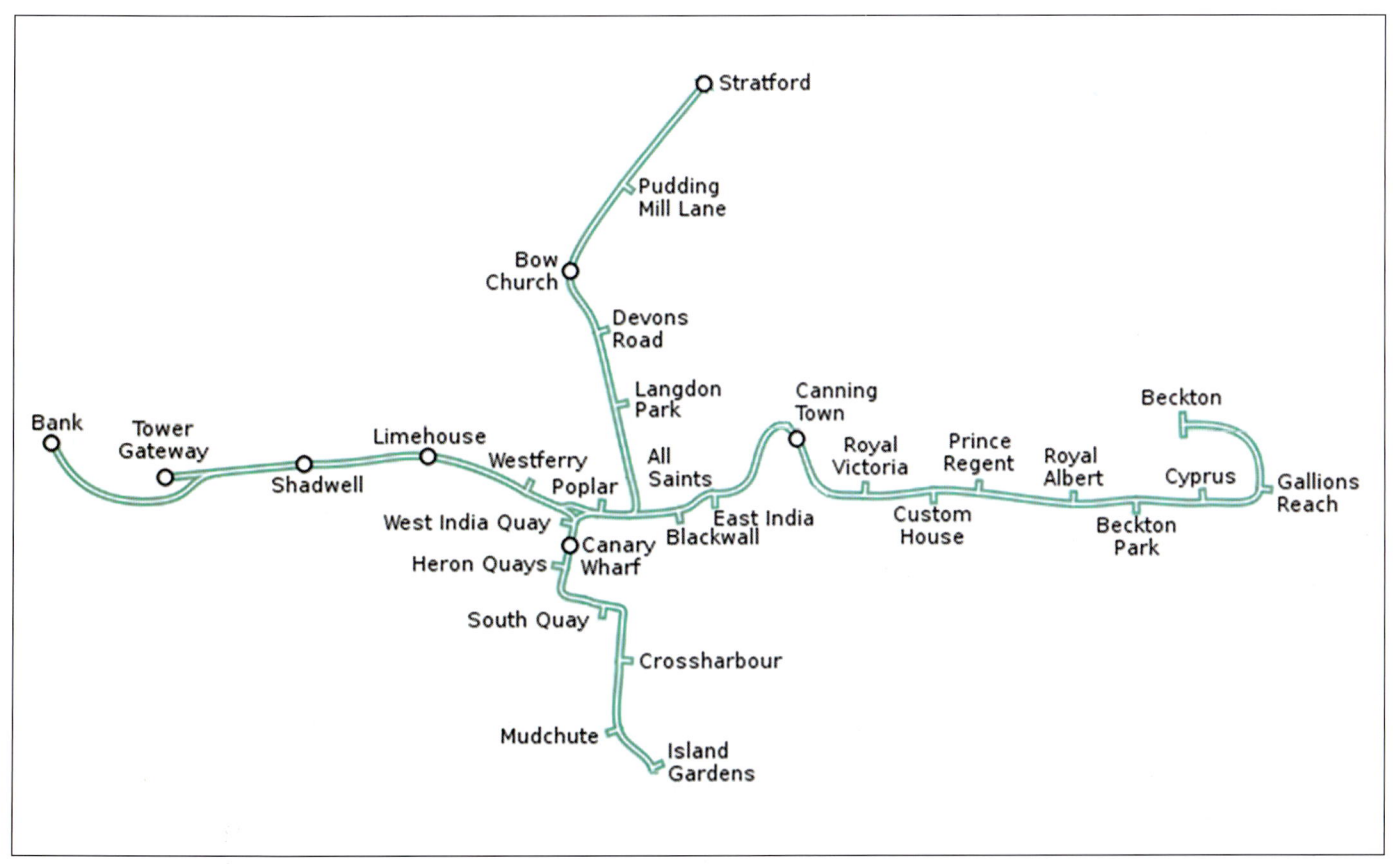

9.5: DLR with Beckton extension.

new stations at Beckton Park and Cyprus. There was also a requirement to allow pedestrians to cross the transport corridor unimpeded. After a lot of thought the innovative design and engineering solution was to site the railway in the central reservation of the dual carriageway and at the stations to elevate the road, to slightly depress the station platforms and to insert between the two a near level pedestrian bridge over the railway. This gave a segregated pedestrian crossing of the road and railway providing step-free access from the housing developments north of the corridor, to the proposed employment areas to the south, at the same time providing access to both sides of the station.

At Gallions the railway left the docks and curved north to an elevated Gallions Reach station, then down to a surface-level station at Beckton. With the expanding railway and the severe constraints on the original depot at Poplar the opportunity was taken to build a second and much larger depot to the east of the railway on land formerly occupied by Beckton gas works.

Station designs on the extension were very different to the initial DLR, particularly the platform canopies, and there was still no requirement for an Environmental Survey of the impact of the railway. However there was an increasing concern, particularly from the point of view of the local authorities, as to how the stations would relate to their local surroundings in terms of pedestrian access, local bus stops, pavements and landscaping. For the first time LT and LDDC took the initiative to produce a 'Context Plan' for each station showing such details to be included in the project.

During the passage of the Bill a new issue arose from the London Borough of Tower Hamlets over concerns about potential increased noise levels with longer and more frequent trains running over the elevated sections of the initial DLR through residential areas. At that time, unlike highways, there was no official noise law or requirements for railways in the UK. An unexpected task for the DLR was to urgently develop a noise policy and reach agreement with the local authority about the noise levels at which trackside barriers and/or secondary glazing could be offered. The necessity to produce the policy for the DLR led to the Department of the Environment setting up the Mitchell Committee which reported in 1991 with new regulations finally

9.6: Beckton Park station.

9.7: Gallions Reach station.

9.8: Beckton depot.

being issued in 1996 covering all new railways in the UK (Ref 9.1). The DLR subsequently went on to construct substantial noise barriers at various sensitive locations along the railway.

Ownership of the DLR

In 1992 during the planning stages of the Beckton extension the Government decided that ownership and management of the DLR should be transferred from LT to the LDDC. At the time the railway was not very reliable and it was felt that the LDDC, whose success in attracting developers hinged on the provision of high quality transport links, would be able to give the problems closer attention. A Parliamentary Bill was required to transfer the assets to the LDDC, which took over the DLR in 1992. Responsibility within Government for the railway therefore passed from the Department of Transport to the Department of the Environment, the funders of the LDDC. When the LDDC took over control of the DLR it appointed a new management team led by Sir Peter Leveen and the American engineering group Brown and Root to take over running the railway and managing its further expansion, for a fee of £30m.

Operations

The Beckton extension opened in 1994. In the same year the then Secretary of State for the Environment, John Gummer, announced the Government's intention

to privatise the whole DLR. In the end this did not go ahead but in 1997 a seven-year franchise was let to Dockland Railways Management Ltd, a consortium of Serco Group plc and a team of ex-DLR managers. The franchisee was responsible for the track, trains and operations, taking income from fares and a fixed annual fee from Government. The franchise was renewed in 2006.

A number of service patterns have been operated on the Beckton branch over the years with currently a train every eight minutes to Tower Gateway in the peak hour. Demand on the branch is generally lower than on the other branches as development has not proceeded as fast as originally anticipated. With a Crossrail interchange station at Custom House both levels of development and DLR passenger flows could change significantly. When there is a major exhibition at the ExCel exhibition centre an additional shuttle service from Canning Town to Prince Regent can be operated.

The DLR Lewisham Extension

The Lewisham extension was first suggested by officers from the borough in 1985 who put pressure on LT and the LDDC to progress the project as soon as the Beckton extension was under construction. The extension was very different from the other routes being designed to provide a link between the major residential areas south of the river and the growing employment opportunities in Docklands, particularly in the Isle of Dogs. If it were possible to provide an interchange with the North Kent line at Greenwich then the extension could be an attractive alternative route into Docklands and even into the City at Bank, avoiding travelling via London Bridge. The benefits of providing a tourist route between the Tower of London and Greenwich were also recognised and it was estimated that an additional half a million people would be living within a catchment of the Canary Wharf development.

The extension left the initial DLR south of Millwall Dock station. The initial railway had risen up to an elevated Mudchute station before running onto the old Millwall Dock railway viaduct to Island Gardens station, formerly named North Greenwich. To avoid demolishing the old viaduct or taking public open space, the extension replaced Mudchute station with a new surface station, then entered a cut and cover section under the park before reaching a new underground station at Island Gardens. The old Millwall Dock railway

viaduct was consequently used from 1870 until 1926, lay abandoned until 1987, was used by the initial DLR for eleven years until 1998, and then allowed to revert to its dormant role as an attractive listed structure.

The extension was also a challenge to the DLR with a number of further hurdles to overcome. It was mainly outside the LDDC's area so funds were unable to be channelled through the organisation. The second hurdle was the tunnel under the Thames – the first railway crossing in East London since Brunel's East London line opened in 1843 – in the uncertain sand and gravel of the Thames and Reading Beds requiring use of a special tunnel-boring machine. The Bank extension had been largely tunnelled through the ideal London Clay.

A deep-level station at *Cutty Sark* was proposed and strongly supported by the borough, which wanted to increase tourism to the historic town of Greenwich. However the closeness to the Thames and restrictions on the works imposed by the borough substantially

9.9 • Mudchute station.

9.10: Island Gardens station.

increased the cost of construction. As a result the Treasury insisted on the station being deleted. However a hurried redesign, shortening the platforms to only accommodate two-car trains, allowing the station to be built by the cut and cover method, rather than by the much more expensive tunnelling and permitting a more profitable over-site development, made the project more affordable.

Tenders for the extension did not include the station, but with agreement from the Minister, Stephen Norris, the bidders were informed that alternative bids including the station would be favourably considered. Three of the four bidders included the station, including the one chosen.

The next major challenge for the extension was the interchange with Greenwich National Rail station. At the east end of the station the BR tracks quickly descended into a tunnel and at the west end Deptford Creek provided another constraint. An underground station was considered but would prove costly as the railway would then probably have had to stay in tunnel for some considerable distance to avoid the creek. In the end an ingenious solution was reached with the DLR tunnel passing as close as possible underneath the BR station approach tunnel and then rising steeply under an extended BR platform to provide surface platforms for the DLR. The DLR was then at an appropriate level to rise over the Deptford Creek and with its single column piers leapfrog from side to side above the water. In a much built up area this required acquisition of small amounts of property for the siting of the columns. The bridge over the South Circular Road at Deptford enabled a station to conveniently straddle the road.

South of Deptford station there was a park through which the railway needed to pass, which not surprisingly caused concern to the borough. However, alongside the park the River Ravensbourne ran in a very unattractive concrete channel. A neat solution was found by diverting the river on a new, much more attractive alignment through the park and constructing the railway in the concrete channel.

9.11: Sinuous route over Deptford Creek.

Along this section there is a major source of domestic fresh water from deep level aquifers in chalk. Thames Water were concerned at the possible pollution from construction of the railway requiring special care during the build.

A surface level station was provided at Elverson Road and the line then ran to Lewisham where a new tunnel had to be constructed through the embankment of the BR line to give a surface station between the two branches of the main-line station.

A significant new requirement for the Lewisham extension was the introduction of an Environmental Assessment – from then on being a statutory requirement for any new railway Bill. This had to be undertaken by expert independent consultants but funded by the promoters who were allowed to comment on the final draft but not make changes to the conclusions. The report made a number of recommendations to mitigate several adverse effects, which had to be taken into account before completion of the project. Parliamentary Powers were obtained for the extension by LT in 1993.

With a new cross-river link between the highly populated areas of South London and the growing employment opportunities north of the river, the passenger forecasts showed the extension would attract

9.12: Alongside the River Ravensbourne.

significant demand.[3] The evaluation showed that the benefit to cost ratio was the highest of all the DLR extensions and that it would generate a healthy financial surplus sufficient to cover the operating costs and make a substantial contribution to capital funding.

A new possible funding mechanism was explored whereby developments of over a certain size in the Isle of Dogs would contribute a percentage of their turnover to close the funding gap of around £50m out of a total cost of around £200m. Unfortunately a UK recession was starting to take hold and the idea had to be abandoned.

Finally 'in February 1995' the Government announced that the private sector was to be invited to finance, build and maintain the 4.2km extension, initially without the costly deep level station at *Cutty Sark*. The Japanese City General Lewisham Railway plc (CGL Rail) won the contract for the construction and then to maintain the infrastructure for twenty-five years. However, as a result of the general capping of fares in London, revenue projections were predicted to be lower than expected and in the end the Department of the Environment accepted to pay the shortfall of £50m. There were also contributions from the London Borough of Lewisham

(£4.8m) and smaller amounts from the London Borough of Greenwich, Deptford City Challenge, University of Greenwich and the National Maritime Museum. The project achieved a much higher percentage of private finance than any other UK public sector project at the time. With strong representation from the London Borough of Greenwich and additional funding secured with the help of English Partnerships, the project was amended to include the *Cutty Sark* underground station.

Initially it was intended to impose an additional 'toll' fare on the river crossing. However with a change in Government in 1997, the Deputy Prime Minister John Prescott gave a grant of £20m to the DLR to remove the toll and pay for additional trains, anticipated to be necessary as a result of increased demand, following removal of the toll.

The Lewisham extension opened in 1999 with DLR operating the services which currently run every eight minutes to Stratford and every four minutes to Bank. Well before these two extensions were open it was realised that further capacity was needed to meet the passenger forecasts. It was time to resurrect the Jubilee Line extension project which had been dormant for more than a decade.

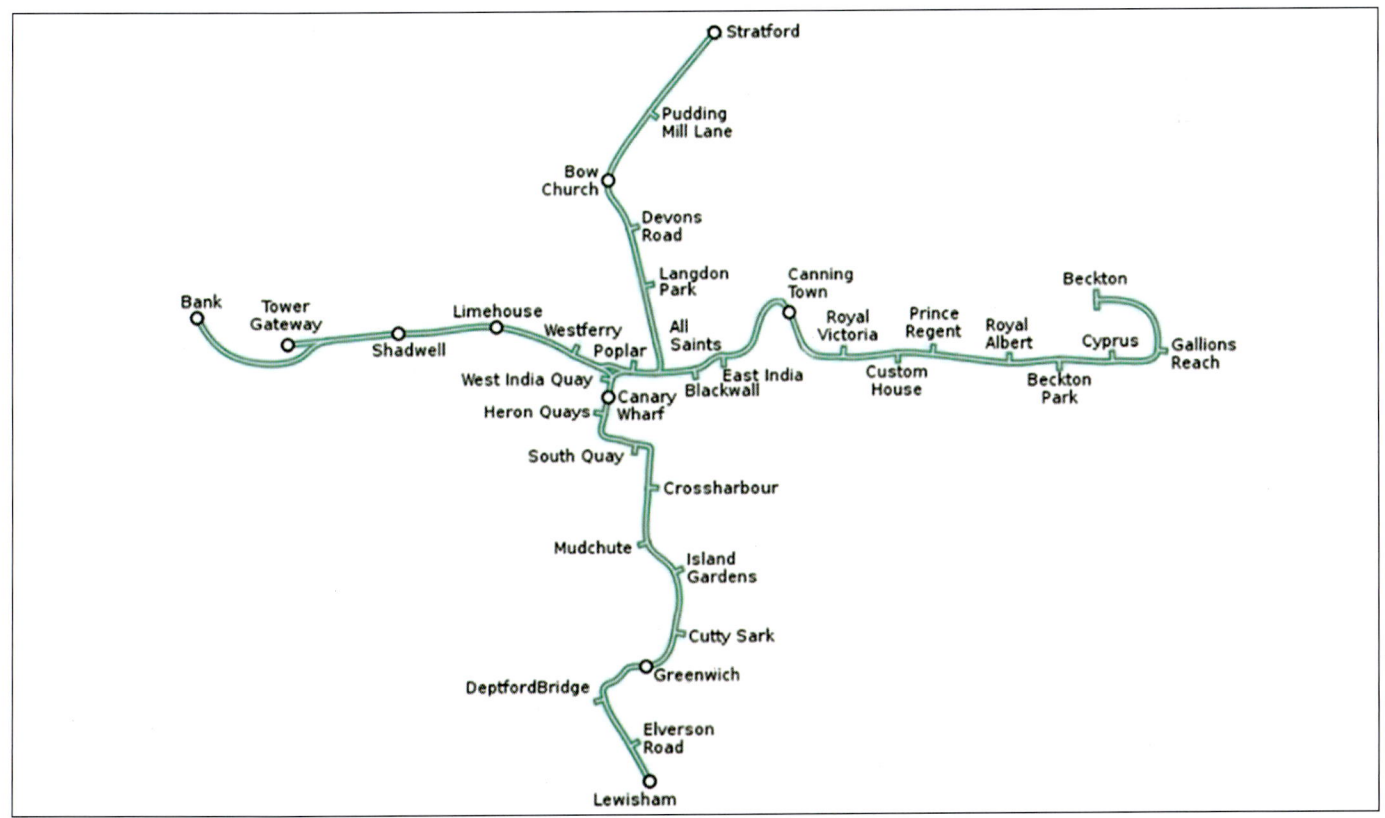

9.13: DLR with Lewisham extension.

9.14 (above): Elverson Road station.

9.15 (left): Bus interchange at Lewisham station.

CHAPTER 10

JUBILEE LINE EXTENSION

The Jubilee Line extension to Docklands, opened just before the millennium, was obviously a major undertaking by LT. The first leg from Baker Street to Charing Cross had been planned some fifteen years before and underground railway design and construction had advanced significantly over the years. Not least was the much increased attention placed on passenger safety and fire prevention following the King's Cross disaster in 1987. My planning team was closely involved in the evaluation of several alignment options for the new line, the location and justification for stations, the project evaluation and the preparation of evidence for the Parliamentary Committees.

Rebirth

By 1988, with the DLR already opened, employment forecasts for Docklands had risen eightfold in eight years, motivating LT to initiate a review of transport provision against likely demand. This brief but significant report, called *Docklands Public Transport Strategic Plan: Discussion Document* (Ref. 10.1), identified four strategic aims for public transport in the area. These were to:

- Provide a wide range of reliable and efficient services to capture the interest of developers and individuals wishing to locate in Docklands
- Provide adequate services capable of carrying the heavy flows associated with the developments presently proposed and for developments that are likely to occur later
- Provide good and preferably direct connections with other major commercial centres and with the local and more distant sources of labour and employment for firms and residents in Docklands and for tourists and other visitors using the various facilities in the area
- Provide public transport services that are sufficiently attractive to ensure that a high proportion of travellers to and from and within Docklands use public transport and that flows on the road network are kept within the capacity available.

The development at Canary Wharf was originally intended to be built in two phases, each of around 0.5m sq. metres and accommodating some 25,000 employees. The expanded DLR at the time could cope with a total of around 65,000 jobs around Canary Wharf but if the anticipated development in the rest of the Isle of Dogs went ahead this number would be exceeded. The second phase of the Canary Wharf development could not realistically go ahead unless further capacity on all modes of transport was available. Also it was realised that unless there was a substantial shift in the modal share in favour of public transport, highway capacity rather than public transport could prove to be the real constraint on development. The report identified the priorities as:

- increased capacity for cross-river access
- new link to Central London
- improved access from areas north and east of Docklands.

Improvements to the existing rail network could provide additional capacity including extensions to the East London line, the DLR to Lewisham and Barking and a new river crossing to Woolwich. However, in order for Docklands to expand to its full potential, the report identified the need for an Underground extension which provided good interchange with all other modes. The Underground was required to increase overall transport capacity as well as support the longer distance journey patterns expected from the growing regional status of the redevelopment. There was also the fact that a second line would increase the choice of routes serving Docklands and provide an alternative in the event of disruption.

The report identified the new Underground link as:

a new South Bank corridor line from Waterloo to Canary Wharf, the Blackwall peninsula and possibly to Stratford or Woolwich which would benefit cross river access, especially to the isolated Rotherhithe

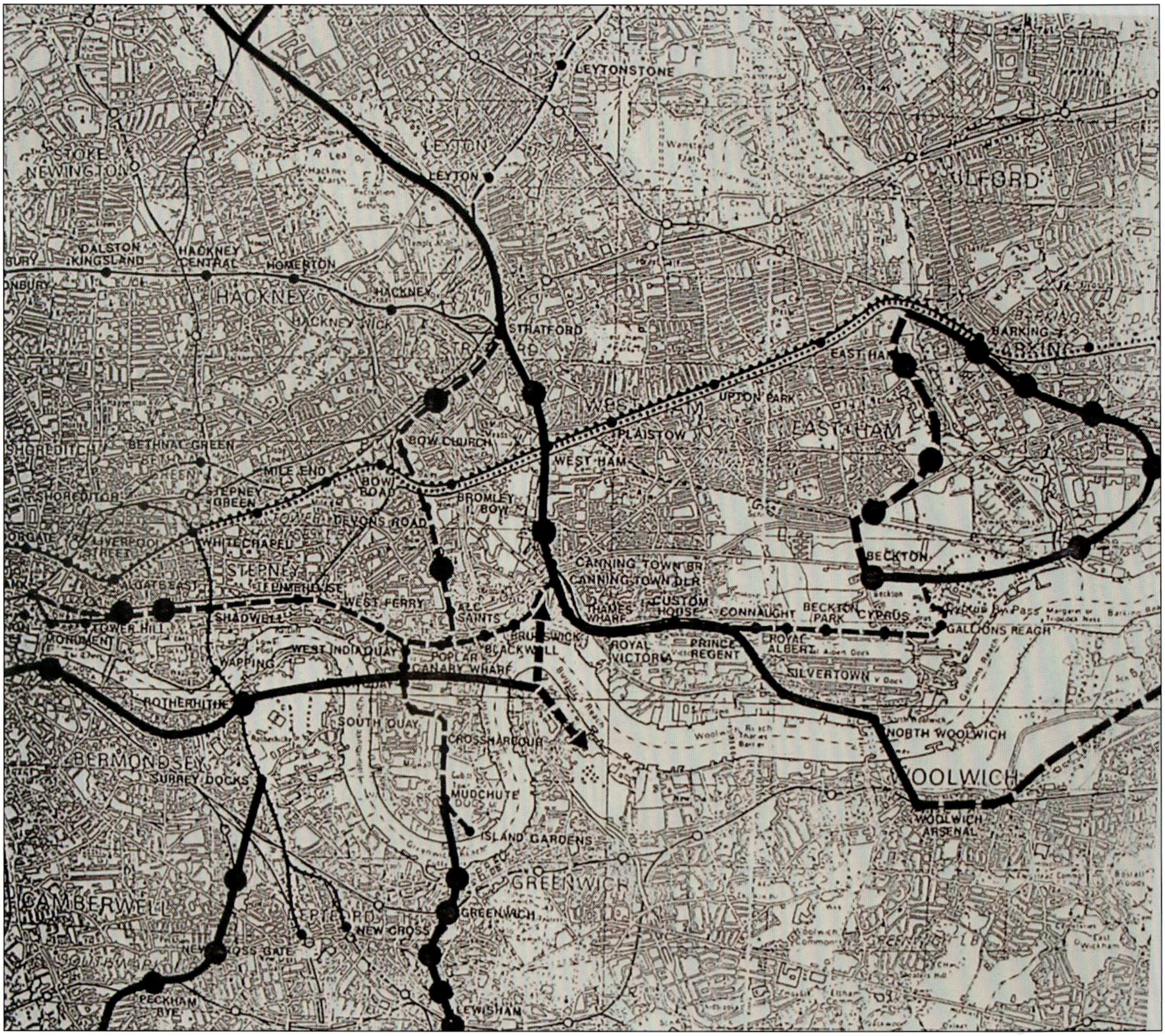

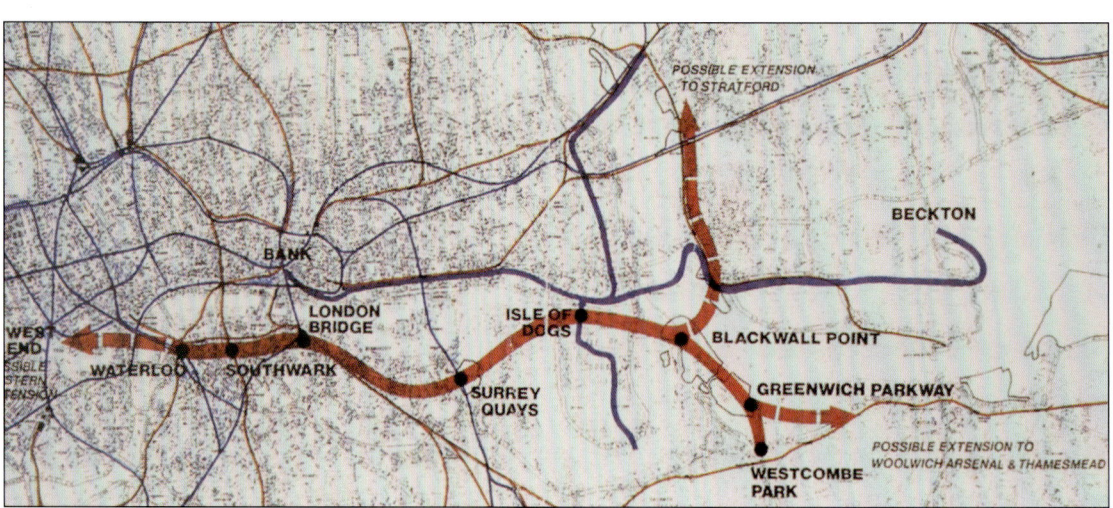

10.1 (above): Strategic Plan options.

10.2 (left): Waterloo and Greenwich proposal.

peninsula, the Isle of Dogs and Blackwall peninsula and provide an additional link to central London and additional capacity to meet future growth.

Developers O&Y were as proactive in their transport ideas as they were in property development, and a momentum quickly developed behind the idea of a Docklands second line.[1]

Several proposals were put forward by O&Y's transport consultants Steer Davis and Gleave, including an extension of the Bakerloo line, but none proved practical from the engineering point of view. Another proposal was for a stand-alone line running between Waterloo and Canary Wharf, then on to Westcombe Park south of the river with a possible extension to Stratford. The main purpose of the Waterloo and Greenwich railway, as it became known, was to carry commuters from the main-line stations at Waterloo and London Bridge to the Isle of Dogs. The developers were convinced that to attract city-type businesses to Docklands, overall journey times from such places as Woking and Sevenoaks should be no longer than to the City. Transport planners would argue that in the longer term the scale of development in Docklands would influence where people would live, but the developers' argument was that people would not have to move home to work at Canary Wharf.

To progress the second line a joint team was set up between the developers O&Y and LT. Considerable effort was put into the design, property issues, environmental impact and community liaison. The railway was the first to be planned following the disastrous fire at King's Cross in 1987 and new fire and safety codes, adapted from the US code of practice NFPA-130, had to be negotiated with HM Railway Inspectorate. Expressions of interest for a Design, Build and Operate contract were obtained from five major consortia and on the basis of this work a proposal was submitted to Government in autumn 1988.

Although extensions at the western end to Paddington and east to Stratford were considered, the initial Waterloo to Greenwich railway would not have been an efficient railway and may not have been justified in social cost-benefit terms. Similar in use to the Waterloo and City Line, the proposed line would have experienced heavy single direction flows to and from Canary Wharf in the peak hours, with little counter-peak or off-peak flows.

To justify public expenditure the line had to be of more benefit for London as a whole and it was LT's view that whilst a free-standing line between Waterloo, London Bridge and Canary Wharf would be beneficial for the developers, in its curtailed version it would do little to improve transport for the rest of the capital. LT favoured an extension of the existing Jubilee Line to provide connections with the main Underground in the central area and to Stratford to link up with the important commuter routes from north-east London. Indeed the chosen route of the Jubilee Line extension has, uniquely, interchanges with *all* other Underground lines.

At the same time as the Waterloo and Greenwich proposal, concern was growing over the rapid growth of employment in the Central Area. Many tube lines in London were becoming overcrowded, especially the Central Line, and O&Y's projections for employment in the Isle of Dogs were also rising. This led the Department of Transport, BR, and LT to agree to jointly commission the *Central London Rail Study* (Ref. 10.2) to examine the issues and propose solutions. The report was published in January 1989. Although pressed by O&Y to deposit a Bill for a Docklands line in November 1988, LT felt this to be premature as the *Central London Rail Study* was to

10.3: *Central London Rail Study* report.

look at a range of options, some of which could impact on Docklands. As a result the deposit of a Bill for a new Docklands line had to wait another year.

The *Central London Rail Study* found that none of the Jubilee Line extensions gave major relief of the critical sections of the Central, Metropolitan and Circle Lines. The report did however identify for further study the possibility of extending the Jubilee Line to Docklands as an alternative to the stand-alone Waterloo and Greenwich railway. As we will see later, the major recommendation of the report was to proceed with a Crossrail project.

To bring the Docklands transport issue to a head, the Department of Transport commissioned a further report in 1989 – the *East London Rail Study* (Ref. 10.3), charged with identifying: 'The best option for further improving access from Central London to Docklands

and east Thameside in order to accommodate the rapid pace of development in Docklands.'

The key issues were:

- Should the line be an extension of an existing line, most obviously the Jubilee Line, or should it be separate from the Underground?
- The route should serve Canary Wharf but there were options both east and west
- In the central area the choice was extending the line from Charing Cross via the City to Docklands or running via Waterloo to Docklands. This second option required the closure of the section of the existing Jubilee Line between Green Park and Charing Cross
- In Docklands, beyond Canary Wharf, the choice was to serve the Royal Docks to Woolwich or

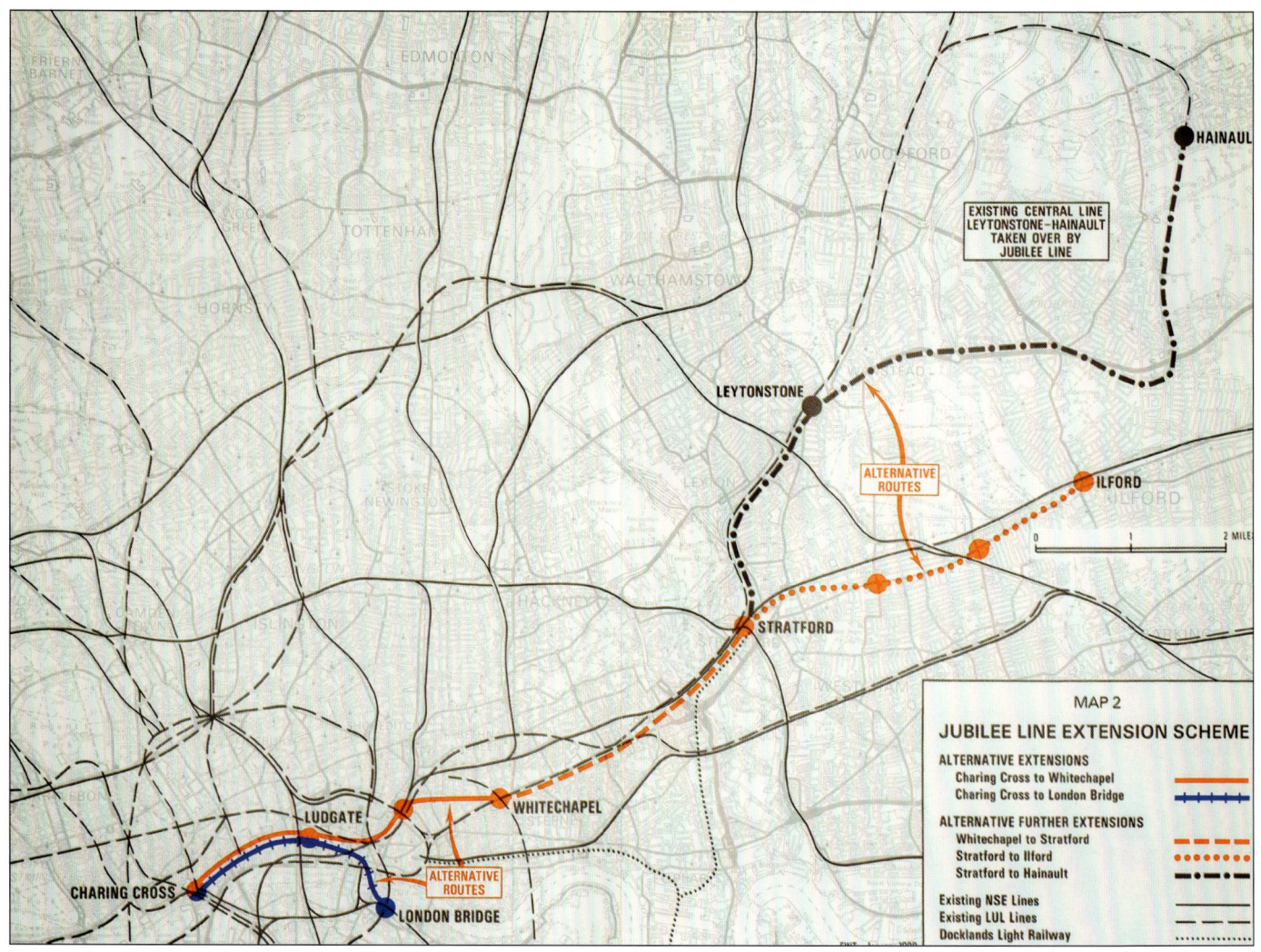

10.4: Jubilee Line extension proposal.

to turn north to Stratford, either via the North Greenwich peninsula or via Brunswick. The Royal Docks were to be served by the DLR Beckton extension, then under construction, so Stratford was more logical and attracted greater relief of the Central Line.

The study concluded that the preferred option was an extension of the Jubilee Line from Green Park, via Waterloo, London Bridge, Canary Wharf and Stratford. Options remained for a route via North Greenwich or Brunswick and whether the line should take over the North London line between Canning Town and Stratford or run alongside it. The report recommended that if resources were available a Bill could be deposited in November 1989.

O&Y's involvement in the design of a new Underground line to Docklands did not cease with the abandonment of the original Waterloo and Greenwich railway. The company undertook numerous studies to confirm the location of the station at Canary Wharf and concluded that it was best sited in the dock between

Canary Wharf and Heron Quay. O&Y agreed to help finance the Bill and a joint team was set up to manage the further design and the Bill preparation. One of the significant pieces of work to be undertaken during the Bill preparation was the production of the 'Environment Statement', *Environmental Assessment of the Jubilee Line Extension* (Ref. 10.4). The joint team worked well and successfully deposited the Bill for the Jubilee Line extension in November 1989.

In the Central Area the route via Waterloo quickly found favour as it served the then proposed terminal of the Channel Tunnel rail link at Waterloo and it would also help to open up the South Bank to encourage more visitors to the area, reducing pressure on tourist hotspots such as Covent Garden.[2]

East of Canary Wharf the route via North Greenwich was chosen as it would open up more development land in an inaccessible area than the route via Brunswick, and also 'with a new bus interchange' serve a wide catchment of south-east London.[3] British Gas, the owners of much of the North Greenwich peninsula, the site of a former gas works, also provided a modest contribution to the route.[4]

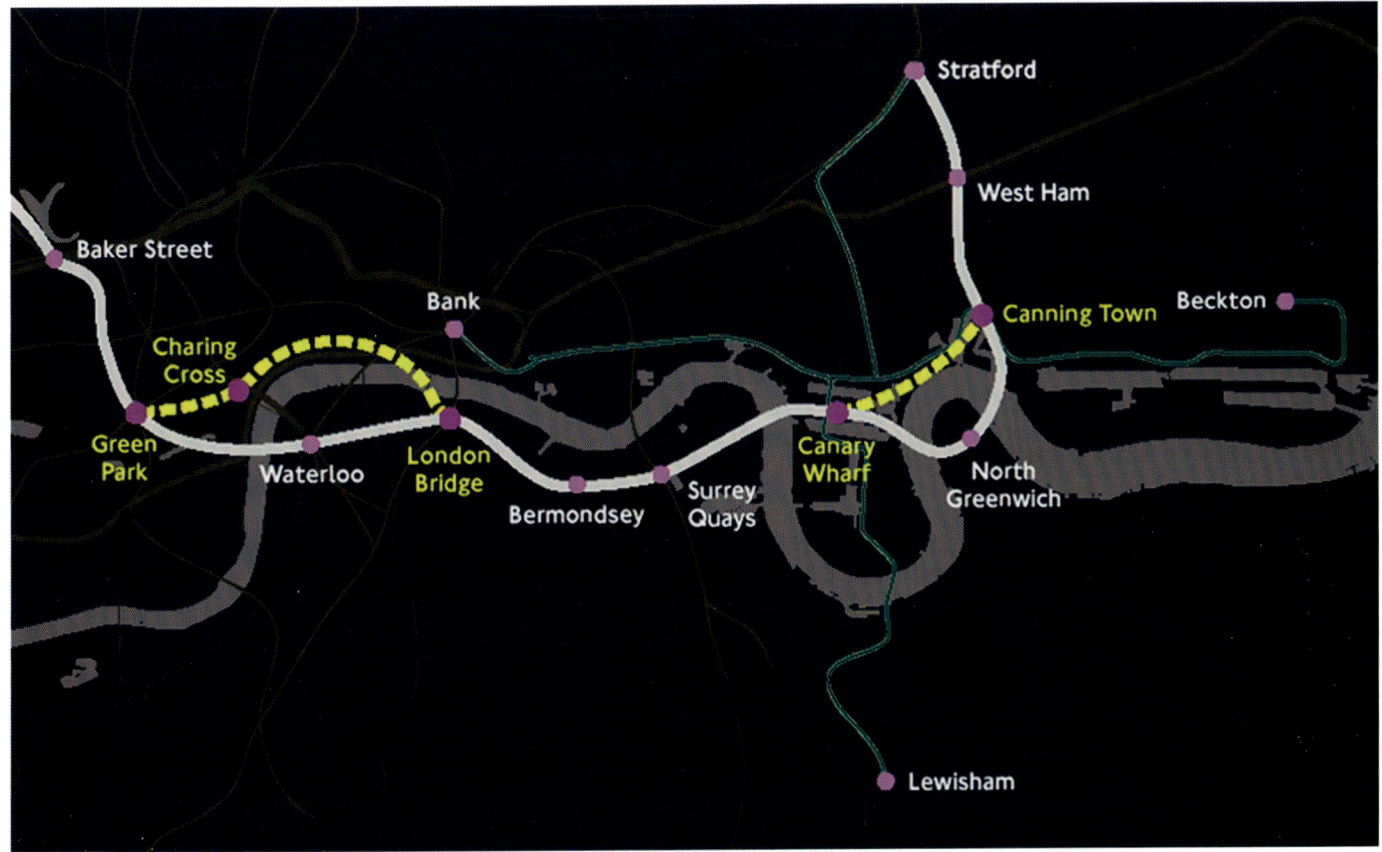

10.5: Extension alternatives.

The main stations on the extension were therefore at Westminster, Waterloo, London Bridge, Canary Wharf and Stratford. A separate justification was developed for the additional stations at Southwark (interchange with Waterloo East BR), Bermondsey, Canada Water (interchange with East London line) and West Ham (interchange with the District and Metropolitan Lines). Surprisingly it was found less costly to run alongside the North Woolwich to Stratford line rather than to take it over. A site for a new depot was also available in the corridor.

Project Appraisal

Forecasting of passenger demand for the Jubilee Line extension using the Department of Transport's London Transportation model gave a maximum of 133m journeys a year with the estimated completion of development in Docklands with 91,000 jobs in the Isle of Dogs. Use of the Jubilee Line as a whole was forecast to increase to 170m journeys a year making it one of the most heavily used Underground lines. The heaviest flow would be between London Bridge and Bermondsey at 18,400 passengers per hour. By the time the Bill was being considered in Parliament in 1992 the cost of the extension was estimated at £1.9bn giving a benefit to cost ratio of 0.95 to 1. To support the case a wide range of additional benefits not included in the normal cost-benefit analysis, such as the creation of more temporary and permanent jobs, was put forward.

Approval and Funding

Following the completion of the *East London Rail Study* in 1989 there was only a very short time before a Parliamentary Bill could be deposited in the November of that year. Massive effort and enthusiasm by all involved achieved the deadline, building on the work already carried out by O&Y. An Additional Provision (a change) to the Bill was lodged in 1990 to alter the originally proposed route via Brunswick to the preferred route via Greenwich. Three Acts of Parliament were required to construct the railway. The main one obtained Royal Assent in 1992, with additional powers for works at Green Park, Westminster, Waterloo and Southwark in 1993 and 1994.

Sixty-nine Petitions were received against the original Bill with a further sixty against the Additional Provision. Most Petitions related to impacts on property and environmental concerns. There were also concerns for the withdrawal of services from Charing Cross and

the decision to route the line via North Greenwich rather than via Brunswick. Most importantly the House of Commons Committee agreed that the route should be via North Greenwich. The Bill passed through the Lords with minimal alteration.

O&Y offered to underwrite a total of £400m to the project, spread over several years, which was eventually accepted by the Department of Transport. Unfortunately by the time the first payment was due in April 1992 a recession was starting to bite and the developers found themselves unable to pay. O&Y went into administration six weeks later and without this contribution the Government was unwilling for the project to proceed. These were difficult times for the project, and for Docklands, whose continued success as a major commercial area depended on the Jubilee Line. Although the improved DLR could comfortably accommodate full occupancy of those buildings already constructed in the Isle of Dogs, it could not sustain much further development. Eventually agreement was reached for Canary Wharf Limited, now owned by a consortium of eleven banks, to emerge from administration. Under a separate arrangement, this provided the key for an initial £98m payment by O&Y to be released, with the remaining £300m to be provided over a twenty-five year period.

Go-ahead for the project was formally signalled by the Prime Minister, John Major, who started the first pile drive at the site of Canary Wharf station in December 1993.

Since the time of the *Central London Rail Study* in 1989 the debate over whether or not the Jubilee Line should have taken preference over the other Central London projects, notably Crossrail which provided higher passenger benefits and a healthier benefit to cost ratio, has remained. The Jubilee Line was anticipated to do more in assisting new development and encouraging regeneration in the Docklands area, but less in terms of relieving congestion. In the end the decision was undoubtedly influenced by the Government's desire to ensure Docklands was a success, and pressure from the developers and their willingness to provide a direct financial contribution to the Parliamentary Process and the capital cost of construction.

Design

As a 16km extension of the Underground, a number of design features were constrained by existing standards, the most significant being the rolling stock gauge. The diameter of the existing Jubilee tunnels was 3.85 metres, however the extension was built 0.5 metres wider at 4.35 metres to allow for a trackside walkway.[5]

Station designs varied markedly between those which formed part of existing stations and those which were new. Of the eleven stations on the extension, three formed part of existing station complexes (Westminster, Waterloo and London Bridge), five were new deep-level stations (Southwark, Bermondsey, Canada Water, Canary Wharf and North Greenwich) and the remaining three (Canning Town, West Ham and Stratford) were at surface level.

An early decision was to allow different architectural practices to design individual stations, a far cry from the days when Charles Holden of LT set the common standards for the station designs on the expansion of the Underground in the 1920s and 1930s. The new underground stations were all designed with access at both ends to comply with the newly adopted station standards for emergency escape. In the case of the anticipated less busy stations – Southwark, Bermondsey, Canada Water and North Greenwich – only one ticket hall was required but at the major station at Canary Wharf a large mezzanine circulation area was provided with three surface access points.

All rises of over 7 metres were mechanically assisted and to avoid the problems at Bank station on the DLR, escalator flights had a minimum of three machines to allow for maintenance. In total 116 escalators were provided on the extension compared to only 243 on the rest of the whole Underground network at the time.

At an early stage of planning it was decided to provide full accessibility for passengers using wheelchairs at all new stations on the extension. The DLR had paved the way in London by providing lifts to all platforms and ensuring near-level boarding of trains. Today we would not consider building a new public facility without such provision but at the time it was a significant decision taken after much debate. Another significant decision was to install platform-edge doors which were starting to be used on other metro systems. In addition to providing extra security for passengers, they reduce noise and significantly simplify ventilation requirements.

As is now normal practice the track was continuously welded throughout and in open sections laid on concrete sleepers on conventional ballast. In the tunnel sections

10.6: Platform-edge doors.

the standard form was to place the rails on resilient baseplates fixed to a concrete deck. In sections close to sensitive buildings, 'floating' tracks on an elastomer support were used.

A new depot was built between West Ham and Stratford housing the engineering and maintenance facilities for the entire Jubilee Line fleet on an 11 hectare site of which 2 hectares was covered by a single open-span train shed.

Trains were to a new design, initially six cars in length (extended to seven cars in 2005) with the latest thyristor controlled motors, utilising regenerative braking for the first time on the Underground. At the planning stage the signalling system was intended to use the latest technology employing a transmission based moving block system with automatic train protection and train control. In practice the system was not considered sufficiently developed to meet the deadline for the opening date in 1999 and a more conventional system was initially installed.

Construction

Construction started in late 1993 with an anticipated six-year construction period. Fourteen major civil engineering contracts were let and by the end of 1996 all four twin-tube crossings under the River Thames (eight separate under-river drives) were complete without any significant problems. Eleven tunnel-boring machines (TBMs) were employed on the project. From Green Park to London Bridge, tunnelling was through the favoured London clay but from Bermondsey to North Greenwich the tunnelling was through the more problematic water-bearing sand and gravel of the London & Reading Beds and Thanet Sands. In the clay section open faced non-pressurised TBMs were used but in the water-bearing areas more expensive pressurised TBMs had to be used.[6]

Constructed in a heavily built-up and historic environment, a critical issue faced by any new tunnelling is ground settlement. Around 4,000 buildings along the route were assessed to determine if damage would occur against a formula based on previous tunnelling experience. Different techniques to minimise the impact during construction were used. Where settlements above specified levels were predicted, compensation grouting was used. The technique uses sophisticated monitoring devices fixed to buildings linked to computers which give the engineers data on how

10.7: Station under Portcullis House, Westminster.

structures are responding. Any movement can then be compensated by the injection of grout before and during the tunnel drive.

A further issue arose with the use of the New Austrian Tunnelling Method (NATM) where essentially larger tunnels are sprayed with reinforced concrete rather than lined with pre-cast rings. The contractors at Waterloo and London Bridge proposed this alternative method as a cheaper and quicker solution as it had been tested for use on the Heathrow Express extension. Work was fairly well advanced on the Jubilee Line stations when a collapse of a tunnel section at Heathrow caused a nine-month delay and £190m additional cost to the project whilst the technique was reassessed and confirmed as sound.

The new stations on the line created a range of challenges. At Westminster the original idea was to build the station below Parliament Square but this was rejected by the Parliamentary Buildings Sub Committee as too disruptive. Fortunately there were plans to demolish a Victorian building on the corner of the Embankment and Bridge Street for new accommodation for Members of Parliament, to be named Portcullis House. The opportunity was taken to construct the station in an open box on this site in advance of the new building. A complication was that the District and Circle Lines ran across the Jubilee Line station box and had to be supported, with the tracks slightly lowered to accommodate the new building. The result is the most dramatic station on the extension with the platforms stacked one on top of each other to maximise the distance between the tunnelling and the somewhat vulnerable Elizabeth Tower which houses Big Ben.[7]

10.8: Westminster station, showing Portcullis House support columns.

Waterloo station is the busiest main-line station in London and the new line had to be built around the working station with minimum interference to passenger movement. This was the first station on the line to use the NATM tunnelling method and as noted above, work was held up for around nine months whilst the safety aspects were examined. Working under the maze of brick built structures required the extensive use of jacks to compensate for any movement, there being insufficient room to use compensation grouting.

Southwark station was constructed under the main railway lines running into Charing Cross which also created particular difficulties. Compensation grouting was used to stabilise the brick viaduct above the tunnels and without the use of this relatively modern technique this station could not have been constructed. Various access arrangements were considered, the chosen solution being three escalator shafts driven between the pillars of the viaduct, requiring precision tunnelling and continuous monitoring of the surrounding structures.

London Bridge station is reputed to be the largest brick built structure in the world. Although a major terminus for suburban services, prior to the Jubilee Line extension the station was only served by the City branch of the Northern Line. The new line has opened up key connections to Docklands and the West End. A significant feature of the construction was the closure of Joiner Street, allowing a new pedestrian route from the Underground station to the main-line station through its undercroft. With the recent major rebuilding of the main-line station this route has been developed as an attractive shopping mall linking the two stations.

10.9: Southwark station.

At Bermondsey station the tunnels entered the Woolwich and Reading Beds, requiring the more complex and costly earth pressure balance tunnelling machines. In such machines bentonite clay is injected ahead of the cutting face to stabilise the ground and this requires men to work in pressurised conditions. In addition the site was very constrained and surrounded by housing which limited twenty-four hour working, resulting in a complex and difficult build.

Canada Water station provides excellent interchange with the historic East London line, made all the more attractive since the East London line has been extended at both the northern and southern ends as part of the London Overground. Construction of the top-down box for the new station required removal of the brick-lined East London line tunnels, leaving at one stage the two exposed tunnel orifices in the face of the box 11 metres below the surface. Although the site had no immediate buildings requiring compensation grouting, the proximity of two residential tower blocks and the neighbouring Canada Water required careful design and noise limitation.

The stations at Canary Wharf and North Greenwich, being some 25 metres below the surrounding water levels, with running tunnels passing under the Thames at either end, required particular engineering consideration. Ideally the station box at Canary Wharf would have been sited under the heart of the development. Unfortunately this option was no longer available as the office development was too well advanced. The station was therefore located in the adjoining south quay – the original West India export

10.10: Canada Water station.

dock. This required the construction of coffer dams to hold back the water, and the construction of massive diaphragm walls and tension piles to avoid the station 'floating' in the water-bearing sands and gravel.

The depth of the platforms and high number of anticipated passengers at the station required a large number of escalators at the three proposed exits. With only one intermediate concourse above the platforms the design resulted in a cathedral-like space, with the main exit requiring a bank of five long escalators emerging under a dramatic curved glass entrance canopy. Normally unseen to the public, beneath these escalators is a similarly large bank of stairs for emergency egress from the station.

10.11: Canary Wharf and North Greenwich station locations.

North Greenwich is the largest station on the Jubilee Line extension and at the time of building was reputed to be the largest underground station in the world, accommodating three tracks and platforms to facilitate the reversing of trains. Initially not planned with the Millennium Dome in mind it eventually became the main means of access to events there and obviously was on the critical path for completion. The land had been previously used as a major gas works and as a result was heavily contaminated. There were also aquifers in the Thanet Sands which had to be de-watered and a massive 2-metre thick base was required to hold the structure down against the uplifting water pressure. The design of the concourse was particularly novel, effectively being hung from the roof structure.

At the eastern end of the station, provision was made for a possible branch extension to the Royal Docks. However, with the construction of Crossrail serving this area, such an extension is never likely to be required.

The first surface station on the extension at Canning Town posed a new range of problems. The North London line ran alongside the site formerly, with a station on the north side of the A13. This had then been rebuilt on the south side as part of earlier road improvements. At the start of planning of the Jubilee Line extension the DLR Beckton extension did not affect the site but following a Petition from the Borough of Newham the Parliamentary Committee required it to be routed via Canning Town. As the site was heavily constrained on one side by a road and on the other by the River Lea, the only way to accommodate all three railways was to demolish

10.12: Canary Wharf station upper concourse.

10.13 (above): Canary Wharf station entrance.

10.14 (left): North Greenwich station.

the partly built DLR station, construct the Jubilee Line station and then rebuild the DLR platforms above those of the Jubilee Line. A further constraint was created by overhead power lines. However the result is an excellent interchange between the Jubilee Line and the DLR and a slightly longer interchange with the former North London line platforms, now also part of the DLR network.

West Ham is the simplest station on the line with no major constructional constraints, built with an island platform giving good interchange with the District and Metropolitan Lines and the London, Tilbury and Southend lines.

Being the terminus of the line, Stratford was to become a significant gateway station providing the main artery from London's north-east suburbs and longer distance commuter areas into Docklands. Although the platform area was a relatively simple build, a major part of the design included a 35-metre wide new subway which had to be thrust-bored under the many main-line tracks and platforms to provide good interchange for passengers using National Rail services and the Central Line.

At an early stage of the planning it was realised that to maximise the benefits of the new line, bus feeder services would need to play an important part in the new transport network of East London. Consequently four stations at Canada Water, North Greenwich, Canning Town and Stratford incorporated major new bus stations which were fully integrated into the Underground station design.

10.16: West Ham station.

10.17: Stratford bus station.

Overall the construction of the Jubilee Line extension involved some of the most complex civil engineering that London had experienced. The variable ground conditions, the many important historic buildings, the need to integrate the stations with the many other railways and the emerging new environmental requirements all required some of the finest engineering skills in the world to solve.

Archaeology

The archaeological work on the line is summarised in the Museum of London's publication, *The Big Dig*

10.15: Canning Town station.

(Ref. 10.5). In the introduction, the then Project Director Hugh Doherty stated:

> In the past, builders and civil engineers have often had an uneasy relationship with archaeologists. This was for the very sound reason that the unplanned discovery of historically important artefacts on a construction site generally brings work to a halt while archaeologists investigate. Inevitably there are delays and a consequent impact on building costs. I am delighted to say that this was not the case with the Jubilee Line Project.

Important finds were anticipated and time built into the programme. With the tunnels generally much deeper than any likely remains, it is at the stations and ventilation shafts where archaeological work was concentrated.

Fragments of Roman buildings were found at Westminster indicating that Romans came to the area. Also parts of gates leading to the Thames from the twelfth and thirteenth centuries were found. Remains of houses along Bridge Street revealed sixteenth-century domestic rubbish, drains and the remains of eighteenth-century buildings. One of the largest excavations took place under Borough High Street as part of the London Bridge station works. Parts of a Roman road, buildings and large numbers of amphorae were discovered together with an area covered in fire debris from around AD 60, possibly as a result of Boudicca's actions. From burial grounds in Southwark, used in the eighteenth and nineteenth centuries, 160 skeletons were removed for examination and later reburial.

Stratford was the other major archaeological site where there were remains of the Cistercian Langthorne Abbey built in 1135, including large stretches of a monastic precinct and part of the stone-built Abbey Church. The burial grounds of important benefactors were uncovered with some stone coffins indicating their status.

The archaeological work undertaken during the construction programme significantly improved the understanding of key areas of London, in particular in Southwark and Stratford.

End of Commission Report

The Jubilee Line extension was originally intended to open in March 1998 but did not actually open until the end of 1999 with a serious cost overspend as well as time overrun. At the time the project was authorised it was anticipated to take fifty-three months to build at a cost of £2.1bn. On completion it had taken seventy-four months, 40 per cent longer, and with costs rising by 67 per cent to £3.5bn. To try to understand the reasons for the delay and cost overrun the Secretary of State ordered an *End of Commission Report* (Ref. 10.6). The report highlighted problems with the original estimates, the difficulties caused by the failure of the NATM tunnelling method at Heathrow, the very complex task of coordinating the electrical and mechanical fit-out of the railway, working with eleven different architecturally designed stations, the revised deadline imposed by the decision in 1997 to site the Millennium Dome at North Greenwich and a number of issues with the form of contracts and documentation.

However the report to the Department for the Environment and the Department for Transport noted in particular: 'the excellence of the infrastructure planning and design which, with its foresight and detail for construction, resulted in no impact on the sensitive built environment along the alignment'.

Operations

Opening at the millennium, passenger use of the line quickly built up as it provided major time savings, for example commuters arriving at London Bridge or Waterloo travelling to Canary Wharf saved around thirty minutes on their journey. Also the transfer of passengers from the DLR was not as high as expected. The forecasts were that the whole line, including the extension, would carry 133m passengers a year with a maximum flow of 20,000 an hour.

Initially the peak service on the line was for twenty-four trains per hour, running with the conventional signalling. After the opening of the line two major projects were planned to increase its capacity to accommodate the anticipated increase in demand. The first was to increase the length of trains from six to seven cars, for which the railway had been designed. Extra cars were purchased and these were introduced into service in 2005.

The second project was for replacement of the conventional signalling with a Thales 'moving block' system. This was eventually installed in 2012 allowing

10.18: Passengers boarding at Canning Town.

thirty trains per hour to run in the peak period through the central section of the line. Ten years after the line opened the annual usage had nearly doubled to 249m and by 2018 had risen to 280m. In view of the continuing increase in usage of the line, even with the completion of Crossrail, plans are in hand to increase the service to thirty-six trains per hour.

All these works resulted in many weekend closures of the line and significant reliability problems causing much frustration to passengers and those promoting new development in Docklands. As with the DLR the seemingly continuing upgrading of electrical systems on the two operating railways has not been an altogether happy story, not reflecting particularly well on our engineering profession. One could cite the nature of planning development in the area with no firm idea for the end state of employment or housing resulting in a continuing need for extra capacity. It is hoped that with the arrival of Crossrail the requirements for the Jubilee Line extension as well as for the DLR will have reached a stable position where further upgrades are no longer required.

Impact Assessment Study

Following the completion of the project LT commissioned the *Jubilee Line Extension Impact Assessment* from the University of Westminster (Ref. 10.7). This major study, costing over £1m, had two aims:

- to understand how the extension had affected London
- to improve appraisal and forecasting techniques.

The study commissioned a number of surveys including:

- land use – within station catchments
- household – questionnaire to 1,600 households
- employer – questionnaire to 600 employers
- agents of change – interviews with fifty key people.

The study's main conclusions are summarised as:

a) It improved accessibility, connectivity and capacity with new bus stations and interchanges.
b) Even in the short three-year period after the line had opened, the changes in the corridor served were many and diverse and it was often difficult to attribute causation.
c) It raised land values in the corridor faster than in London as a whole but it was difficult to quantify this.
d) It stimulated development that might not have otherwise been expected.
e) It allowed the Canary Wharf development to continue to grow, thus making a major contribution to London and the national economy.
f) It was the catalyst for a rapid increase in the rate of residential development in its catchment area.
g) It had a favourable impact on the level of employment around most stations but appeared to have had little effect on local unemployment levels.
h) It was the dominating influence on the development of the Greenwich peninsula allowing the Millennium Dome to be built and speeding the redevelopment of the rest of the area.
i) Although passing through some significantly deprived areas, in the time since it opened there is no strong evidence to show that the project improved local economies.

The study was undertaken within a relatively short time after opening when interest in the project was high and funds were available. Whilst it gave an initial snapshot of the impact of the investment, it would require a repeat exercise say ten or twenty years later to provide a comprehensive understanding of the impacts. Many projects are not subject to a post-opening impact study as funding for such exercises is always problematic. In addition, many other changes will have occurred in the corridor of impact since the project opened making the determination of change that much more difficult.

University of London – *Mega Projects*

In 2012 the Bartlett School of Planning, University College London, published the results of a study analysing selected large-scale transport infrastructure projects: *Mega Projects – Lessons for Decision Makers* (Ref. 10.8). The work looked at some thirty projects from ten different countries. In the UK the projects were the Channel Tunnel Rail Link, the M6 toll road and the Jubilee Line extension. A primary purpose of the study was to foster institutional learning worldwide concerning decision making in the planning, appraisal and delivery of major transport projects.

Many projects act as 'agents of change' affecting regeneration and new development, or having wider social and economic impacts. The study concluded that often these factors are not always appreciated by the decision makers and can sometimes lead to unexpected results. The work advocates closer examination of these wider impacts of projects as a key part of the planning phase.

In answer to the question 'What constitutes a successful Mega Transport Project?' the report states:

> … this simple question demands many varied and interrelated responses. In the context of MTP [Mega Transport Project] planning, appraisal and delivery, these include a view on: understanding how well risk, uncertainty and complexity has been treated; and acknowledging the importance of context in decision-making and most importantly in making judgements about 'success'.

In the conclusion to an annual lecture to MSc students studying MTPs at University College London (2014–18) the author identified the following key agents of change which, in his opinion, influenced the regeneration of Docklands:

1. Initial DLR – improved accessibility and put Docklands on the map as a potential development area.
2. Government influence – Changed planning regime – Created the Enterprise Zone – Deregulated the banks.
3. Developer influence – Required open offices not available in the old City – Contribution to transport infrastructure costs.
4. London as world city – Importance of service sector. Dramatic change in population and employment forecasts. Major growth areas identified. Importance of the Docklands – City – West End – Heathrow linkages.
5. Overcrowded network – Significant extra capacity required.
6. In Docklands buses and DLR improve local accessibility.
7. Jubilee Line improves Central Area accessibility.
8. Crossrail provides the strategic link for Docklands to the Central Area, Heathrow Airport and the outer suburbs.
9. All three Docklands rail projects improve capacity allowing Docklands and London to grow.

Even with the Jubilee Line extension and the plans emerging for Crossrail, the expansion of the DLR was not over – two further projects at the eastern end of Docklands were underway.

CHAPTER 11

DLR CITY AIRPORT, WOOLWICH AND STRATFORD EXTENSIONS

In 1997 DLR Ltd commissioned consultants to review the potential for further extensions and to develop a ten-year strategy for the development of the railway. The study, named *DLR Horizon 1998* (Ref. 11.1), was asked to address three broad questions:

- What role will DLR play in the future?
- Is the current system best placed to serve that market?
- Are there improvements, enhancements to the existing railway, or further extensions or involvement in other complementary modes which would enable DLR to exploit new opportunities to increase passenger volumes and maximise revenues?

A wide range of options was drawn up including extensions at the eastern end to Thamesmead, Woolwich and Barking, extensions to the north to Stratford and beyond, an extension from Lewisham to Catford and extensions beyond Bank into the Central Area. Improvements to interchanges and possible new bus feeders were also included. The idea was to identify extensions which were technically and economically viable.

The first stage of the study recommended for further analysis:

- DLR spur from Prince Regent station to London City Airport
- improvements to interchanges at Shadwell and Lewisham
- DLR extension to Woolwich
- DLR to take over main-line service from North Woolwich to Stratford
- DLR extension to Thamesmead over the proposed Thames Gateway Bridge
- DLR extension to the proposed Stratford International station.

The results of the evaluation showed that only the spur to London City Airport, the improvements at Shadwell and the link to Thamesmead would have a positive benefit to cost ratio. However the alternative of linking Gallions station to Thamesmead using intermediate modes (guided buses or trams), then under investigation by LT, instead of a DLR extension, was to be preferred. The core recommendations were therefore for an extension to London City Airport; a further extension to Woolwich Arsenal; to convert the existing North London line running from Canning Town to Stratford; and then a final extension of this to serve the Stratford International station.

City Airport Extension

The first project to be taken forward was the extension to London City Airport. Three options were further investigated: a branch from close to Gallions Reach on the Beckton branch across the Albert Dock, the spur from Prince Regent requiring a crossing of the Victoria Dock and the branch from Canning Town along the alignment of the former Silvertown Tramway. The latter was a more expensive option but would provide the shortest journey times to the airport and not require any crossings of the docks. It would also serve existing industry and significant potential new development areas closer to the river. It had the highest benefit to cost ratio of the alternatives.

The extension would run at an elevated level with intermediate stations at West Silvertown and Pontoon Dock. By this time passenger numbers at the airport had grown to around 4m per annum, helping to justify the investment and in 2005 the Government gave the go-ahead for the DLR extension to the airport and a short distance beyond to a new station at King George V. Unfortunately the works required the demolition of a 100-year-old primary school which was on the alignment. However a new school was built nearby.

11.1 (above): Pontoon Dock station.

11.2 (left): City Airport station.

The cost of the extension was £115m and in 2002 DLR let a contract to an AMEC/RBS consortium to design, build and maintain it for a thirty-year period. Construction started in 2003 and the line opened in 2005. After only a year of operation over 4m passengers used the extension, with nearly 50 per cent of passengers travelling to the airport using public transport, the highest proportion for any UK airport.

Woolwich Arsenal Extension

Earlier in 2000 the newly created TfL, together with DLR and Railtrack, re-examined rail alternatives between Stratford, the Royal Docks and Woolwich. The work concluded that a DLR service would be able to deliver greater benefits at lower cost and was capable of more rapid implementation.

In 2004, under Ken Livingstone's second period of responsibility for TfL as Mayor, a new programme of investment in public transport was unveiled which included the extension under the river to Woolwich Arsenal. DLR was authorised to obtain authority for the works through a Transport and Works Act and in 2005 a contract was let to a 50:50 consortium of AMEC and RBS to build the 2.5km extension under a £240m Private Finance Initiative (PFI). AMEC undertook the design, engineering and construction of the extension and its long-term maintenance for the thirty-year concession period. The extension opened in 2009.

11.3: Woolwich Arsenal station.

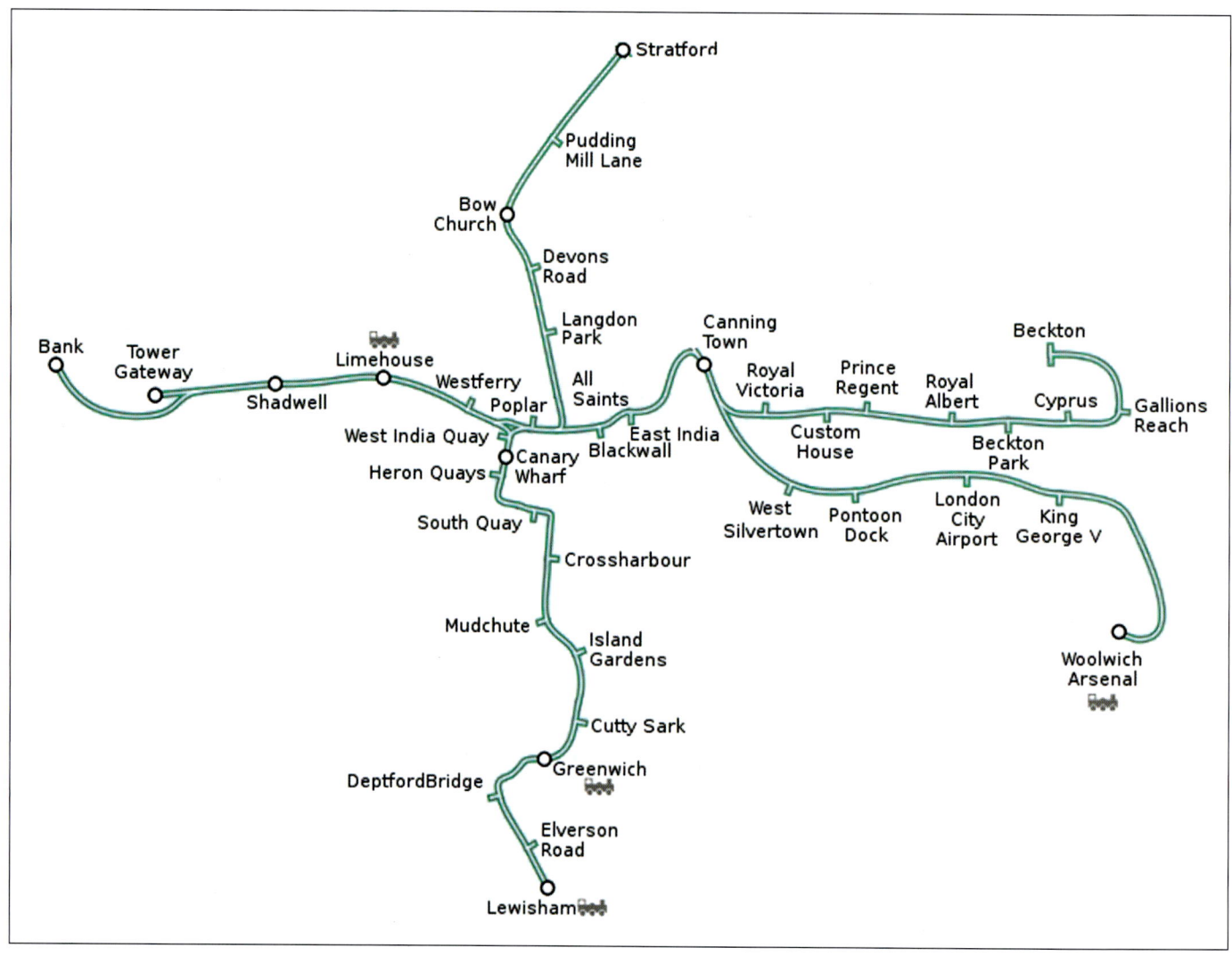

11.4: Extension to London City airport and Woolwich.

Stratford International Extension

The final part of the DLR jigsaw in this part of Docklands was to take over the old North London line from North Woolwich to Stratford. Following the Horizon Study in 1998 the Government asked DLR to develop the scheme further with an extension beyond the Stratford regional station to the International station. This was to take into account the emerging thoughts about the redevelopment of the former railway lands north of the regional station, including part of the site being used for a possible London Olympics.

In 2005 TfL sought a Transport and Works Act for the extension which was granted by the Department for Transport in 2006. VolkerRail, in a joint venture with Skanska, with design provided by Mott Macdonald, were appointed as principal contractors by DLR to deliver this 4.6km extension. The contract included the detailed design and construction of works, converting the former Network Rail formation to DLR standards, the renovation of the existing stations at Canning Town and West Ham and the construction of four new stations at Star Lane, Abbey Road, Stratford High Street and Stratford International. In 2006 the North London main line services ceased to run to North Woolwich and were first curtailed at Custom House and then diverted to new northern platforms at Stratford. The new DLR service, opened in 2011, provided an important connection during the 2012 London Olympics between the events in the Olympic Park at Stratford and the Excel Arena in the Royal Docks.

Also during this period the GLA and TfL asked DLR to investigate an extension from Gallions Reach

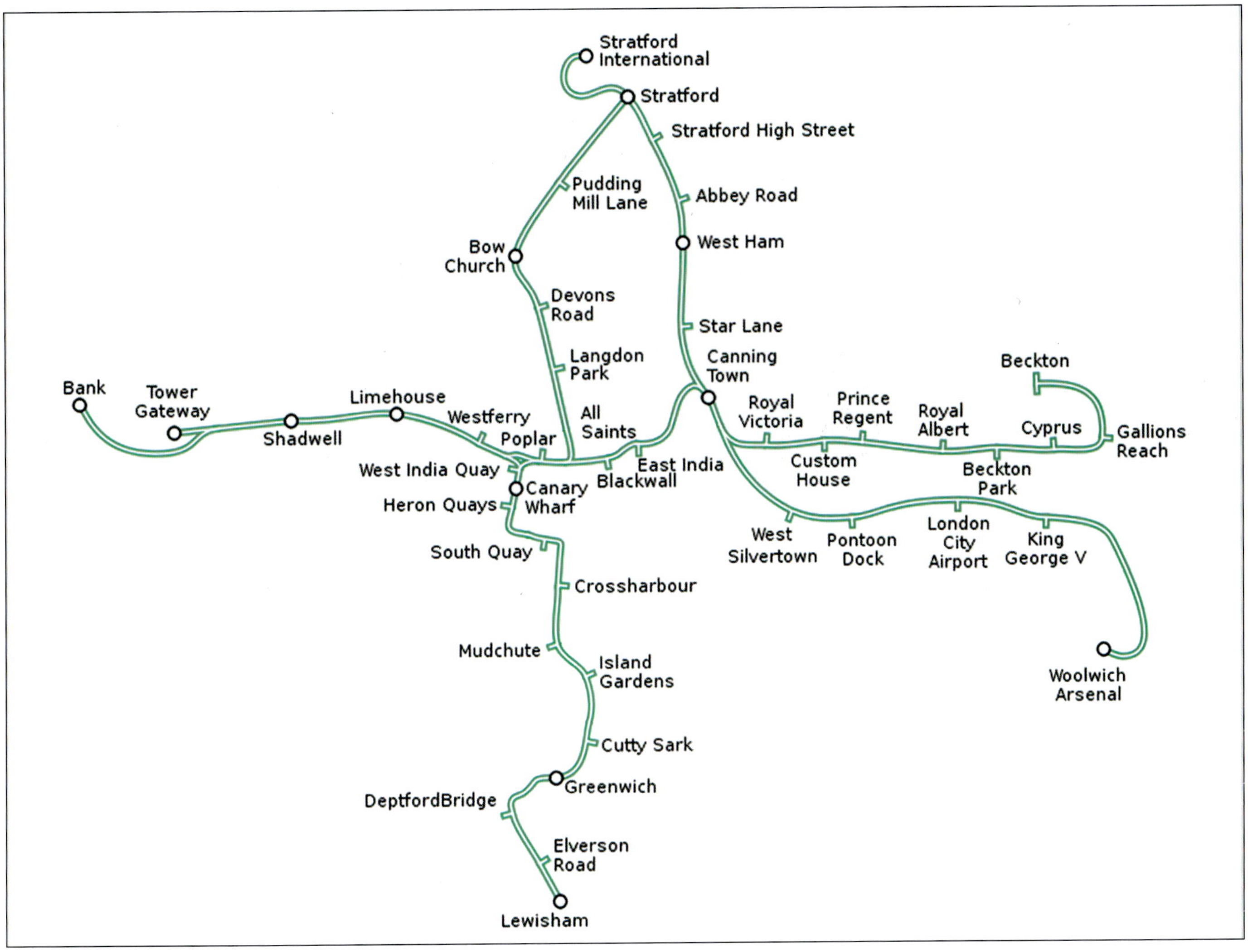

Stratford
International

Stratford

Stratford High Street

Pudding
Mill Lane

Abbey Road

Bow
Church

West Ham

Devons
Road

Star Lane

Langdon
Park

Canning
Town

Beckton

Bank

Tower
Gateway

Limehouse

Westferry

All
Saints

Royal
Victoria

Prince
Regent

Royal
Albert

Cyprus

Gallions
Reach

Shadwell

Poplar

West India Quay

East India

Custom
House

Beckton
Park

Heron Quays

Canary
Wharf

Blackwall

South Quay

West
Silvertown

Pontoon
Dock

London
City
Airport

King
George V

Crossharbour

Mudchute

Island
Gardens

Woolwich
Arsenal

Cutty Sark

DeptfordBridge

Greenwich

Elverson
Road

Lewisham

11.5 (above): Extension to Stratford International.

11.6 (right): Star Lane station.

11.7 (left): Stratford High Street station.

11.8 (below): Stratford International station.

to Barking Riverside, earmarked for the building of 11,000 new homes. Following further work and consultation the favoured option was to terminate the line at Dagenham Dock giving interchange with mainline services. A Transport and Works Act application was made in 2008 but subsequently withdrawn the following year due to lack of funding and delay in the housing proposals. In the end a decision was taken to extend the increasingly successful London Overground to Barking Riverside, rather than the longer and more expensive DLR. A contract has been let for this 4.5km extension leaving the existing line between Barking and Dagenham Dock stations with a new station in the heart of the development. At the time of writing construction has started and the line is expected to be open in 2022.

DLR – The Future

In 2005, DLR commissioned a second Horizon report from consultants Ove Arup & Partners (Ref. 11.2) to look at the potential further development of the railway over the period from 2012 to 2020. Its starting position was the projects already in the pipeline including the extensions to Woolwich and Stratford International and the stations and service upgrades. It also included assumptions about other projects which would potentially have an impact on DLR usage including upgrades to the Jubilee Line, construction of Crossrail and the development of the London Overground, taking over the East London line. In 2005 DLR was carrying 51m passengers a year which was forecast to increase to 140m by 2030 if all extensions were built.

A range of extensions was analysed using the Department for Transport's new *Transport Appraisal Guidance* (Ref. 11.4) under five main objectives: Economy, Environment, Safety, Accessibility and Integration. Extensions from Bank to either Liverpool Street or Shoreditch had high benefit to cost ratios at 9.6 and 4.6 to 1.0 respectively. Extension to Crossharbour from

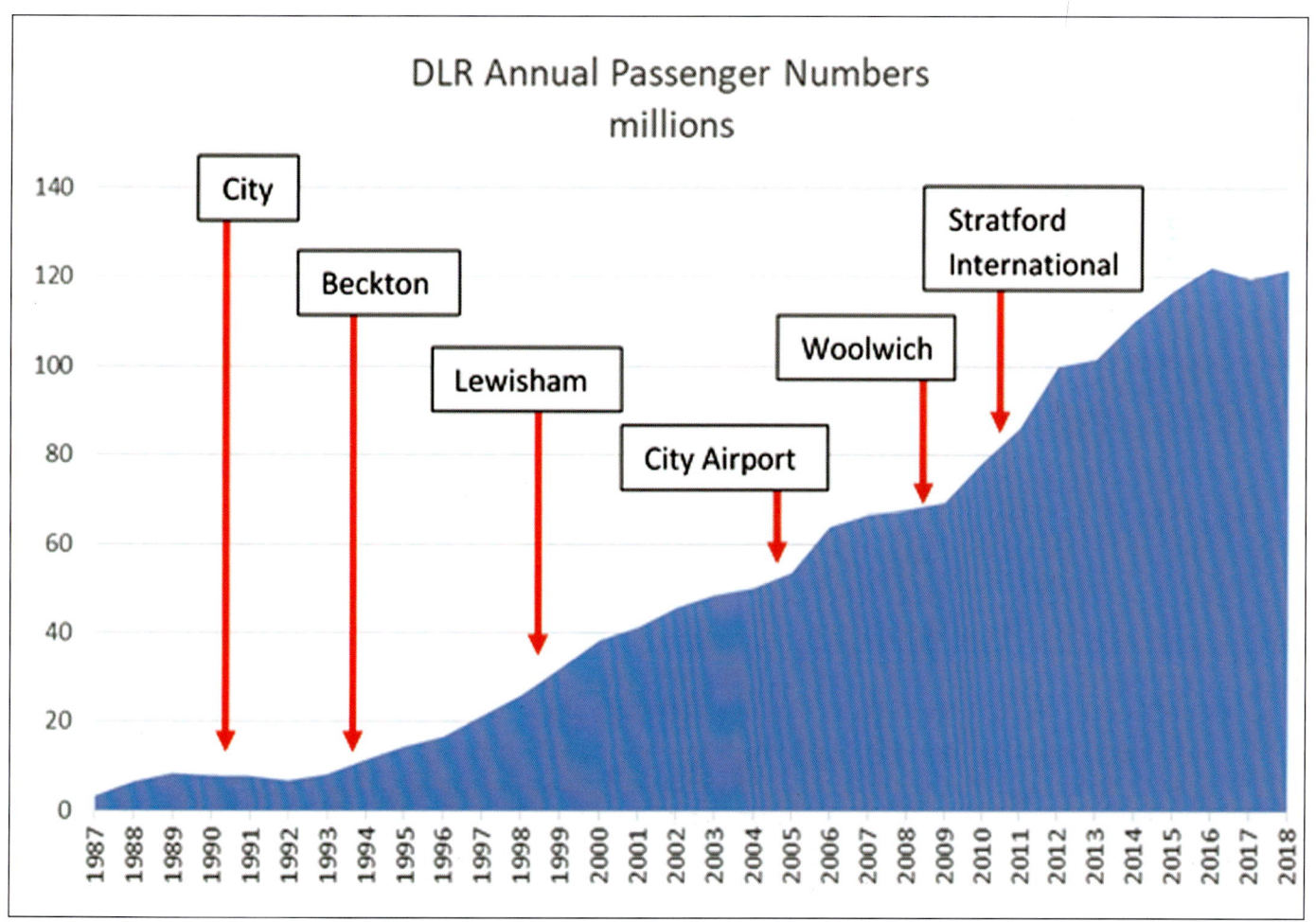

11.9: Growth in DLR passenger numbers.

All Saints and from Gallions Reach to Dagenham Dock had benefit to cost ratios of around 3.5 to 1.0. Extensions to Farringdon, Catford, Charing Cross, New Cross and to the Lea Valley all had ratios around 2 to 1.

At the time of writing TfL and DLR have been asked to look at the extension of the DLR to Thamesmead and general service upgrades to improve capacity. The proposal for the Thames Gateway Bridge was cancelled by Boris Johnson when he was Mayor so any extension across the river would need to be in a tunnel.

In 2011 TfL announced that it was proposed to take over the two companies which held PFI contracts to finance, build and maintain extensions to the DLR network. City Airport Rail Enterprises plc held the thirty-year concession covering the 4·4km extension from Canning Town to London City Airport and King George V, which opened in 2005. Woolwich Arsenal Rail Enterprises Ltd held a similar contract for the 2·4km extension to Woolwich Arsenal which opened in 2009.

TfL stated that current market conditions and the 'unique circumstances of TfL's ability to raise finance' meant that replacing private borrowing with public sector borrowing would bring 'ongoing savings' of up to £250m over the remaining life of the concessions. Both companies appointed Colas Rail to maintain the new infrastructure and these contracts remain in place. The PFI contracts ceased in 2012.

11.10: Mock-up of new DLR train.

The number of passengers using the railway has risen from over 3m a year when it was initially authorised and opened in 1987 to around 120m in 2020. The figure shows the growth in demand over the years and marks the opening dates of the various extensions. Today, little of the initial DLR is recognisable. The DLR is no longer a 'Mickey Mouse' railway but an incredibly sophisticated and well used transport system carrying many times its original forecast of passenger numbers. It can claim to be the most complex light rail system in the world, running completely automatically and reliably with intelligent trains which know where they are and how close they are to the train in front. They can even run in the wrong direction! It has won several industry awards and has come a very long way in its thirty plus years of operation.

To date the DLR currently has forty-five stations, 38km of track and fifty-six trains. Forty-three new 'walk-through' air conditioned trains have been ordered from the Spanish company CAF (Construcciones y Auxiliar de Ferrocarriles).

In December 2020 the DLR was awarded £28m from the Government's Housing Infrastructure Fund, aimed at unlocking many more homes in Docklands. The DLR funds will enable the purchase of an extra fourteen trains in addition to the forty-three already ordered. Beckton depot will be expanded and Poplar depot partly roofed over allowing for the construction of 1,700 new homes. Also included is funding for the new station at Thames Wharf south of Canning Town, as part of a deal to construct 18,000 more homes in the area.

With the continued redevelopment and renewal of East London, the DLR's role in providing a high quality local transport service complementing the role of the Jubilee Line is almost certainly not yet complete. Whilst the extended DLR network and the Jubilee Line extension could cope with significantly increased population and employment forecasts in East London, London's growth as a whole is set to continue and jobs in the Isle of Dogs could double to over 200,000. Yet more capacity will be needed in Docklands. It is fortunate that the revival of Europe's largest railway project, Crossrail, designed principally to relieve congestion in the Central Area, could be adapted to also serve Docklands.

11.11: Pontoon Dock elevated track.

CHAPTER 12

CROSSRAIL – ELIZABETH LINE

Following the creation of the GLA in 2000, chaired by the Mayor, Ken Livingstone, with responsibility for transport in London, the Government's Strategic Rail Authority (SRA) and TfL joined forces to form Cross London Rail Links to develop the Crossrail Project. I was seconded from TfL to this group as Head of Planning, seeing the project through its reincarnation, assessing a wide range of options and making a recommendation on the way forward.

Early Beginnings

The historic constraints imposed by the Royal Commission in 1845 on London's main-line terminals has ever since required many passengers wishing to cross London to be inconvenienced by the need to change stations and trains, necessitating transfer to other means of transport such as buses, taxis or the Underground.

In the 1860s there was a brief sojourn into the City by the Great Western Railway (GWR) with trains running

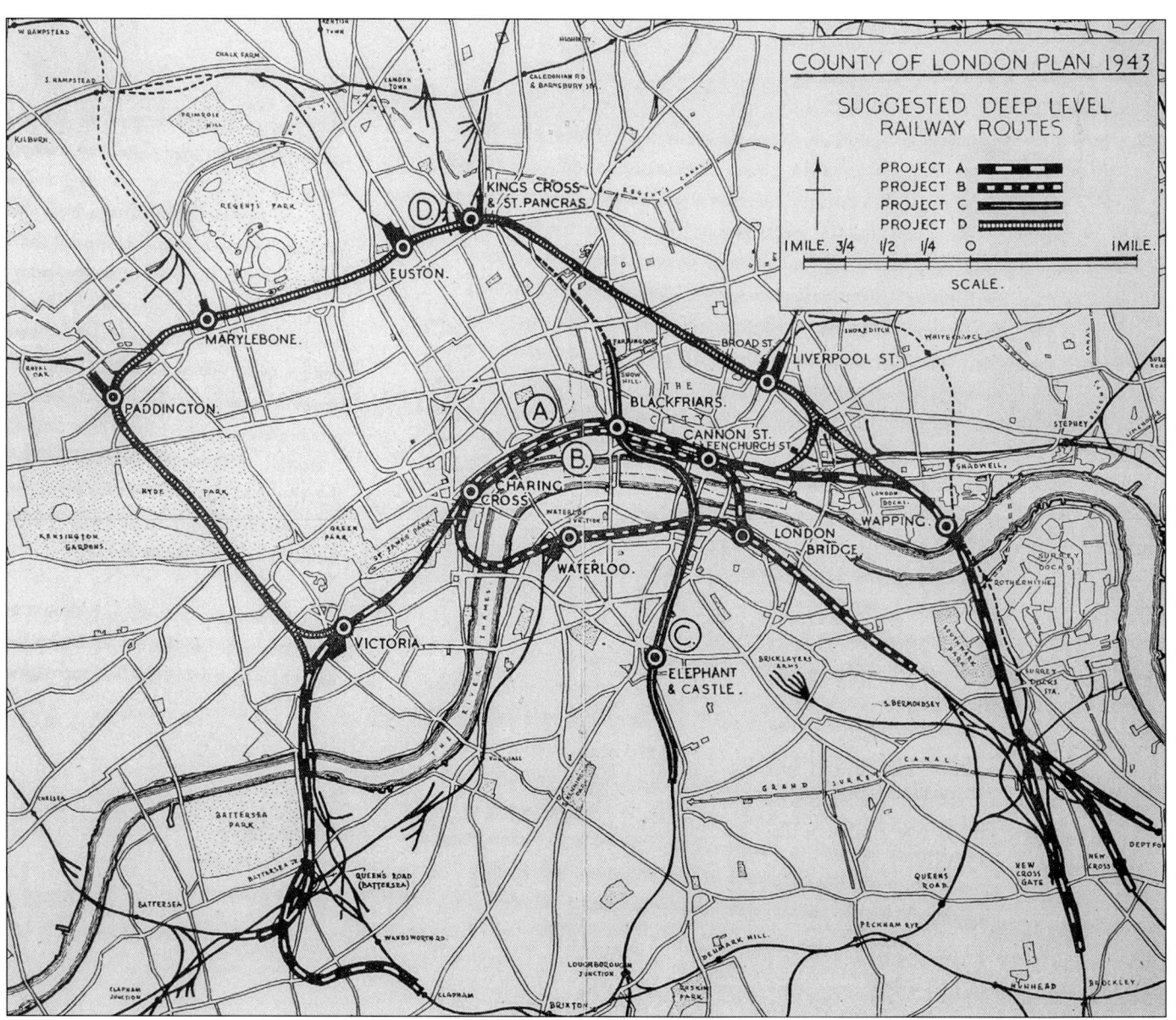

12.1: *County of London Plan.*

onwards from Paddington over the Metropolitan Line to Moorgate. Another early cross-city London link was built by the London, Chatham and Dover Railway (LCDR) in 1864, connecting services south of the river with the Metropolitan Railway on the north side. This comprised a new Thames bridge at Blackfriars and a tunnel running from close to Ludgate Circus to Farringdon with an intermediate station at Snow Hill. Services ran from south of the river to the Midland line at King's Cross until 1916, although freight services continued to run until 1970.[1]

However it was not until 1943 that ideas for a major new east to west cross-London link first emerged as part of the *County of London Plan* (Ref. 3.1) and the *Greater London Plan* – the Abercrombie Plan – following the Second World War. The latter also included a number of proposals for new Underground lines. The plans led to the setting up of a Railway Committee and in 1948 the newly formed British Transport Commission produced *A Railway Plan for London* (Ref. 3.3). This included thirty-four new miles of large bore tunnelling under Central London designed for the through running of main-line trains, including both north-south and east-west alignments. Funding after the war was very scarce and there was little enthusiasm for new railways. However the origins of the Fleet line, later called the River, then Jubilee Line, the Victoria Line and Crossrail can all be traced back to this work.

The London Rail Study

As described in Chapter 3 in relation to ideas to extend the Underground to Docklands, the 1974 *London Rail Study* (Ref. 3.7) set up by the GLC and the Department of the Environment also examined a range of options for the through running of suburban trains being developed in a number of cities including Munich and Paris. Its main recommendations were:

- to extend the Fleet line from its terminus at Charing Cross, then under construction, to East London, taking over parts of the East London line
- to safeguard the north-south Chelsea-Hackney line
- to reopen the Snow Hill tunnel and
- to propose a deep-level line between Victoria and London Bridge and a similar east-west through running line from Paddington to Liverpool Street.

With the first phase of the Fleet line under construction, fears started to materialise about the decline of London's population and economy and there was little support for major expenditure on new railways. However, money was earmarked for the safeguarding of the east-west route, which proved to be very important for the future alignment.

Cross London Rail Link

By the end of the 1970s the Government had abandoned the 'Relocation of Offices' policy and London's population and employment had slowly started to increase. In 1980 BR, under the chairmanship of Sir Peter Parker, produced a discussion document, *A Cross London Rail Link* (Ref. 12.1) which, after looking at a number of options, proposed a new cross-London route between Victoria and Euston with, for example, long distance main-line trains running from Birmingham to Brighton. It found little support, particularly from the new Government and its new Prime Minister Margaret Thatcher, who allegedly did not favour railways.

By the early 1980s London's population was still growing and there were increasing concerns over congestion on the Underground. As a result the Secretary of State Paul Channon initiated the *Central London Rail*

12.2: Cross London Rail Link logo.

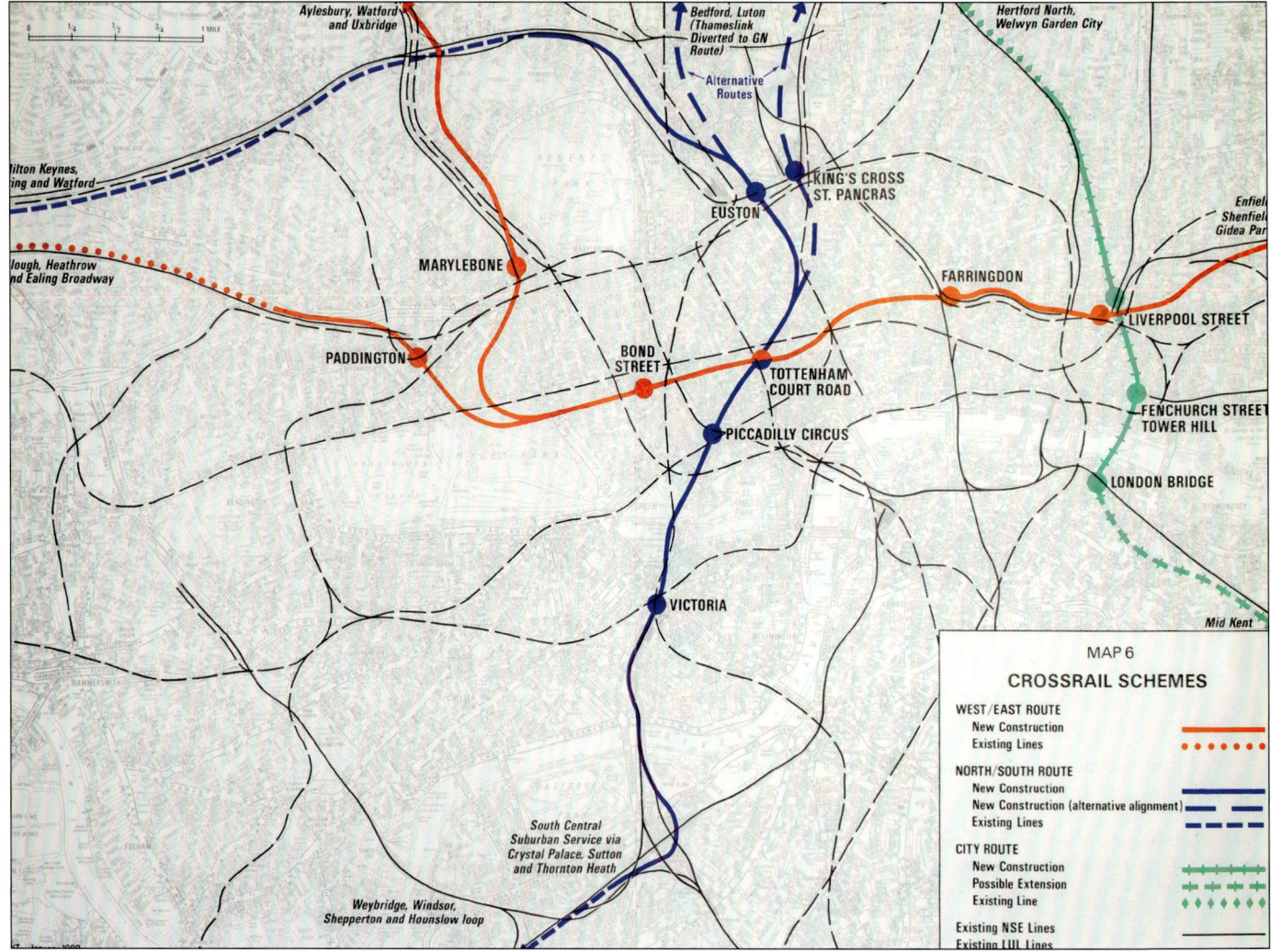

12.3: Central London Rail Study Crossrail proposals.

Study (Ref. 10.2). This was prepared by officers from the Department of the Environment and the GLC. The initial report was published in 1988 and included a version of Crossrail.

The work led to the setting up of a more formal committee charged with producing a Central London Rail Plan to be undertaken by the Department of Transport, BR, LT, now renamed for a short time London Regional Transport (LRT), and LU. This was to assess options against a background of increasing economic activity particularly within London's inner suburbs and as a result of the 'Big Bang' deregulation of the banks in 1986. The final report was published in 1989.

The study concentrated on Central Area issues but recognised that the former docks were being transformed, with the DLR up and running and the Canary Wharf

developers already active. Further improved transport for Docklands was also being considered in the separate *East London Rail Study* (Ref.10.3), being undertaken at the same time.

Passenger arrivals in Central London had risen by 35 per cent since 1980 and were forecast to increase by a further 60 per cent or more by the end of the century. Off-peak passenger numbers on the Underground had increased by 80 per cent in the eight-year period. The result was increasing congestion at stations, with major problems at twenty-five stations, forecast to increase to thirty or forty stations by the year 2000.

The report considered what contribution upgrading the existing rail networks could make to easing congestion, including expansion of stations, new trains and signalling. However the modelling showed that overcrowding would still occur, particularly on the Central, Victoria and Northern Lines. It then examined the effect of new lines and extensions, including various extensions of the Jubilee Line, the Chelsea-Hackney line and extension of the Bakerloo Line. A range of 'Crossrail' options were also examined.

The term 'Crossrail' was defined as:

> … proposing BR (British Rail) – gauge tunnels under central London to link existing rail services on either side … This would allow many suburban areas to be linked direct to central London destinations for the first time. Crossrail would relieve congestion at the main line terminals and on some of the most crowded sections of the Underground … It would also release valuable capacity at BR terminals, which could be used for longer distance commuter trains.

The study looked at four main Crossrail options:

- North-South Crossrail – linking Euston/King's Cross to Victoria
- East-West Crossrail – linking Paddington to Liverpool Street
- City Crossrail – linking London Bridge to Fenchurch Street and Liverpool Street
- Thameslink Metro – linking King's Cross to Blackfriars and London Bridge.

The analysis showed the East-West Crossrail had the highest benefits, slightly higher than the Chelsea-Hackney line. It concluded that to provide a full solution to London's congestion would need a £1.5bn upgrade of the Underground and construction of both the East-West Crossrail and the Chelsea-Hackney line at a cost of £2bn. In October 1990 the Government finally gave the go ahead to develop the Crossrail project.

The First Crossrail Bill

In 1991 a Private Bill was submitted to Parliament for the East-West Crossrail project including a new line underground from Paddington to Liverpool Street. Decisions were taken at this stage, including the diameter of the tunnels at 6 metres and the length of the trains at up to twelve cars long, requiring double-ended stations in the tunnel section, all of which have been retained in the final project.

The Bill was promoted by LU and BR, and supported by the Government. An amendment or 'Additional Provision' was submitted in 1993 and the second reading of the Bill commenced in June of that year. Some 314 Petitions were received against the Bill mainly relating to property impacts particularly from the owners of expensive dwellings in Mayfair. In addition there was great concern from the Borough of Tower Hamlets where construction of the project would have a significant impact with little benefit for the residents and businesses of the area. The eastern portals of the central tunnel were designed to emerge in one of the few green spaces in the area. The borough employed consultant Jim Steer from Steer Davies and Gleave to argue on its behalf that the project was not being developed within a wider strategy for London and in particular did little for Inner London, Docklands or access to Heathrow Airport. Funding was also not in place.

The Commons Committee for the Bill sat over eighteen months until May 1994 under the chairmanship of the MP for Northampton North, Tony Marlow, and carried out a thirty-two day thorough, wide-ranging examination of the project, looking at everything from finance, to the London job market, the effect on existing train services and the environmental benefits. Their conclusion was to reject the Bill. At the time there was already a growing feeling that the Government was becoming lukewarm to the project. The Treasury was against it and the UK was entering a recession and public transport use was falling, undermining its basis. The Committee refused to give its detailed reasons for the decision but concerns raised during the proceedings suggested that financing the project was top of the list.

Crossrail was originally conceived as a public sector project but the Government thought that the private sector should be involved. This would be difficult to achieve as a large part of the revenue earned from the line would be abstracted from other operators. There was also a concern about the forecasts of passenger demand. London was entering another recession and peak-hour demand on the railways had fallen 20 per cent since the project had been initiated. The consultant acting for the London Borough of Tower Hamlets argued that London needed an overall strategic plan before individual schemes such as Crossrail could be considered. A major problem was that the abolition of the GLC in 1986 meant that London lacked a strategic body capable of undertaking such a plan.

Other reasons cited by various people were that the line did not link with the Channel Tunnel, then under construction, and the pressure from O&Y, the owners of the Canary Wharf development, on the Government, leading them to give the go-ahead for the Jubilee Line extension in October 1993. These two projects were seen as higher priority than Crossrail and with Government funding required for both, additional finance could not be made available. There was also increasing pressure to bring the Underground up to date before further new lines were considered.

Crossrail was effectively rejected by the Private Bill Committee on the grounds that a case had not been made. However the government issued 'Safeguarding Directions', protecting the route from any development that would jeopardise future schemes. The Minister of Transport at the time, Stephen Norris, expressed his disappointment in the House: 'We were disappointed that the Private Bill Committee did not find the preamble of the Bill proved and I know that this sense of disappointment was widely shared by Hon. Members on both sides of the House.'

With the apparent dismissal of Crossrail, work on the project did not come to a full stop. A small team was established from LU staff to safeguard the project – mainly examining a plethora of planning applications all along the route to see if they impinged on the works. The city was expanding and deep piled foundations for increasingly tall buildings were becoming the norm. The team sought to negotiate changes to designs to allow for the future tunnels, thereby avoiding foundations. They also initiated a number of ground and soil surveys. Both of these actions significantly facilitated the actual project build.

Project Revival

Construction of the Channel Tunnel finished in 1994 and the Jubilee Line extension in 2000. That year also saw the setting up of a new strategic authority for London, the GLA, by the Labour Party now in government after victory in 1997.

The new London Mayor, Ken Livingstone, could speak for London and could produce a Transport Strategy with responsibility for transport under the new organisation, TfL. John Prescott, the Deputy Prime Minister, expressed an interest in Crossrail and asked the newly formed Strategic Rail Authority (SRA) to look at the potential for new rail links. The Government produced a 'Transport 2010' strategy (Ref. 12.2) which included Crossrail and a number of light rail projects, all assumed to be capable of being built with substantial private sector funding.

In 2000 the SRA produced the 'London East-West Study' (Ref. 12.3) which recommended improving the network for both passengers and freight. It looked at both Crossrail and Chelsea-Hackney options and its analysis favoured the Crossrail project. Government was supportive and asked the SRA and the newly formed TfL to set up a joint project group to develop it further.

The GLA reviewed planning forecasts for the capital indicating significant growth both in population and employment. Congestion on the Underground and the privatised National Rail network was by now growing rapidly and the forecasts suggested that significant investment both in improving existing rail services and new lines was necessary in order for London to function efficiently in the future. The new Mayor's Transport Strategy identified the three major rail projects Thameslink 2000, the Chelsea-Hackney line and Crossrail as the core proposals to support the increasing population and employment forecasts.

With the Government's and the Mayor's blessing a new company, Cross London Rail Links Ltd (CLRL), was set up between TfL and the SRA. Its purpose was to develop two new rail lines across London. Crossrail line 1 would run on an east-west alignment and would be planned and taken forward to implementation. Crossrail line 2 would run north-east to south-west across the city and was to be planned in principle.

The broad objectives for CLRL were stated as:

to support the continuing development of London as a world city and its role as the key financial centre of the UK and Europe, to support economic growth and regeneration areas by tackling the lack of capacity on the existing network and to improve rail access into and within London.

The specific objectives for Crossrail 1, agreed between the Minister, the Mayor and the Chairman of the Strategic Rail Authority, were as follows:

- Support the wider transport, planning, social and environmental objectives of the Government's ten-year plan, the Mayor's Strategies for London, the Strategic Rail Authority's Strategic Plan and Regional Planning Guidance
- Relieve congestion and overcrowding on the existing National Rail and Underground networks and support the development of a network of strategic interchanges
- Facilitate the improvement of London's primary finance and business service activities, which are now located in both the City and Docklands
- Facilitate the improvement of London's international links, including Heathrow
- Facilitate the regeneration of priority areas, such as the Thames Gateway and the Lea Valley
- Provide improved east-west rail access into and across London from the East and South-East regions.

The basis for the development of the project assumed that the other major rail elements of the Mayor's Transport Strategy would be implemented, including Crossrail 2, the completion of Thameslink, the West London Tram and the extensions of the East London line.

The first task was to identify what was termed the 'Core Route' for the project. To start to meet the objectives this included the safeguarded underground route between Paddington and Liverpool Street with extensions to Heathrow in the west and to Stratford and the Isle of Dogs in the east.

Next a long list of options was drawn up. To the west they were:

- Maidenhead and possibly beyond
- Uxbridge
- High Wycombe
- Watford
- Amersham and possibly beyond.

To the east they were:

- via Charlton or the Royal Docks
- Shenfield and possibly beyond
- Grays and possibly beyond
- Ebbsfleet.

Eleven different service options were considered on these routes and discussed with key stakeholders. The developers of Canary Wharf were obviously in favour of a route via their site and in particular the direct link through to Heathrow Airport. The City saw Crossrail in terms of improving access for the vast armies of clerks they traditionally relied on. When the route to Canary Wharf was proposed their first instinct was to oppose it but this quickly died down when UK blue-chip companies began building headquarters on the Wharf.

Following consultation a comprehensive sifting process was undertaken based on six criteria:

- capital and operating costs
- economic impacts including effects on development, congestion relief, regeneration and social impact
- environmental impacts
- statutory consents
- engineering feasibility
- operational feasibility.

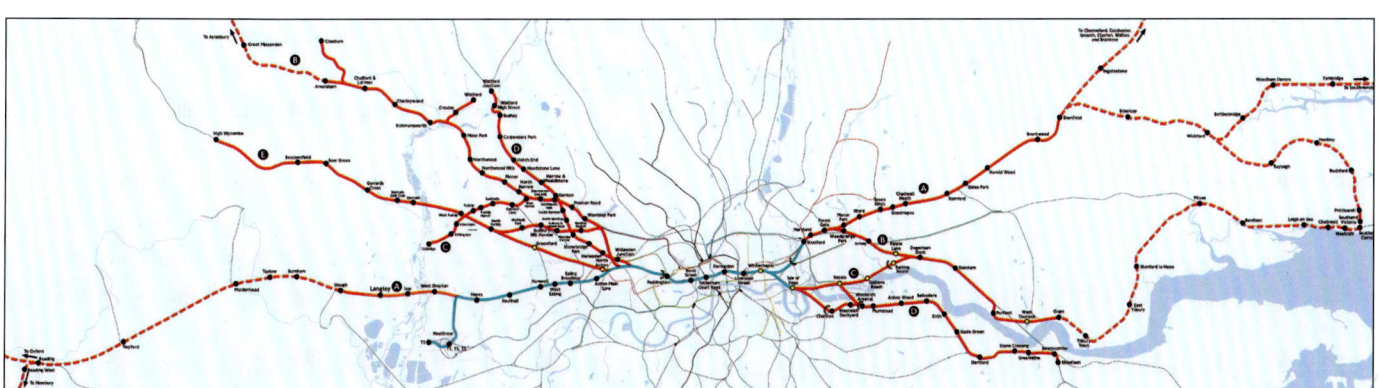

12.4: Long list of Crossrail options.

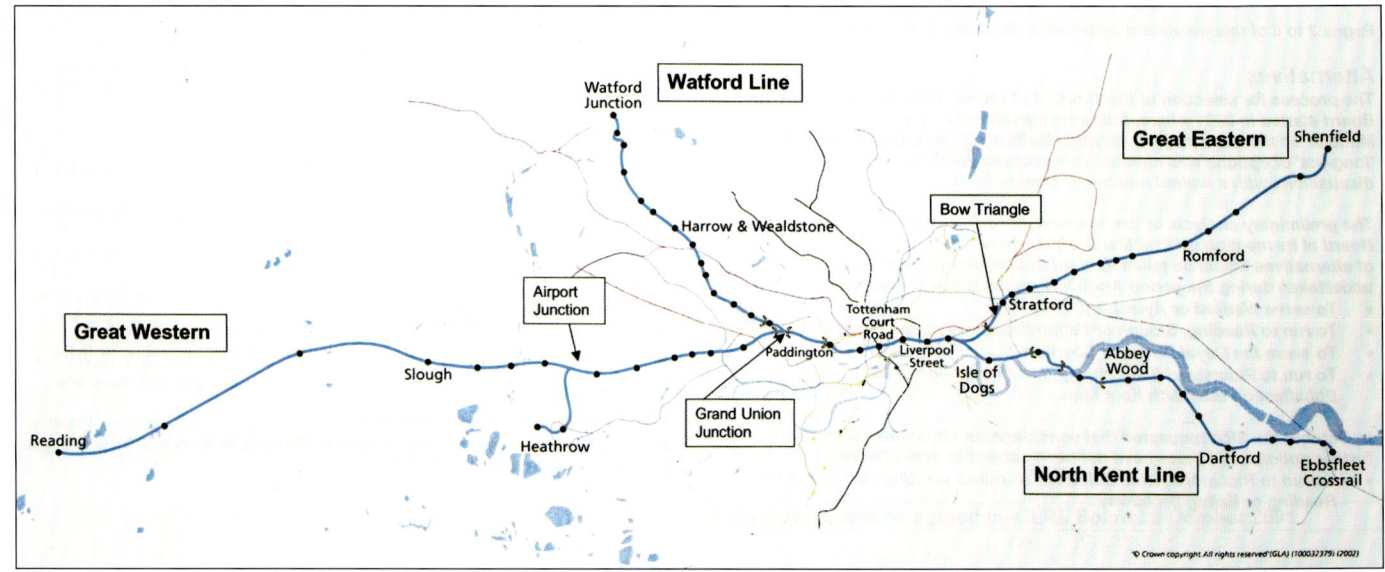

12.5: Initial recommended routes.

The result was a shortlist of routes and services which were then the subject of wider public consultation and appraisal in a multi-criteria appraisal process based on the Government's 'New deal for Transport' under the headings of Environment, Safety, Economy, Accessibility and Integration. Following the completion of the consultation and the detailed assessment at the end of 2002, the recommended proposal for Crossrail was a route from Paddington to Whitechapel with western branches to Reading and Watford and eastern branches to Shenfield and Ebbsfleet.

The first report on *The Case for Crossrail* was presented to the CLRL Board in November 2002 (Ref. 12.4). However before the report was submitted to Government the SRA expressed concern about the operability of the route to Watford and an alternative proposal to take the route to Kingston was assessed and consulted on. The final proposal submitted to Government in July 2003 was therefore a central route from Paddington to Whitechapel with western branches to Reading and Kingston and eastern branches to Shenfield and Ebbsfleet. This was estimated to cost £10.7bn and have a benefit to cost ratio of 1.99 to 1.

The case for the project had widened from its original remit to tackle congestion and now included the stimulation of the growing importance of the financial sector in the UK, in the City and Docklands, improved access to Heathrow and the regeneration of the Lea Valley.

The Montague Review

As the £10.7bn Crossrail Project was not part of the Government's Ten Year Plan for Transport (2001–11), immediately after the CLRL submission the Minister for Transport requested a review and asked the businessman and Chief Executive of the Private Finance Initiative Task Force at the Treasury, Sir Adrian Montague, to undertake it. His terms of reference for the review were:

a) To establish the full cost of the CLRL proposal and to assess
b) Whether they are likely to deliver to time, scope and budget
c) Whether the Business Case proposals will offer value for money
d) The extent of Government money that can be justified
e) The proportion of the funding required from non-Government sources
f) To identify any means of delivering a Crossrail project which performs better than the Business Case proposals against test (a)-(d) above
g) To report to the Secretary of State as soon as practical.

The review analysed a number of options against the CLRL Baseline proposal including dropping the Kingston branch, running only a few services on the Great Western main line and curtailing the south-eastern branch to Abbey Wood. A new station at Whitechapel was also examined.

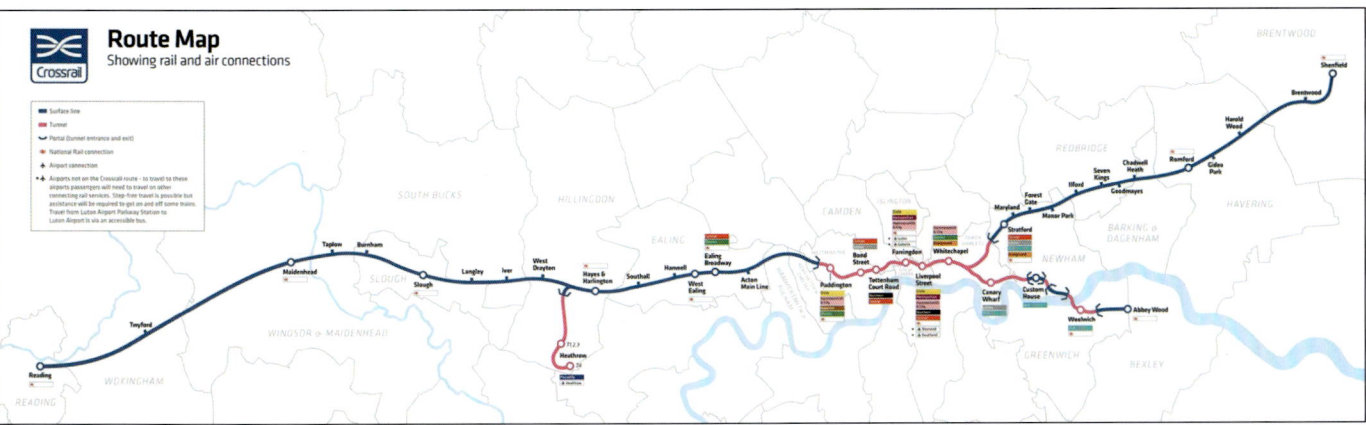

12.6: Final agreed route.

The report was completed by 2004 (Ref.12.5). In summary its key findings were:

that the Baseline project appears to be value for money, but there are uncertainties about the scale of the benefits; the costs were broadly right with the whole-life cost estimated at £11.2bn and London businesses could make a significant contribution to the cost.

However the review had some doubt about whether or not the Baseline Scheme could be delivered in practice. It identified concerns about the level of services that the scheme could support and whether the construction market had sufficient capacity to build the project. The major concern was a funding gap of £7–8bn. Most significantly the report concluded that it would not represent value for money to utilise private finance for the construction of the railway.

The review stated that the option serving Heathrow, Maidenhead, the Isle of Dogs and Shenfield had much to commend it with a whole-life cost of £8.5bn. However this still had a funding gap of between £4.5–5.5bn. The report also identified a significant extra amount of work that needed to be completed before the deposit of a Parliamentary Bill could be considered.

The report also reviewed a lower cost alternative proposal termed 'London Regional Metro' put forward by a private sector consortium which would link the Great Western and Great Eastern main lines using a similar Central London alignment and a possible branch to Canary Wharf. The review concluded that the project would be unlikely to deliver some of the wider benefits of the CLRL proposal and not be significantly

more easily funded or constructed. The review also considered a conventional metro idea put forward by Canary Wharf Ltd but concluded that this would have limited effect on overcrowding on the network and not bring many wider benefits.

In 2004 the Secretary of State for Transport, Alistair Darling, gave the go ahead for deposit of a Hybrid Crossrail Bill based on the reduced proposal identified in the Montague Report.

Project Evaluation

To support the Bill process in 2005 CLRL commissioned a report by consultants Steer Davies and Gleave on *The Transport Case for Crossrail* (Ref. 12.6) based on the defined objectives.

In summary the report found that with the ten-year forecasts for population and employment growth, even with the already planned network improvements, future levels of crowding on the rail network would exceed tolerable levels and that Crossrail would:

- increase capacity of the London Rail Network, allowing more people to travel to, from and across London and remove constraints on future economic development
- relieve crowding on the existing rail networks, including National Rail, Underground and DLR services
- reduce journey times for journeys to, from and across London.

In addition the Economic Appraisal of the project was updated. This examined both the conventional transport benefits and gave an evaluation of the wider economic impacts, following the Department for Transport's appraisal guidance.

The conventional transport benefits assessed time savings on public transport and upon the roads, highway vehicle operating cost savings and a reduction in accidents, improved comfort from reduced congestion and benefits to mobility-impaired passengers.

Against a Base Cost of £13bn Net Present Value (NPV), user benefits were estimated at £16.1bn NPV. In addition net rail revenue amounted to £6.1bn. With a net cost to Government of £9bn the benefit to cost ratio was calculated at 1.8 to 1.

Wider economic benefits of the project were assessed around the need to facilitate the continued development of London's finance and business services in three key areas of London – the West End, the City and the Isle of Dogs. The argument was that higher productivity results from the benefits of agglomeration, particular in the financial sector[2] (Ref 12.7). The main impacts of improved transport access, which are now included in the Department for Transport guidance, include: the benefits arising from a move to more productive jobs; the agglomeration benefits – increase in productivity following increase in employment density; the increase in labour force participation; and the benefits of reducing imperfect competition. Together these wider economic benefits were estimated at £7.1bn NPV and if included in the cost-benefit calculation raised the ratio from 1.8 to 2.6 to 1.

The Hybrid Bill

The Crossrail Bill was deposited in Parliament under the Hybrid Bill process. In a Hybrid Bill the Government votes on the principle of a project via a Second Reading before it is referred to a Select Committee, effectively giving it approval in principle. Railway projects deemed as 'National Significant Infrastructure Projects' are now taken through this process, most other projects being subject to a Transport and Works Order.[3] The Crossrail Bill was submitted in 2005 and by this time it had been agreed between Government and the Promoters that the proposed route would serve Heathrow and Maidenhead in the west and Shenfield and Abbey Wood in the east. An enormous amount of work remained to be completed before the Bill could be considered by the House, including an

Environmental Impact Assessment and despatching over 4,000 Land Owner Notices.

Delayed by a general election, the Second Reading of the Bill took place in July 2005. Three hundred and fifty-eight Petitions, mostly objections, were received to the Bill. The House of Commons Select Committee first met on 17 January 2006 and sat for a total of eighty-four days. Over the course of the Bill the Promoters gave a large number of undertakings to the Petitioners, mainly concerning the impact on property during construction or operations. Interestingly one petition about the impact on church buildings and religious services along the alignment mimicked a similar petition against the first dock railway some 150 years previously. Another petition concerned the temporary relocation of allotments, several opposing the extension of the route to Shenfield from Stratford and another advocating the use of the Crossrail tunnels by freight.

As originally designed the Crossrail route excluded a station at Woolwich, the Promoters not seeing this as economically viable as the area was already served by the North Kent line and the DLR. A number of Petitions in favour of the provision of a Woolwich station were received and the Committee was minded to ask the Government to reconsider its position. Initially the SRA had wanted the Thames Tunnel to accommodate freight trains between Custom House and Abbey Wood but the shallow gradients required by freight trains made providing a station very expensive if not impossible. When this requirement was dropped an affordable station became a possibility although the Government refused to fund it. Eventually the station was achieved by Berkeley Homes constructing the station box and paying towards its fitting out in return for Greenwich Council allowing increased density in Berkeley's Woolwich Arsenal development.

In January 2008 the Bill passed to the House of Lords where the Committee received 113 further Petitions. Issues again related to impact on property, noise, dust and vibration and lorry movements. Some repeated their House of Commons Petitions and others wanted to strengthen the agreements that the Promoters had already given them during the House of Commons Committee.

Royal Assent was obtained to the Crossrail Act on 22 July 2008 which included a description of the works to be undertaken and where they were to be carried out and identified the land needed temporarily or permanently. It gave permission for the railway to be built, operated and maintained. However there remained the question of money.

Funding

Prime Minister Gordon Brown, although still keen on the project, was anxious that there would be a significant contribution from the private sector. At the time of the funding deal in 2008 the cost of the railway had risen to £15.9bn. TfL and Central Government would contribute £1.9bn and £4.8bn respectively. The GLA would contribute £3.5bn via a Business Rate supplement of 2p in the pound for every premises in London with a rateable value of £55,000 or more over the period from 2010 to 2039. Network Rail would contribute £2.3bn to pay for the upgrading of the sections of the project using its tracks. Other contributions were £250m from the City Corporation, £45m from Berkeley Homes for the station at Woolwich, £70m from the owners of Heathrow and £150m from Canary Wharf. In addition revenue from over-site development was estimated at around £1bn. In practice if the net effects on public funds were to be fully assessed only a very small proportion of the cost of the project was actually paid for by the private sector. At the same time as the Funding Agreement in December 2008 Crossrail became a subsidiary of TfL as part of the Development Agreement.

Construction began on 15 May 2009 with work commencing at the new Crossrail Canary Wharf station. A further update of the case for the project was produced in 2010 (Ref. 12.8). The agreed project, by 2011 officially a subsidiary of TfL, runs from Abbey Wood and Shenfield to the east of London to Maidenhead and Heathrow in the west. However, following external pressure and further analysis the Government announced in March 2014 that limited services should be extended to Reading. The separate National Rail project which included the major upgrading of Reading station and electrification of the Great Western line had significantly reduced the cost of this option.

Tunnelling

Although the route through the Central Area had long been safeguarded, the challenge to develop the detailed alignment through London's maze of Underground

12.7: Tunnel-boring machine.

lines, pipes, services and building foundations was a complex task.

Fortunately the accuracy at which modern TBMs can be driven forward allowed the engineers to find a route which kept the line as close as possible to the surface, in some cases passing above, rather than below, other Underground lines. This kept interchange and exit times to a minimum, shortening escalators, etc. At one point the distance to a Northern Line tunnel was only about 600mm. In some cases it was also possible to site the station platforms at the top of a rise in the track level,

aiding de-acceleration and acceleration of the trains as they enter and leave the platforms.

The tunnelling was accomplished with eight TBMs over the period May 2012 to May 2015 working on ten drives. These were built in Germany and shipped to the UK in 2012. Six were of the earth pressure balance type for use in the London clay, sand and gravel in west London. Two were of the mix shield slurry type for use in the wet chalk and flint under the Thames in East London. Each was capable of tunnelling up to 100 metres a day.

12.8 (above): Typical precast tunnel lining.

12.9 (left): Sprayed concrete lining.

A total of 21km of the tunnels were lined with 6.2 metre diameter precast concrete linings. Six large underground caverns were constructed using sprayed concrete linings incorporating fibre reinforcement and waterproof membranes as were station platforms and passages. Ground settlement occurs as earth is extracted, so surface or building movement was carefully measured utilising some 75,000 measuring points along the route. Compensation grouting was used at several stations to counteract any significant movement.

Some 7m tonnes of waste was removed from the construction and reused in a variety of places, including landfill restoration, a golf course, nature and bird reserves. Some 3m tonnes of earth contributed to the creation of a 1,500-acre wildlife habitat at Wallasea Island near the Essex coast. This will become the largest and most important coastal habitat scheme in the UK.

Over 10,000 people have worked on the Crossrail tunnels including over 700 apprentices. As part of the project a Tunnelling Underground Construction

12.10 (above): Wallasea Island.

12.11 (right): Track-laying machine.

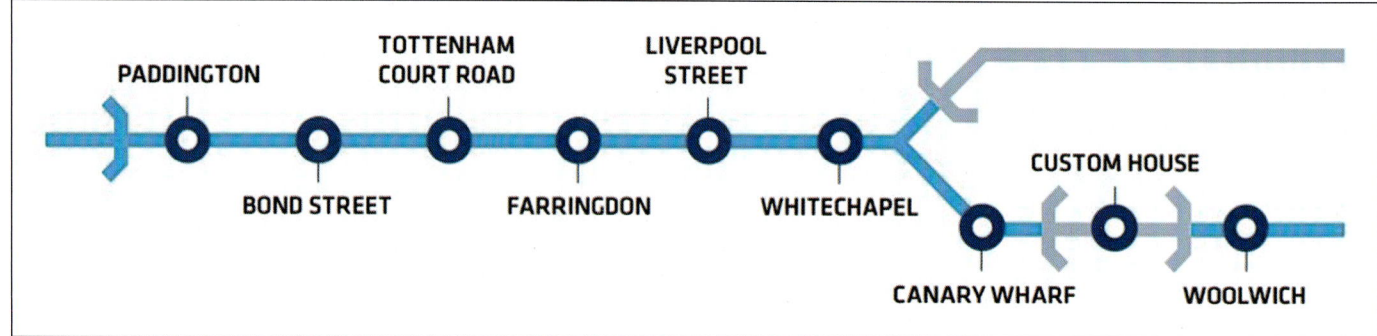

12.12: Central Area stations.

Academy (TUCA) was set up to help train existing and future engineers. Over 15,000 men and women have since been trained at the academy.

Many major international companies were involved in the construction. A consortium of Bechtel, Halcrow and SYSTRA was engaged as Programme Delivery Partners for project management of the central section. For the tunnelling and stations, Crossrail let a number of design contractors, the output of this then being handed to the construction contractors. For the trains and railway, systems contracts were let for design, construction and maintenance.

Station Designs

The 118km long line will serve forty stations with 31km of sub-surface tunnels and eight new sub-surface stations. Custom House in the Royal Docks and Abbey Wood are the two new surface stations.

The Crossrail publication *Platform for Design* (Ref. 12.9) sets out the rationale for the design of the stations. Unlike the Jubilee Line extension, where different architects were involved in each station, Crossrail employed a single set of architects to work on all the lower-level platforms, passages and concourses and separate architects for the upper levels.

A common set of parts, including seating, signage, communication equipment, lifts, escalators and fire safety equipment, was also developed to provide a consistent theme across the railway. Passengers using Crossrail will experience a very different travelling environment, in stark contrast with many parts of the Underground.

Also a significant difference for Crossrail is the extensive use of sprayed concrete, not only for some parts of the running tunnels but also for connecting passages, lower concourses and platforms. This construction technique allows for a more flexible design, avoiding sharp corners and permitting much larger cross-sections. The sprayed concrete walls are generally finished with glass fibre reinforced concrete panels.

At platform level, as on the Jubilee Line extension, there are platform edge doors to enhance safety and reduce wind effects but on Crossrail the screens extend to the roof of the tunnels and incorporate sophisticated heat extraction, fresh air fans and ducts. The screens will also be used for lighting and passenger information screens, reducing the clutter typically found above most Underground platforms.

Following completion of the basic infrastructure a major part of the project was to install the station finishes and all the complex electrical and mechanical systems, including escalators and communication systems.

On opening of the project it will be renamed the 'Elizabeth Line'. As passengers will become familiar with the names of stations and services on the Elizabeth Line, from this point forward the new name is used to describe these aspects of the project.

Stations

Although this book is focused on Docklands the following section briefly covers the route and its stations as many passengers will travel to and from Docklands using other Elizabeth Line stations and indeed many will make their whole journey just using the line. Design and construction details of all the Central Area stations can be found on the Crossrail Learning Legacy website (Ref. 12.10).

Starting in the west, Reading station completed in 2015 a separate major rebuilding project, with the addition of five more platforms giving a total of fifteen as part of the GWR upgrading and electrification. All fourteen intermediate stations between Reading and Paddington have had a facelift with the addition of lift access where necessary to provide full access for disabled people. Entrances and ticket halls at stations at West Drayton and Hayes and Harlington have been rebuilt with greatly improved passenger facilities.

At Old Oak Common, adjacent to the Elizabeth Line train depot, a major new interchange station with HS2 is under construction. The first phase of HS2 is currently planned to open around 2030 in advance of the connection to Euston. It is envisaged that Elizabeth Line trains, initially terminating at Paddington, will be extended to terminate at the new interchange at this time. The Elizabeth Line is therefore likely to experience high passenger interchange flows before Euston opens.

The first station on the new tunnel section is Paddington with the line diving under the main-line station from the northern side of the approach tracks to a sub-surface station on the south side. The taxi rank at this location was relocated to the far side of the station close to a rebuilt Hammersmith & City line ticket hall.

With a site relatively clear of underground obstructions the opportunity was taken to build the Elizabeth Line station from the surface, allowing daylight to penetrate right down to platform level. An underground passenger link is provided to the Bakerloo Line with passengers transferring to the District, Circle and main-line services using a new entrance into the main-line station, alongside Platform 1. The glass ceiling of the station is decorated with a 'cloud' installation by the artist Spencer Finch. This is one of a number of art installations at the new stations, contributed to the project by the City of London and others.

The next station has its western entrance at Bond Street, fully integrated with the existing station serving the Jubilee and Central Lines. This will provide a major interchange with these lines and consequently, in anticipation, the existing station has been subject to a significant upgrade.

12.13: Hayes and Harlington station.

12.14: Paddington station.

12.15: Bond Street station.

Although there are only two Elizabeth Line stations serving the busy Oxford Street shopping area at Bond Street and Tottenham Court Road, as the platforms are 240 metres long, each station with two entrances effectively provides four spaced out stations along the street. Bond Street's second entrance is located a few paces south of Oxford Street in the corner of Hanover Square.

It is often asked why a station at Oxford Circus, where there is interchange with the Victoria Line as well as the Bakerloo and Central Lines, was ruled out. This station is very busy and a complex mesh of small platforms, passages and escalators. With the very large flows anticipated with the Elizabeth Line the station would have been completely overwhelmed if trains had stopped there. The area is also heavily constrained by buildings and roads. The solution would have necessitated an incredibly difficult, complex and costly rebuild. This was ruled out at an early stage as impractical.

The station at Tottenham Court Road will have two entrances, the first sited at Dean Street along Oxford Street and the second at St Giles Circus close to the Centre Point building forming part of the existing Northern Line station. This has been rebuilt with a wide new entrance and a replacement of the former very cramped and claustrophobic ticket hall. The construction required the demolition of the old Astoria theatre and concert venue, however a new theatre is planned by Crossrail oversite partners together with a much improved pedestrian plaza.

Farringdon is the next station along the line which will become a major interchange between the north-south Thameslink and the east-west Elizabeth Line station. Farringdon will have two platform tunnels, each 245 metres long, between new ticket halls to the east and west ends. At the western end, the entrance has been combined with a new ticket hall for Thameslink services on Cowcross Street, opposite the existing Metropolitan Line station entrance. A separate east ticket hall has an

12.16: Tottenham Court Road station.

12.17 (left): Farringdon station.

12.18 (below): Liverpool Street station.

entrance onto Long Lane at the corner with Lindsey Street. Over 130 trains on the three lines will stop at Farringdon in the peak hour, which is destined to become one of the busiest stations in London. Services from the station will also directly serve three of London's airports.

Liverpool Street has again two separate entrances at each end of the platforms. The eastern entrance and ticket hall will link to the existing main line and the Underground station whilst the western entrance and ticket hall will interchange with Moorgate station. Moorgate is the London terminus for services to Hertfordshire operated by Great Northern and Underground services on the Circle, Hammersmith & City, Metropolitan and Northern Lines. The station will therefore become another important interchange with Elizabeth Line east-west services.

12.19 (above): Whitechapel station aerial view.

12.20 (right): Whitechapel station.

Whitechapel station, the first on the line to directly serve the Docklands area, will also become an important interchange as the station is also served by the Hammersmith & City Line and by London Overground, which now provides services to the north to Dalston and Highbury and Islington and south to Clapham Junction and Croydon. Access to all lines will be from a spacious, new ticket hall above the Victorian railway,

with a sedum-clad green roof. Entry to the station will be through the refurbished original entrance on Whitechapel High Street. A new second entrance to the same ticket hall will be provided at the northern end of the station.

Just east of Whitechapel the line divides at Stepney Green Junction, the northern branch leading to Stratford and stations to Shenfield and the southern branch to

12.21 (above): Stepney Green Junction.

12.22 (left): Romford station.

Docklands and Abbey Wood. Stratford station received a major upgrading with the Jubilee Line extension, the DLR extensions and the London Overground, all completed in time for the London Olympics in 2012. As with stations on the western branch of Elizabeth Line, all stations from Stratford to Shenfield are being upgraded with access for disabled people provided where necessary. In order to accommodate the tunnel portal west of Stratford, Pudding Mill Lane DLR Station had to be rebuilt on a new alignment, replacing the original station which was on a single track section of the route.

Similar to the Jubilee Line, the Canary Wharf Elizabeth Line station has to be in a deep box as the railway has to pass under the River Thames at either end. It is sited in the former North Dock in juxtaposition to the Jubilee Line station in the former South Dock.

In a deal with the project, Canary Wharf Ltd took responsibility for the construction and preliminary fitting out of the station for a total of £500m. Although similar to the Jubilee Line station an alternative construction technique had to be used as the box was much closer to occupied buildings, ruling out percussion piling. Alternative machinery and crew were brought in by Canary Wharf to complete the task before handing over to the Crossrail to fit out the railway and all its systems.

Unlike the Jubilee Line station, which is all below ground with only ticket hall and platform levels, the Elizabeth Line station has been built with seven levels, only three of which are above ground, incorporating a number of restaurants and bars. On the top level a magnificent public garden has been provided.

12.24: Canary Wharf station.

12.23: Cross section of Canary Wharf station.

12.25: Canary Wharf station roof garden.

12.26: Canary Wharf ticket hall.

12.27: Custom House station adjacent to Excel exhibition centre.

Custom House and Abbey Wood are the only new surface stations on the line. When the Beckton extension of the DLR was built, it ran parallel to the North London line tracks at Custom House. In 2006 the NLL service was withdrawn with the DLR taking over the service between Canning Town and Stratford, leaving the former NLL alignment available for the Elizabeth Line between Royal Victoria and the Connaught tunnel.

A surface station is provided at Custom House, albeit on a rather constrained site. It is anticipated that bringing the Elizabeth Line to the Royal Docks will stimulate further development in the area.

12.28 (above): Custom House station.

12.29 (right): Connaught tunnel entrance.

12.30: Woolwich station.

Beyond Custom House the line follows the old North Woolwich line alignment into the Connaught tunnel which passes under the link between the Victoria and King George V docks. Originally the dock railways crossed the gap with a swing bridge but this was replaced by the tunnel. This posed a major challenge to the Crossrail engineers as it required enlargement to accommodate the larger Elizabeth Line trains and the overhead wires. The solution was to replace the whole roof of the tunnel below the dock passage which necessitated the temporary construction of coffer dams so that the water above the tunnel could be drained.

Woolwich is a deep-level station providing interchange with the North Kent line and the DLR. It was initially argued that as Woolwich was already well served by rail, including the DLR, an Elizabeth Line station would be difficult to justify. As mentioned earlier, after protracted negotiations it was included in the project with contributions from the borough, developers and the GLA.

The final station on this branch is at Abbey Wood, constructed alongside the North Kent Line station.

Unfortunately the original plan to site the Elizabeth Line platforms between the main-line tracks to allow cross-platform interchange has not been implemented but even so the interchange is expected to attract many passengers wishing to travel to the City and West End.

Trains and Services

Seventy nine-car Elizabeth Line trains are required to run the service which have been built by Bombardier in Derby. They are 200 metres long and have space for up to 1,500 people, but with only 450 seats. As the trains will be carrying very heavy loads in the peak periods through Central London the designs reflect more metro-type trains than those found on the main lines.

At the time of writing, in the peak periods twelve trains per hour will run from Shenfield to Paddington and twelve will run from Abbey Wood, with six of these running to Heathrow and six to Maidenhead, with four of the latter being extended to Reading. Thus twenty-four trains per hour will run through the central section which will be automatically

12.31 (above): Crossrail train at Reading station.

12.32 (right): Train interior.

controlled. Outside the Central Area trains will be manually driven. When the Old Oak Common interchange with HS2 opens it is likely that all the trains terminating at Paddington will be extended to the new station.

Archaeology

As with the Jubilee Line extension the construction through Central London opened up, literally, major opportunities to uncover London's earlier life. The Crossrail and Museum of London publication *Tunnel – the*

Archaeology of Crossrail (Ref. 12.11) provides a detailed description of the finds, only very briefly summarised here. The then Chairman of Crossrail Sir Terry Morgan, in introducing the book, described the *Archaeology of Crossrail* as: 'The story of London uncovered beneath the streets of the city will be one of the greatest legacies of the Crossrail project, to be enjoyed for years to come.'

Most of the tunnels are too deep to disturb the archaeology but the numerous shafts giving access to stations and the platforms as well as for services and ventilation offered up substantial rewards.

At the eastern end in the Woolwich area the Thames used to be much wider. Evidence of seasonal camps were found from the Mesolithic period some 6–8,000 years ago. In the Royal Docks and Isle of Dogs area, remains of buildings associated with ship-building, slipways and iron works of the nineteenth century have been discovered.

At Canary Wharf a piece of amber estimated to be 55m years old together with a fragment of a jawbone of a woolly mammoth from the last Ice Age were found. At Stepney Green, where the two eastern branches of the Elizabeth Line join, the remains and household items of a fifteenth-century moated manor were found, later to be known as 'Worcester House'.

The construction of Liverpool Street saw some of the most significant archaeological finds. Sections of a Roman road showing wheel ruts, a Roman cemetery with eight decapitated burials, numerous skulls, coins

12.33: Roman coin found at Liverpool Street.

and artefacts were discovered. Above the Roman layer the New Churchyard later known as Bedlam and used until 1739 revealed over 3,000 burials, most likely deaths from the Great Plague of 1666.

The Position in 2021

The Elizabeth Line was originally due to progressively open from late 2018 and be fully open in late 2019. However, early in 2020 it was announced that delays in fitting out the stations and the testing of trains had imposed up to a two-year delay. In 2019 Elizabeth Line trains had taken over stopping services between Reading and Paddington and in 2020 local services to Heathrow. Also in 2021 Elizabeth Line trains are now running between Shenfield and Liverpool Street.

Later in 2020 it was announced that following intensive trial running of trains in 2021 the central section from Paddington to Abbey Wood would not open until the first part of 2022. Through running to Shenfield and Reading would follow on later. The complexity of the project and the Coronavirus pandemic restrictions were cited as the main causes of delay.

In October 2020 the governance of the project moved to sit directly within TfL with a special committee chaired by the Deputy Mayor. Costs of the project had also risen up to £1.1bn above the financing package agreed in 2018. This to be initially funded by the Greater London Authority borrowing up to £825m from the Department for Transport which will be given by the GLA to TfL as a grant. The GLA will repay this loan from the Business Rates Supplement and Mayoral Community Infrastructure Levy. Completion of the project is estimated to generate £42bn for the UK economy.

Impact on Docklands

The Elizabeth Line is the third major rail network to serve Docklands following the Jubilee Line, and the six stages of the DLR, each one progressively following the success of its predecessor. The three Elizabeth Line Docklands stations at Whitechapel, Canary Wharf and Custom House will improve access for people working in the area from many parts of London, particularly from the west, the north-east and the south-east and reduce any constraints on further development in the area for a long time. It will provide a much quicker and more comfortable journey for those living in the

12.34: Rebuilt Pudding Mill Lane DLR station.

area travelling to the City and West End. The impact on further development in the Royal Docks area could be significant, this being an area not as attractive to developers as originally anticipated.

An extension beyond Abbey Wood to Ebbsfleet has been mooted as has a second branch to the west beyond Paddington.

Further Information

This chapter has only sought to provide a brief summary of this incredible project – the largest railway project at the time in Europe. Others have given many more and deeper insights into the difficult and highly complex processes this project has been through. The Crossrail website (www.crossrail.co.uk) provides a wealth of information on the project with many videos and images covering many different aspects of the project. There is a separate Learning Legacy website (www.learninglegacy.crossrail.co.uk) with more technical information aimed at sharing the lessons from delivering Crossrail for the benefit of future projects. Excellent publications produced by the project cover the details of design, construction and archaeology. Another recommended publication is Christian Wolmar's *The Story of Crossrail* (Ref. 12.12), which comprehensively covers all aspects of the project from its concept, through its tortuous political and funding process, in far more detail than possible here.

The Crossrail story goes on. In early 2020 all work stopped on the project as a result of Coronavirus and work only recommenced when additional safe working arrangements had been implemented. Work restarted later in 2020 under strict Covid precautions. Intensive trial running commenced in spring 2021 with the line expected to open in the first half of 2022.

CHAPTER 13

180 YEARS OF DOCK RAILWAYS

Over the past 180 years Docklands and its Isle of Dogs focus has witnessed two major periods of railway development. The major docks to the west of the River Lea built in the early part of the nineteenth century functioned without rail access for nearly fifty years, relying on the horse and cart and the Thames lighters to carry the goods to and from the ships. The coming of the railways in the mid-nineteenth century rapidly expanded the catchment of the docks allowing goods to be transported to and from the docks and all over the country. The later Royal Docks had the advantage of being built with rail access in mind, providing a direct link between rail and ship and avoiding the need for extensive local storage. Direct rail links into city depots also reduced the need for road transport.

The first dock railway network grew in the fury of mid-century rail mania. Companies competed for space and business and tracks and depots spread like amorphous tentacles, especially in the Isle of Dogs. Agreements of inter-running were slowly established and by the time the PLA took over the running of the docks in 1909 it inherited an extensive railway network of over 100 miles in length. Forty years later, on the nationalisation of railways in 1948, the only passenger services still operating were between North Woolwich and Stratford and on the East London line.

The rapid expansion of the Underground and London's suburban rail network in the late nineteenth and early twentieth century had largely passed Docklands by. As dock workers had traditionally lived close to their work, improved passenger services to Central London and commuter links into the area were not required. The last freight line from Victoria Park to Poplar Docks ran in 1971 leaving only the North Woolwich line with a half-hourly passenger service to Stratford and the rather neglected East London line. Apart from a few local bus services Docklands had again largely become an inaccessible place. Large areas were closed to the public with abandoned ships, cranes, rail tracks and warehouses. It was a desolate, contaminated and a dangerous place.

The year 1973 saw the publication of one of the first reports suggesting the area could be extensively redeveloped. The rest of that decade saw a plethora of studies from the Government, GLC, local authorities and LT, and reports into what might potentially happen in terms of the development of housing and businesses and what might be the appropriate means of transport to serve them. Buses, busways, minitrams, light rail and metros were all considered but with little agreement between the local, London and Government authorities on what type and scale of development was required, progress was minimal.

The decision of the Secretary of State Lord Heseltine to proceed with the setting up of the LDDC in 1981 and the construction of the modest initial DLR was a visionary step forward. Taking away the powers from the local authorities and creating the LDDC resulted in virulent opposition from them as well as from local residents, but the construction of a new railway service was welcomed by both. In time the LDDC realised they had to work together and with financial support in areas such as training the wounds were gradually healed.

With the Government only allowing very modest funds for transport the only way to build a segregated system was to make maximum use of the former railway rights of way. Without these alignments, still in public ownership, the DLR could not possibly have been built for its out-turn cost of £77m. Some 90 per cent of the initial DLR took over former railway alignments and indeed with its expansion over the last thirty years from the initial 11km to its current 38km, around 50 per cent of its route is on former railway rights of way.

London's deregulation of the banks, the need for a new style of trading floor, restrictions on the rebuild of City office space, the availability of land with Government grants not too far from the centre and the improved accessibility resulting from the construction of the initial DLR, effectively combined to provide the stimulus for the unprecedented redevelopment focused on Canary Wharf. It can well be argued that without the DLR being under construction, Docklands would not have been in the eye of the developers and without the former railway alignments being available and reusable the DLR would not have been built. Docklands would undoubtedly have been a very different place from what it is today.

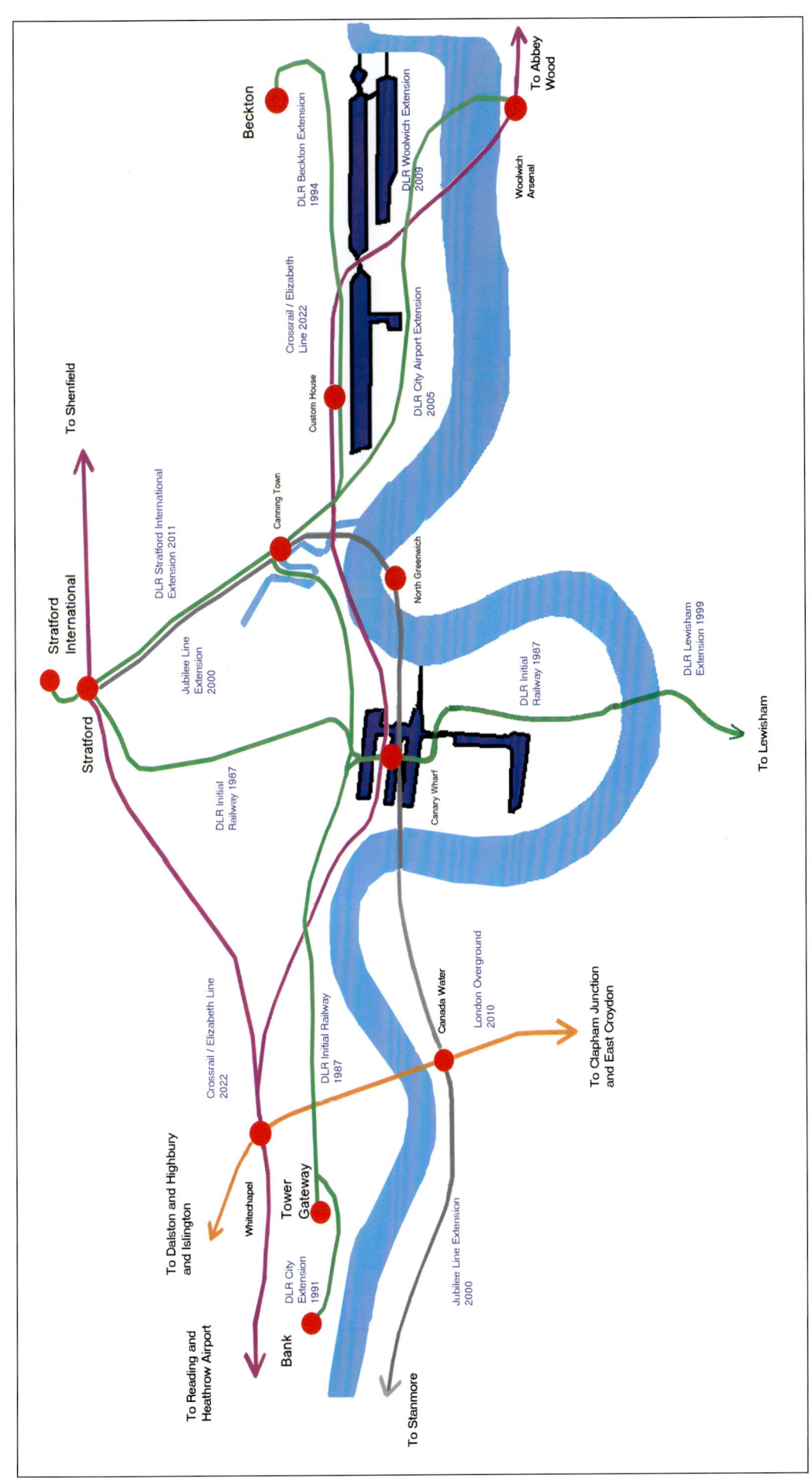

13.1: Docklands New Railways.

The comparison between the early dock railways serving worldwide trade and the modern systems also serving many worldwide but rather different businesses is obvious.

With forecasts of jobs in the area rising from initial figures of 25,000 in the mid-1980s to well over 100,000 by the millennium and possibly in the future to over 200,000 this is not an ideal scenario in which to plan and provide transport provision. Massive and disruptive expansion of the DLR, the construction of the Jubilee Line extension and now the Elizabeth Line have all been driven by these forecasts. If we had known at the beginning what we know now, it is interesting to speculate what might have been. Almost certainly the DLR would not have been built, with just the Underground extension and the Elizabeth Line serving the area, most likely with more frequent stations. This would be a pity as the DLR provides such an excellent local service for people living and working in the area, significantly quicker and more reliable than buses which would have been the alternative.

An early consideration for Docklands was the limit on road capacity to serve the growth of the area. New roads have been constructed but it was quickly recognised that travel patterns typically found in Central London with over 90 per cent of people travelling to work by public transport had to be achieved in Docklands if the massive growth was to be accommodated. Although by no means planned from the start, the combination of local bus, river, light rail, metro and regional metro services serving Docklands has produced a high quality public transport network to rival anywhere in the world.

The justification and funding arrangements for all the many individual railway projects in Docklands is worth a book in itself. The latest economic and environmental appraisal techniques are a far cry from those of the 1980s used for the initial DLR. A limited cost-benefit appraisal was carried out but there was no requirement for an Environmental Assessment or Appraisal. However a new technique assessing the likely number of jobs created by the various options was an important indicator in the decision-making process. Moving on to the DLR expansion, the Jubilee Line extension and the Elizabeth Line, an increasing range of sophisticated techniques for assessing a range of financial, economic, environmental and social impacts has evolved. Techniques developed for the

Crossrail project assessing wider economic impacts on city agglomerations have now been adopted within the Department for Transport's standard appraisals.

However it can be argued that a major component of the economic impact of new railways, missing from the current evaluation process, is the impact on land values. After the working docks ceased operations much of the residual land was contaminated and effectively had a negative land value, substantial investment being necessary to just bring the land up to a developable state. From the early days when estate agents put up site billboards on developable land stating 'close to the new Docklands railway' all the public investment has seen a massive uplifting of land values. Some of this was realised by the LDDC but much remained outside its portfolio. At least one landowner later admitted that he had benefited by several million pounds since the Jubilee Line extension had opened. Unlike in the early days of railways and in several countries abroad, railway promoters in the UK cannot accumulate land if it is not required for construction or operations.

London has had limited success in encouraging property owners to contribute to the cost of new railways. The City extension of the DLR, the Jubilee Line extension and the Elizabeth Line have all received modest financial support from the private sector. The Elizabeth Line has managed to take a further step forward with the Mayor of London introducing the 2p levy on non-domestic properties with a rateable value of over £55,000. It would require a significant change in the law if railway promoters were to be allowed to purchase land which would benefit from their investment.

In 2014 TfL commissioned a report from property consultants Jones Lang LaSalle to assess the increase in land values around two stations, Canary Wharf and Southwark (Ref. 13.1). The conclusion estimated that the increase around Southwark station was £800m and around Canary Wharf station £2bn.

In 2017, TfL and the GLA published the results of a technical study into *Land Value Capture* (Ref. 13.2). This report investigated ways in which the Government could work together with the Mayor of London and TfL to improve the ability to capture land value uplift to fund transport investments in the capital. The research revealed that land values arising from the Jubilee Line extension have risen by 52 per cent, from the DLR extension to Woolwich by 23 per cent and the incorporation of the North London line into the London Overground resulted in a 6 per cent increase. The report, which has been produced to stimulate discussion and debate, suggests a number of ways in which this value could be captured. It would take a major change in Government policy to bring such suggestions into effect.

The story of recent railways in Docklands has not always been straightforward. All three recent rail systems have had their problems. The problem with the initial DLR was caused by a relatively untried automatic control system and the extensive upgrading of the railway as soon as it was opened, causing many months of unreliability. The Jubilee Line had problems with completing the station equipment and services within an enforced deadline of the millennium. The Elizabeth Line was all going well until it was realised that delays to the track and station systems installations effectively prohibited the proper testing of trains. Also the temporary halt to construction during 2020 will have further delayed its completion.

Railways are now one of the most complex engineering systems of the modern world. Tunnelling with high-tech machines has become relatively straightforward. Multiple systems for signalling communications, safety and passenger information are now essential but involve increasingly complex components, many needing to closely integrate with each other. New aircraft and warships are of similar complexity but can be built and tested in a secure place. Railways are one-offs, and cannot be tested until built. Those in densely urban areas such as London have to contend with myriad interfaces, often unknown and unexpected, both during construction and operation. New-build railways always bring new challenges to

13.2: Isle of Dogs, aerial view.

engineers. There is sometimes a tendency to go for unproven technological improvements and sometimes lessons of the past are forgotten.

Is this the end of railway development serving Docklands? Perhaps not. DLR extensions from Woolwich to Thamesmead and from Lewisham southwards and from Bank westwards have been mooted. As have the restoration of the earlier proposal for extending the Elizabeth Line from Abbey Wood to Ebbsfleet and possible extensions to the west to better balance services on the line. Extending the Bakerloo Line to the Isle of Dogs and Greenwich has also been suggested. All of these will be dependent on further growth in East London. With the uncertainties created by the withdrawal of the UK from the European Union, the downturn in the global economy and the effects of the pandemic, it may well take a few years before this is known.

In May 2021 the Government announced its proposed reorganisation of the National Rail system, bringing fundamental changes to the management and operation of the UK network within a new body called 'Great British Railways'. These changes will not affect the Docklands services described in this book as they will remain under the control of TfL and the London Mayor. The proposed franchising of services planned for the national network reflects that very successfully implemented by TfL for the DLR and Overground networks.

POSTSCRIPT

This book was finalised during the pandemic created by Coronavirus. The country was in lockdown and travel was restricted to essential journeys. Passenger numbers on the Underground had fallen by 80 per cent and commuter services into London severely curtailed. Many people were working from home.

More than thirty years ago the transport planning profession was questioning whether future demand for travel would be affected by the spread of the internet. Until recent times this proved not to be the case. However, now, in 2021, after over a year of travel restrictions, there is growing evidence that home or hybrid working is feasible and that there are advantages for companies which can save costs in office space and rentals and advantages for individuals as travel time is eliminated.

There is also evidence that the productivity of some people who work from home improves but others miss the camaraderie of the office and find remote working relationships difficult. Whilst demand for travel will obviously significantly return once the crisis is over, the forced growth of home working in the current circumstances may have already changed attitudes to five day nine to five office working. Most recent projects have been based on the assumption that demand for travel, particularly in the peak hours, will continue to grow. Estimating future demand for London's railways will be increasingly problematic and several projects in the pipeline may well be paused to be reassessed when things have settled down. This may well take several years. Transport planners will inevitably have a much more difficult time in assessing future projects.

APPENDICES

Principal Docklands Railway Statutory Approvals

1. Railway from the Minories to Blackwall, with branches, to be called 'The Commercial Railway', Act 1836.
2. Numerous Dock Railway Acts (1836–1900).
3. The London Docklands Development Corporation (Vesting of Land) (Port of London Authority) Order 1981.
4. London Docklands Railway Act 1984 (DLR Tower Gateway to Island Gardens).
5. London Docklands Railway Act 1984 (DLR Poplar to Stratford).
6. London Docklands Railway Act 1986 (DLR City extension).
7. London Docklands Railway Act 1989 (DLR Beckton Extension).
8. London Regional Transport Act 1989 (DLR Pudding Mill Lane station).
9. London Docklands Railway Act 1991 (DLR works at North Quay Junction).
10. London Underground Act 1992 (Jubilee Line – Green Park to Stratford).
11. London Underground Act 1993 (Jubilee Line – Westminster, Waterloo and Southwark stations).
12. London Docklands Railway Act 1993 (DLR Lewisham extension).
13. London Docklands Railway Act 1993 (DLR powers transfer to LDDC).
14. London Underground Act 1994 (Jubilee Line – Green Park station).
15. Transport and Works Act Order 2002 (DLR City Airport extension).
16. Transport and Works Act Order 2002 (DLR Silvertown and City Airport Extensions).
17. Transport and Works Act Order 2004 (DLR extension to Woolwich Arsenal).
18. Transport and Works Act Order 2005 (DLR Capacity improvements).
19. Transport and Works Act Order 2006 (DLR extension to Stratford International).
20. Transport and Works Act Order 2007 (DLR capacity enhancement and Games preparation).
21. Crossrail Act 2008.

London Docklands Key Dates

	Open	Closed
DOCKS		
Surrey Docks (Howland Dock)	1696	1979
West India Docks	1802	1975
London Docks	1805	1968
East India Docks	1827	1975
St Katharine's Dock	1828	1968
Victoria Dock	1855	1970
Millwall Docks	1868	1975
Albert Dock	1880	1981
King George V Dock	1921	1981
DOCK RAILWAYS		
London to Blackwall Railway	1840	1958
North Woolwich line (Beckton)	1846	1971
North Woolwich line (Woolwich)	1846	2006
East London line	1865	2007
Millwall Extension Railway	1870	1926
North London line (Blackwall)	1870	1966
DOCKLANDS RAILWAYS		
Initial Dockland Light Railway	1987	
DLR City extension	1991	
DLR Beckton extension	1994	
DLR Lewisham extension	1999	
Jubilee Line extension	2000	
DLR City Airport extension	2005	
DLR Woolwich extension	2009	
London Overground	2010	
DLR Stratford International extension	2011	
Crossrail/Elizabeth Line	2022	
AUTHORITIES		
London County Council	1889 to 1965	
Port of London Authority	(1908 to 1981 (?))	
London Docklands Development Corporation	1981 to 1998	
LT	1933 to 1999	
GLC	1965 to 1986	
Greater London Authority	2000–	
Transport for London	2000–	

AUTHOR'S NOTES

About the Author

1. A particularly daunting process but perhaps even more daunting was being asked by my boss, in his absence, to chair a planning meeting of the 'Millennium Night Transport Group', involving the heads of the many London organisations involved such as the police and the transport operators, not forgetting the Minister for Transport in London. Thankfully, there were no major problems on the night. I was 4,000 miles away celebrating with friends in India, some five hours before London.

Chapter 2

1. The environmental concerns over noise and vibration raised by their Lordships were similarly raised by petitioners against Docklands Light Railway Bills on exactly the same route around 150 years later.
2. Coincidentally about the same order of magnitude which used the Docklands Light Railway running on the same alignment and serving roughly the same stations, when it opened nearly 150 years later.
3. Later this created a significant engineering challenge for the Crossrail project which has used the tunnel alignment.
4. At the time of writing Greenwich power station is still operational, providing peak loads for the Underground.
5. It would be nearly half a century later before trams returned to London with the opening of Croydon Tramlink in 2000.

Chapter 3

1. The author remembers it taking up to one and a half hours to travel by public transport from Central London to the Isle of Dogs, taking the District Line to Mile End and then by local bus.
2. Looking back at the choice of options and some of the results of the evaluation does rather question some of the techniques used. The dismissal of any form of light rail at an early stage is also surprising. One speculation is that London Transport was adverse to anything remotely connected with a tram, it being only just over twenty years since their wholesale dismissal as an appropriate form of transport for the capital.
3. Fortunately the road was not seen as a top priority and the light railway bagged the viaduct. When the LDDC later decided to progress a new road linking the Isle of Dogs to The Highway, a very much more expensive route, running beneath Limehouse Basin, had to be adopted.

Chapter 5

1. At one stage, the author, who was working for the GLC at the time, held a number of 'clandestine' meetings with officers of the LDDC to try and mutually move transport options forward.
2. Approximately the same number of people originally working in the Isle of Dogs docks.

Chapter 6

1. David and I went on to produce a report with the title *Light Rail for London?* which formed the basis for the Croydon Tramlink, opened in 2000.
2. This decision by BR was taken in a climate of falling passenger demand and BR was prepared to give up two running lines from Limehouse to Fenchurch Street. Later, particularly after privatisation, when demand was rising, it is understood that this decision was deeply regretted.
3. It would be another twenty years before this was rectified.
4. Has a new railway ever been approved so quickly by Government? Many years later, at an event celebrating twenty-five years of the Canary Wharf development, the author asked Lord Heseltine how he had persuaded the Government go ahead with the project in spite of the Department of Transport reluctance. His answer was unequivocal: 'I simply announced it at the Tory party conference.'
5. The Victoria Line, opened in 1968, was automatically driven but still required a 'motorman' in the driving cab.

6. Or even transport planners, as the author was later to find out!

7. To produce this information necessitated an act of sheer bravery by a consultant who had to explore and seek out the owners of the many and various properties under the old viaducts of the former railways, inevitably homes to some very 'alternative' businesses often guarded by fierce Alsatian dogs.

8. Unlike in some other countries, the procedure did not allow the promoters to acquire any extra land outside the immediate requirements for construction and operation. Therefore the promoters could rarely benefit from any increase in land values as a result of their investment.

9. The station was seen as providing access to a rather remote industrial area and has never attracted many passengers. It has now been rebuilt on a new twin track alignment to accommodate the Crossrail tunnel approach, but ironically was closed during the London Olympics for fears of overcrowding.

10. Over time the name 'Docklands Light Railway' has shortened to the initials DLR, these being now used for example, for all announcements on the London rail network.

11. This section of the railway was badly damaged by an IRA bomb in 1996. It was rebuilt to the same alignment. Later, when three-car trains were introduced, South Quay was rebuilt as a new station further to the east on a straighter alignment.

12. The author was responsible for the passenger demand forecasts for the line and had an anxious week or two before these figures were confirmed.

Chapter 8

1. Initially a direct link was proposed which would have resulted in the longest escalator in London. In the end a combination with new escalator connections to the Northern Line was built.

2. Today the sophisticated signalling system has, to a degree, overcome this problem by allowing bidirectional working of trains.

3. At the time of writing an idea has emerged to allow the expansion of Fenchurch Street main-line station over the land occupied by the DLR Tower Gateway station, replacing this with a new DLR

interchange station at Tower Hill on the underground section.

Chapter 9

1. When this occurs the promoters are given a very short time – often only a few hours – to decide whether or not to accept the decision of the Committee. There is a real danger of losing the Bill if the promoters decide not to accept the amendment.

2. At an early point the LDDC had considered a proposal to 'straighten' the tortuous bend in the River Lea to produce more developable land. The potential silting of the River Thames ruled out the proposal. A similar proposal some 150 years earlier to cut a new route for the River Thames across the Isle of Dogs was similarly ruled out as impractical.

3. At a public meeting in the Isle of Dogs at which the author presented the plans for the extension, a number of residents surprisingly expressed opposition to the project. On questioning their reason the response from one resident, loudly cheered by others, was 'because we don't want those bloody southerners coming over and taking our jobs!'

Chapter 10

1. The other four proposals identified in the plan – the DLR extension to Lewisham, the East London extension to Peckham, the development of the North London line with a river crossing to Woolwich and DLR to Barking, have all been taken forward in one form or another. In the event, London Overground has taken over and extended the East London line. DLR has been extended to Woolwich and an alternative London Overground extension to Barking Reach is under construction.

2. The then Director of the Tate Gallery was quoted as saying that the fact that the Jubilee Line was to be routed via the South Bank was a significant factor in the decision to go ahead with the construction of Tate Modern within the remains of the former Bankside power station.

3. This was contested during the Parliamentary Proceedings by the owners of a development site in the Brunswick area, north of the river. The promoters argued that the route via North Greenwich

would open up a much larger area of development and 'via a bus interchange' serve a wide existing residential catchment.

4. The Millennium Dome did not influence the routing of the railway, the decision to site the Dome at North Greenwich coming after the choice of route was made.

5. The author sometimes reflects on the decision to extend an existing small-bored tube railway, seeing how much better designs and comfort levels can be achieved with modern full-sized rolling stock, as now used on London's sub-surface lines, Crossrail and many metros around the world. With the continued growth of London the relatively small additional cost would probably have been justified. It could have interchanged with the existing line at Charing Cross and could have been readily extended to Paddington or Baker Street and beyond.

6. The extent of the London Clay largely determined the historic development of the Underground. Modern railway tunnelling machines, as first demonstrated in London with the Lewisham extension of the DLR, now mean the restrictions on the development of the Underground network are largely removed.

7. During tunnelling of the line through Westminster, movement of the tower was carefully monitored by consultant Prof. John Burland of Imperial College. Compensation grouting was injected into the ground when movement over a certain level was detected. John Burland went on to mastermind the stabilisation of the Leaning Tower of Pisa.

Chapter 12

1. In 1988 following studies by the GLC and BR new cross-London services began to run through this link under the Thameslink name.

2. This analysis, now applicable to major projects in a few of the larger UK cities, was developed by an economic consultant, Paul Buchanan, employed by Crossrail.

3. The procedure was changed from the Private Bill process to the Transport and Works Act process in 1992, partly because of the significant number of railway Bills, particularly in London, being submitted, taking up too much Government and Committee time and procedures.

REFERENCES, BIBLIOGRAPHY AND FURTHER READING

Chapter 1

1. Greeves, Ivan, *London Docks 1800–1980. A civil engineering history.* Thomas Telford, 1980.
2. SK AlNaib, *Docklands - An illustrated historical survey of life and work in east London.* North East London Polytechnic, 1986.
3. L M Bates, *The Spirit of London's River,* Grensham Books, 1980.
4. Fiona Rule, *London Docklands – A History of the Lost Quarter,* Ian Allan, 2009.
5. Peter Stones, *The History of the Port of London – A Vast Emporium of All Nations,* Pen and Sword Books, 2017.
6. Alan Palmer, *The East End – Four Centuries of London Life,* John Murray, 1989.
7. www.pla.co.uk/ *A Brief History of the PLA.*
8. www.thehistoryoflondon.co.uk/ *the-port-of-london-in-the-age-of-steam.*
9. www.british-history.ac.uk/survey-london.
10. XXXX

Chapter 2

1. Christopher, John, *The London and Blackwall Railway – Dockland's First Railway,* Amberley Publishing, 2013.
2. Brennard D, *London's East End Railways – Part 2 Branch Lines to the Docks,* Booklaw Publications, 2013.
3. Alan Palmer, *The East End – Four Centuries of London Life,* John Murray, 1989.
4. C R L Coles, *Railways Through London,* Ian Allan, 1983.

Chapter 3

1. London County Council, *County of London Plan,* Macmillan & Co., London, 1943.
2. Railway (London Plan) Committee, *Report to the Ministry of War Transport,* HMSO, London, 1946.
3. British Rail and LT Boards, *A Railway Plan for London – Preliminary Report by a Working Party of British Rail and LT,* British Rail, London, 1965.

4. LT, *The Case for the Fleet Line,* LT, London, 1971.
5. Llewelyn-Davies, Weeks Forestier-Walker and Bor, *South East London and the Fleet Line Revisited – a study of land use potential,* LT Executive, London, 1973.
6. Travers Morgan, *Docklands Redevelopment Proposals for East London,* DoE and GLC, London, 1973.
7. Department of the Environment and GLC, *The London Rail Study,* HMSO, London, 1974.
8. Docklands Joint Committee, *A Strategy for Docklands: Setting the Scene,* Docklands Development Organisation, London, 1975.
9. Docklands Joint Committee, *The Docklands Spine – Tube, Bus or Tram?,* Docklands Development Organisation, London, 1975.
10. Docklands Joint Committee, *Docklands Strategic Plan,* Docklands Development Organisation, London, 1976.
11. GLC, *1988 Olympic Games Feasibility Study,* GLC, London, 1979.
12. GLC, *Jubilee Line Stage II – Report to Planning and Resources Committee,* GLC, London, 1979.
13. LT, Docklands Development Organisation, Department of Transport, Department of the Environment, GLC, *A Study of Lower Cost Alternatives to the Jubilee Line in Docklands,* GLC, London, 1978.
14. GLC, *Transport Packages for Docklands,* GLC, London, 1980.
15. Department of the Environment, *The Thames Gateway Planning Framework,* HMSO, 1995.

Chapter 5

1. London Docklands Development Corporation, *Transport in Docklands,* LDDC, 1989.
2. London Docklands Development Corporation, *London Docklands Transport – The growing Network for the 1990s,* LDDC, 1991

3. London Docklands Development Corporation, *Starting from Scratch – The Development of Transport in London Docklands*, LDDC, 1997.
4. London Docklands Development Corporation, *Attracting Development, Creating Value – Establishing a Property Market in Docklands*, LDDC, 1998.
5. Brownill, Sue, *Developing London's Docklands – Another Planning Disaster*, Paul Chapman Publishing, 1990.
6. Bentley, James, *East of the City – the London Docklands Story*, LDDC, 1997.
7. Kenneth Powell, *City Reborn – architectural and regeneration in London from Bankside to Dulwich*, Merell Publishers Ltd, 2004.

Chapter 6
1. GLC, LT and LDDC, *Public Transport Options for Docklands – summary of the assessment of schemes*, London, GLC, 1982.
2. Catling D and Muir R, *The Possible Role for Intermediate Capacity Guided Transport Systems in London*, LT Executive, 1980.
3. Willis Jon, *Docklands – Planning the Initial DLR*, Journal of the Institute of Highways and Transportation, IHT, 1987.
4. Docklands Light Railway, *Official Handbook*, DLR, Capital Transport, 2006.

Chapter 7
1. Olympia and York, *Canary Wharf – Transport Development*, Marketing Brochure, 1990.
2. Prof. S.K. Al Naib, *London Canary Wharf and Docklands – Social, Economic and Environmental*, Research Books, 2003.

Chapter 8
1. Transport for London, *Transport and Works Order Bank Station Upgrade*, HMSO, 2015.

Chapter 9
1. Department of Transport, *Report on railway noise and the insulation of dwellings*, The 'Mitchell' report, 1990, HMSO.
2. London Docklands Development Corporation, *Starting from Scratch – The Development of Transport in Docklands*, Frontline Graphics, 1997.

3. Louise Butcher, *Railways: Docklands Light Railway (DLR)*, Standard Note SN/BT/415 House of Commons Library, 2010.
4. Docklands Light Railway, *Official Handbook*, DLR, Capital Transport, 2006.
5. LT, *The Docklands Public Transport Strategic Plan— Discussion Document*, LT, 1988.

Chapter 10
1. London Regional Transport, London Docklands Development Corporation, British Rail, *Docklands Public Transport Strategic Plan: Discussion Document*, 1988.
2. British Rail, LT and the GLC, *Central London Rail Study*, London, 1989.
3. Department of Transport, *East London Rail Study*, London, 1989.
4. Environmental Resources Ltd. *Environmental Assessment of the Jubilee Line Extension*, LT, 1989.
5. Museum of London, *The Big Dig – Archaeology and the Jubilee Line Extension*, Museum of London Archaeology Service, 1998.
6. Ove Arup & Partners, *Jubilee Line Extension - End of Commission Report*, London, 2000.
7. University of Westminster, *Jubilee Line Extension Impact Assessment*, University of Westminster, London, 2004.
8. Bartlett School of Planning, *Mega Projects – Lessons for Decision Makers*, University College London, 2012.
9. Willis Jon, *Extending the Jubilee Line – the Planning Story*, LT, 1997.
10. World Tunnelling, *Jubilee Line Extension – Underground Construction*, Laurence Williams, 1996.
11. New Civil Engineer, *The Jubilee Line Extension*, NCE, 1994.
12. New Civil Engineer, *The Jubilee Line Extension*, NCE, 1996.
13. Mitchell R, *The Jubilee Line Extension – from Concept to Completion*, Thomas Telford, 2003.

Chapter 11
1. Docklands Light Railway, *DLR Horizon 1998*, DLR, 1997.
2. Docklands Light Railway, *DLR Horizon. Study Business Case Appraisal*, Ove Arup, 2005.

3. Railtrack, British Rail, LT, London Docklands Development Corporation, *The Woolwich Rail Tunnel – Thames Gateway Metro*, LT, 1996.
4. Department of Transport, *Transport Appraisal Guidance*, 2018.

Chapter 12
1. Peter Parker, *A Cross London Rail Link*, British Railways, 1980.
2. HM Government, *2010 Transport Strategy*, London, 2000.
3. Strategic Rail Authority, *London East-West Study*, London, 2000.
4. Cross London Rail Links Ltd, *The Case for Crossrail*, Crossrail, 2003.
5. Adrian Montague, *Crossrail Review*, Department of Transport, 2004.
6. Steer Davies and Gleave, *The Transport Case for Crossrail*, Crossrail, 2005.
7. Department for Transport – *Transport Analysis Guidance*, DfT, 2013 and updates.
8. Crossrail, *Crossrail Business Case Update,* Crossrail, 2010.
9. Hugh Pearman, *Platform for Design, Crossrail*, 2016.
10. Crossrail Learning Legacy: https://learninglegacy.crossrail.co.uk/.
11. Crossrail, *Tunnel – the Archaeology of Crossrail*, Crossrail, 2017.
12. Christian Wolmar, *The Story of Crossrail*, Head of Zeus Ltd, 2018.
13. Crossrail, *Stakeholder Consultation*, Crossrail, 2002.
14. Transport for London, *Transport Vision for a Growing City*, TfL, 2005.
15. Greater London Authority, *London Mayor's Transport Strategy*, GLA, 2010.
16. Crossrail, *Crossrail Business Case Technical Report*, TfL/Crossrail, 2011.
17. Greater London Authority, *The London Plan – the Mayor's Spatial Development Strategy*, GLA, 2012.
18. Greater London Authority, *London Infrastructure Plan 2050 – Transport Supporting Paper*, GLA, 2014.
19. House of Commons Select Committee on the Crossrail Bill *First Special Report of Session*, 2006–07.
20. Institute of Civil Engineers, *Crossrail Project – Designing and Constructing the Elizabeth Line*, ICE, 2017.
21. Crossrail, *Breakthrough – Crossrail's tunnelling story*, Crossrail, 2015.

Chapter 13
1. Jones Lang LaSalle, *Land & Property Value Study – Assessing the Change in Land & Property Values Attributable to the Jubilee Line Extension*, LT, 2014.
2. Transport for London, *Land Value Capture*, TfL, 2017.

IMAGE SOURCES

Preface
P.1 ©Alamy

Chapter 1
1.1 ©Alamy
1.2 ©Alamy
1.3 ©Alamy
1.4 ©Alamy
1.5 ©Alamy
1.6 ©Alamy
1.7 ©Alamy
1.8 ©Alamy
1.9 ©Alamy
1.10 ©Alamy
1.11 ©Alamy
1.12 ©Alamy
1.13 The Author

Chapter 2
2.1 The Author
2.2 ©Alamy
2.3 ©Alamy
2.4 Author's Collection
2.5 Author's Collection
2.6 Author's Collection
2.7 Wikimedia Commons
2.8 ©Alamy
2.9 ©TfL from the LT Museum collection
2.10 Author's Collection
2.11 Author's Collection
2.12 Author's Collection
2.13 Wikimedia Commons
2.14 Author's Collection
2.15 Author's Collection
2.16 Author's Collection
2.17 The Author

Chapter 3
3.1 LT
3.2 LT
3.3 ©TfL from the LT Museum collection
3.4 ©TfL from the LT Museum collection
3.5 GLC
3.6 The Author
3.7 LT
3.8 GEC Ltd.
3.9 GLC
3.10 Docklands Joint Committee
3.11 Docklands Joint Committee
3.12 GLC
3.13 Docklands Joint Committee
3.14 Docklands Joint Committee
3.15 ©TfL from the LT Museum collection
3.16 GLC

Chapter 4
4.1 GLC
4.2 Author's Collection
4.3 The Author
4.4 The Author
4.5 The Author
4.6 © ©Miles Willis
4.7 ©Transport for London

Chapter 5
5.1 London Docklands Development Corporation
5.2. London Docklands Development Corporation
5.3 The Author
5.4 The Author
5.5 London Docklands Development Corporation
5.6 ©Canary Wharf Ltd.

Chapter 6
6.1 GLC
6.2 GLC
6.3 GLC
6.4 GLC
6.5 Wikimedia Commons: Ed g2s & James D Forrester
6.6 The Author
6.7 The Author
6.8 The Author
6.9 The Author
6.10 The Author
6.11 The Author

6.12 The Author
6.13 The Author
6.14 ©Alamy

Chapter 7
7.1 The Author
7.2 ©Canary Wharf Ltd.
7.3 ©Canary Wharf Ltd.
7.4 ©Canary Wharf Ltd.
7.5 ©Canary Wharf Ltd.
7.6 The Author
7.7 The Author

Chapter 8
8.1 The Author
8.2 The Author
8.3 LT
8.4 The Author
8.5 The Author
8.6 Wikimedia Commons: Ed g2a & James Forester
8.7 The Author
8.8 The Author
8.9 ©Transport for London

Chapter 9
9.1 The Author
9.2 The Author
9.3 ©Miles Willis
9.4 ©Miles Willis
9.5 Wikimedia Commons: Ed g2s & James D Forrester
9.6 The Author
9.7 The Author
9.8 ©Transport for London
9.9 The Author
9.10 The Author
9.11 The Author
9.12 The Author
9.13 Wikimedia Commons: Ed g2s & James D Forrester
9.14 The Author
9.15 The Author

Chapter 10
10.1 LT
10.2 ©Canary Wharf Ltd.
10.3 GLC
10.4 LT
10.5 LT

10.6 The Author
10.7 LT
10.8 The Author
10.9 The Author
10.10 The Author
10.11 ©Canary Wharf Ltd.
10.12 The Author
10.13 The Author
10.14 The Author
10.15 The Author
10.16 The Author
10.17 The Author
10.18 The Author

Chapter 11
11.1 ©Miles Willis
11.2 The Author
11.3 The Author
11.4 Wikimedia Commons: Ed g2s & James D Forrester
11.5 Wikimedia Commons: Ed g2s & James D Forrester
11.6 ©Miles Willis
11.7 ©Miles Willis
11.8 ©Miles Willis
11.9 The Author
11.10 ©Transport for London
11.11 The Author

Chapter 12
12.1 London County Council
12.2 ©Crossrail
12.3 LT
12.4 ©Crossrail
12.5 ©Crossrail
12.6 ©Crossrail
12.7 ©Crossrail
12.8 ©Crossrail
12.9 ©Crossrail
12.10 ©Crossrail
12.11 ©Crossrail
12.12 ©Crossrail
12.13 ©Crossrail
12.14 ©Crossrail
12.15 ©Crossrail
12.16 ©Crossrail
12.17 ©Crossrail
12.18 ©Crossrail
12.19 ©Crossrail

12.20 ©Crossrail
12.21 ©Crossrail
12.22 ©Crossrail
12.23 ©Canary Wharf Ltd.
12.24 The Author
12.25 The Author
12.26 ©Crossrail
12.27 ©Crossrail
12.28 ©Crossrail
12.29 The Author
12.30 ©Crossrail
12.31 The Author

12.32 The Author
12.33 ©Crossrail
12.34 ©Miles Willis

Chapter 13
13.1 The Author
13.2 ©Alamy

Note Wiki commons licence: https://commons.
wikimedia.org/wiki/Commons:GNU_Free_
Documentation_License,_version_1.2

INDEX